ORSAY
Sculpture

ORSAY

Sculpture

Anne Pingeot

Conservateur Général at the Musée d'Orsay

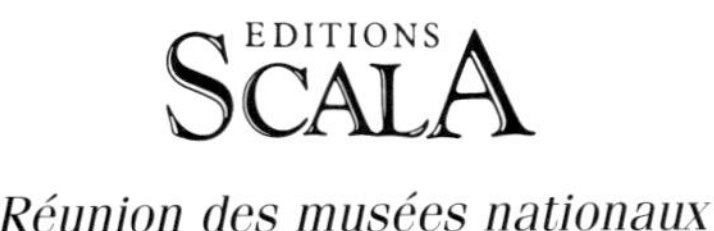

Réunion des musées nationaux

26, rue de Charonne - 75011 Paris
Design : Jérome Faucheux
Cover design : Philippe Hubert
Plans : Thierry Renard

Front cover : Aristide Maillol, *Méditerranean* or *Thought,*
1905-1927 (detail). © RMN, © Adagp, Paris 1998
Back cover : View of the interior of the Musée d'Orsay. © RMN

Contents

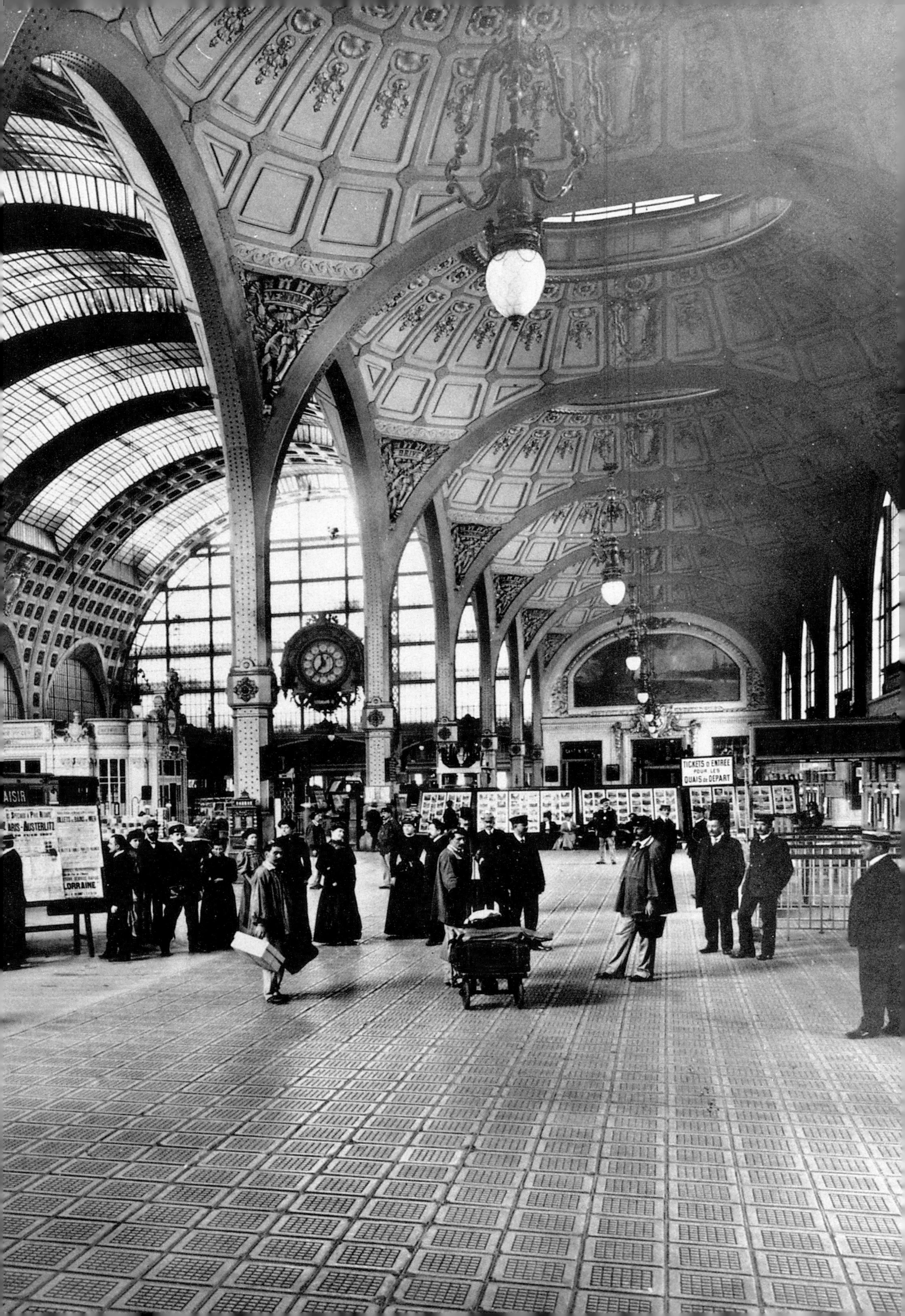
AISIR
LORRAINE
TICKETS D'ENTRÉE
POUR LES
QUAIS DE DÉPART

Sculpture in the Musée d'Orsay: a Short History

The 19th century was a period of excess for sculpture, which was adopted by a triumphant bourgeoisie eager to adorn its dwellings and immortalize its image. Political regimes also made use of it. The sculptor's task was to fix messages, figures and symbols for all eternity – on behalf of ideals, beliefs and powers which were not themselves eternal, and which therefore shifted continuously.
Just as nature is prodigal in order to achieve a single success, this proliferation of sculpture commissions inevitably produced a few masterpieces. But are masterpieces the key to art history? Should they be winnowed out and then displayed as being representative of all artistic creation during their century (or half-century, in the case of the Musée d'Orsay)? The perspective given would be false, because focused solely on what we, at the end of the 20th century, consider a 'work worthy of exhibition'. Less false, in our view, however, than the one prevailing between 1945 and 1975, when three-quarters of the production under consideration here was relegated to attics, cellars and rubbish dumps. We believe our perspective to be broader than that of those vengeful years, when 'experts' secure in their own judgments gave spectators no chance to make their own.
The Musée d'Orsay, opened to the public in December 1986, is housed in a converted railway station built in central Paris to serve the World's Fair of 1900, and contains a major selection of all French sculpture dating from the second half of the 19th century. In order fully to appreciate this collection, it might be useful to understand a little of its history.

A great antecedent: the Luxembourg Museum

The allies who defeated Napoleon I following the 'Hundred Days' reclaimed the plundered art works stored in the Louvre. The gaps this left were filled with paintings from the Luxembourg Palace. The problem then was how to fill the gaps at the Luxembourg – the solution, with works by living French artists. The first exhibition was held on 24 April 1818. In 1852 a scanty collection of 25 paintings and sculptures was augmented with prints and engravings. When the initially royal, then national, Luxembourg Museum became imperial in 1852, its collections began to move with the times: four sculptures were acquired at the Salon of 1852 and five at the Salon of 1853 (the Salon being the annual official exhibition during which artists won glory for themselves and customers for their works). In 1863 the Luxembourg's curator, Philippe de Chennevières, submitted two requests to Beaux-Arts superintendent Alfred-Emilien de Nieuwerkerke for approval:
– allocation of a special room in the museum for non-French artists, so that the foreign schools represented at the Louvre could be extended into the 19th century; this request was rejected, and the Musée d'Orsay collections still suffer from that contemporary lack of hospitality to foreign works;
– retention of works by deceased artists for a period of five years following their death, so that posterity's judgment might be more objective; however, even when extended to ten years, this waiting period proved insufficient for reliably winnowing the wheat (for the Louvre) from the chaff.
The year 1863 also marked the opening of the Salon des Refusés (where works rejected by the official Salon were shown); the reform of the Ecole des Beaux-Arts; and Charles Garnier's commission to the sculptor Carpeaux for a *Dance*

Interior of the Gare d'Orsay, photograph c.1910.

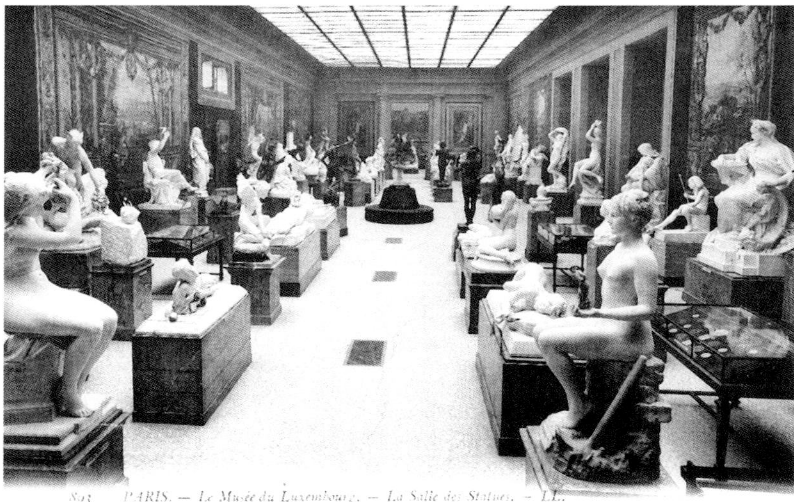

Postcard showing a sculpture sampler at the Luxembourg Museum. Left: Hector Lemaire's *Morning* (1887), transferred to Arbois, 1935. Right: Gérôme's *Tanagra* (1890), exhibited in the Musée d'Orsay ballroom.

of the Bacchae to adorn his opera house – with the Carpeaux sculpture and all the studies for it ultimately finding a home at the Musée d'Orsay.

By 1870 the Luxembourg was beginning to run out of space, and Philippe de Chennevières suggested to minister Jules Simon that the entire palace be used for living art – a museum, a school of decorative arts, and meeting rooms for learned societies. Following the Paris Commune, there were plans to construct a new building or restore older ones: the ruins of the Tuileries Palace (which had the advantage of proximity to the Louvre); the ruins of the Cour des Comptes; the Palace of Industry; the Champ de Mars; School for Deaf-Mutes, etc. However, none of these was implemented. Although the newly 'national' Luxembourg Museum continued to house mythological works dedicated to the glory of the imperial regime (such as *Sleeping Hebe* by Carrier-Belleuse), the Franco-Prussian War of 1870–71 opened the way for patriotic works. In 1875 the sculpture catalogue listed 72 works, including 'engravings on medals and precious gems'. The most important novelty, however, was the listing of 'sculpted studies'. Previously, the Luxembourg had accepted only finished works in marble. The first bronze sculpture, Francisque Duret's *Young Fisherman Dancing the Tarantella* (1833, Louvre), finally appeared in the catalogue of 1850, a revolutionary step made possible by the death of Barye. As a result of his advanced age, the doors of the Academy had been opened to him, and a posthumous sale of his works convinced museum administrators that the preliminary studies were also worth acquiring. This was recognition of the pre-eminence of the creative act. The catalogue of 1876 listed the further acquisition of 'preliminary models for casting' and 'studies in wax' by Barye.

In 1879 the Marquis de Chennevières was succeeded as curator by Etienne Arago, who noted that the museum's foreign collections had come to a standstill, 'just when the World's Fair of 1878 has shown us what striking progress [foreign artists] are making'. Buying 'French' from the Salon continued and, when that institution was reorganized and taken over by the artists themselves, the latter naturally enough called themselves the Société des Artistes Français.

In 1884 the Librairie Baschet published a *Livret illustré du musée de Luxembourg* containing 47 sculpture reproductions. The supplement to this catalogue, published in 1885, listed Rodin and his *Saint John the Baptist Preaching.* The Nation had purchased his first work in bronze, *Bronze Age*, from the Salon of 1880 after it won a 3rd-place medal. This concluded a scandal that had made headlines in 1877, when the plaster version of the work exhibited in Brussels and then in Paris was accused in both capitals of having been moulded from life.

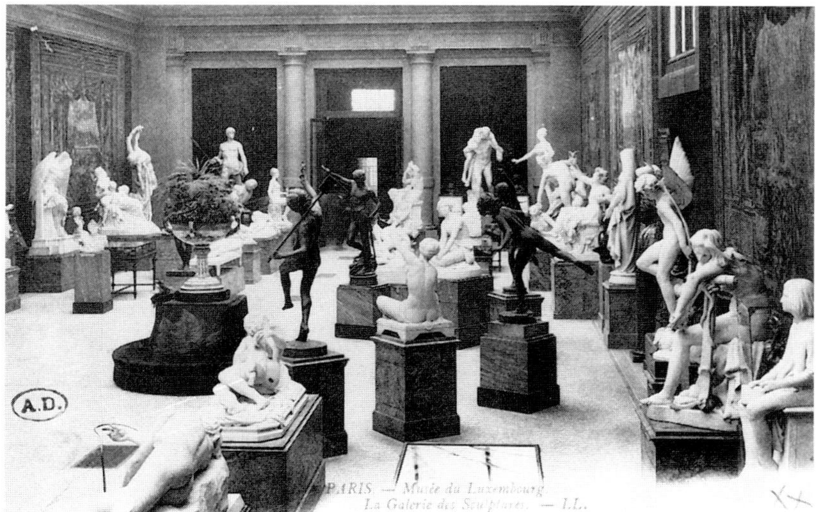

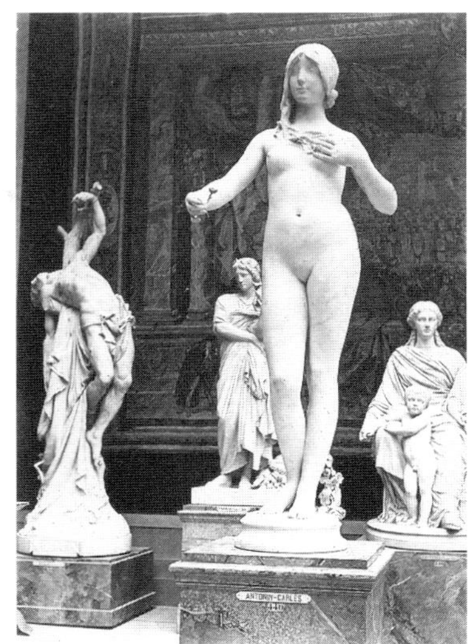

Sculpture Gallery, Luxembourg Museum. Although Mercié's *David* (1871), Moulin's *Find at Pompeii* (1863) and Barrias's *Spinner of Megara* (1870), shown in the centre of the photograph, are at the Musée d'Orsay, Chapu's *Joan of Arc* (1872) and d'Injalbert's *Hippomenes* (1886) are at Amboise.

Among the sculptures exhibited at the Luxembourg, only Becquet's *Saint Sebastian* (1884) was sent to Mans in 1927. Three other marbles went to the Musée d'Orsay after 50 years in storage at the Louvre: G.J. Thomas's *Virgil* (1861); Carlès's *Youth* (1885); and Cavelier's *Cornelia, Mother of the Gracchi* (1861).

In 1879 the French Senate, which had fled to Versailles during the Franco-Prussian War, returned to its home in the Luxembourg Palace. Coexistence with the museum proved difficult. France was criticized for being virtually the only country in which contemporary art had 'no home of its own'. The Senate offered to hand over its Orangerie and to enlarge it, and the new construction was inaugurated on 1 April 1886 by Jules Grévy, President of the Republic, who noted in his remarks: 'The Senate has recognized with enlightened patriotism that the more a love of the Fine Arts spreads among the masses, the less this love should be refused the means to express itself expansively under a republican government.' The enlarged Orangerie was thus the first fine arts museum in Paris to benefit from new construction, although the Le Havre museum had been inaugurated 46 and the Amiens museum 20 years earlier. Visitors entered by crossing a small courtyard facing the rue de Vaugirard. In 1886, the year of Jean Moréas's Symbolist Manifesto, there were 95 sculptures at the Luxembourg. By 1887 there were over a hundred.

The first non-French sculptures were acquired in 1890. It had taken 27 years for Philippe de Chennevière's wish to be realized, through Belgian Constantin Meunier. Two of the latter's bronzes were acquired from a new Salon held by the Société Nationale des Beaux-Arts – an avant-garde offshoot of the Société des Artistes Français – whose first Salon was held in 1890.

In 1892 Etienne Arago was succeeded by Léonce Bénédite, who had served as his assistant since 1886. Bénédite remained in charge until his death in 1925, and in 1893 he proudly opened the museum to *objets d'art*, in order, in his words, to 'extend to the Luxembourg, in a fitting way, the marvels of the Gallery of Apollo'. Two masterpieces were acquired that year, Rodin's *Danaïd* and Daumier's *The Old Campaigner*. There were some problems with the latter: the committee was reluctant to exhibit 'this interesting figure whose particular merits nonetheless are inconsistent with the aesthetic character of the Luxembourg Museum'. In 1905 the museum acquired its first work by Bourdelle, a bronze *Head of Beethoven* (1903).

A Transit Museum

The works of living artists replaced those of recently deceased artists, but where were the latter works to go? Allocation was based on perceived quality. At the conclusion of the extended ten-year grace period, those judged best went to the Louvre, and the rest were returned to the National Depository. The best of these were then donated to provincial museums, and the second-

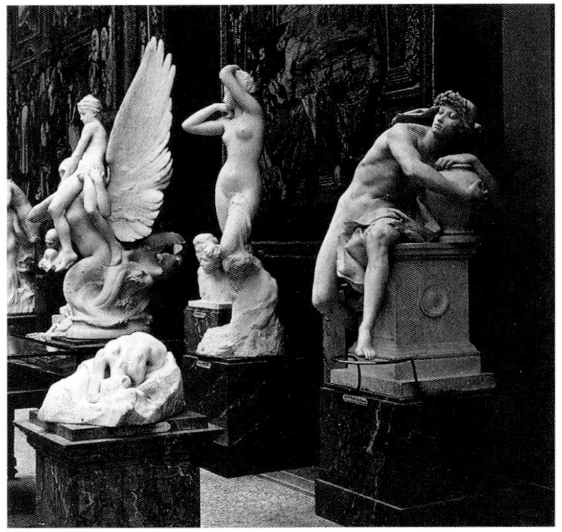

A gallery at the Luxembourg Museum. Denys Puech's *Siren* (1890) was sent to Bort-les-Orgues in 1953; Gustave Michel's *In a Dream* (1898) to Longwy; Saint-Marceaux's *Genius Guarding the Secret of the Grave* (1879) is exhibited at the Musée d'Orsay; and Rodin's *Danaïd* (1890), left foreground, was sent to the Rodin Museum in 1919.

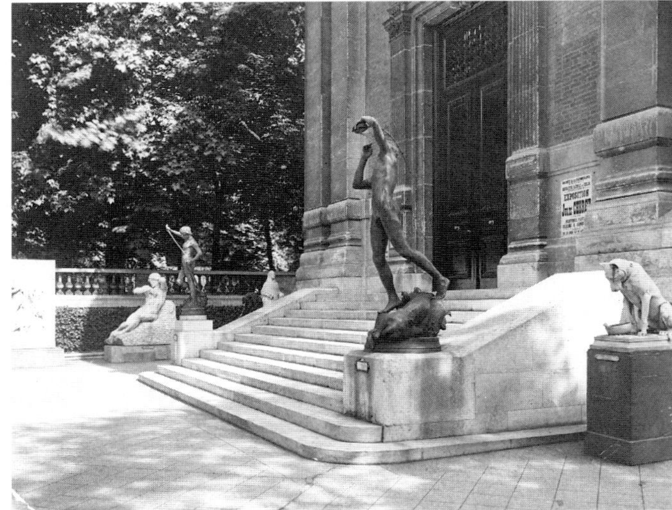

In order to free space, sculptures were transferred outdoors, either in the gardens or, as here, in the courtyard of the Luxembourg Museum. Only one is still at the Musée d'Orsay. From left to right: Georges Bareau, *Humanity Awakens* (1906), Barentin; Mercié, *David* (1871), Orsay; Henri Peinte, *Orpheus Lulling Cerberus to Sleep* (1888), Cambrai; Stanislas Lami, *Great Dane* (1892), Miramas.

best to public properties such as city halls and municipal parks, or sent through the National Trust to French embassies abroad. The relatives of deceased artists strongly objected to any location other than the Louvre, but grudgingly accepted the Tuileries Gardens.

Despite this periodic 'dispersal', the problem of space became crucial, even though the National Museum Advisory Committee in 1886 limited the number of works per artist to three. 'A fourth acquisition will replace one of the three others, which will then be sent to the provinces bearing the distinguished label: «Formerly displayed in the Luxembourg Museum».'

Another solution, skimming off some of the cream, explains the existence of the Rodin Museum.

Paris, the Rodin Museum

Despite the three-works-per-artist rule, Rodin had 38 at the Luxembourg during his lifetime. Almost all were subsequently transferred to the Rodin Museum, opened in 1919 in the town house built by Jacques Gabriel and Jean Aubert for Abraham Peyrenc de Moras in 1728. The Austrian poet Rainer Maria Rilke introduced Rodin to this masterpiece of rococo architecture standing in a 'neglected garden where innocent rabbits gambol among the trellises as if in some antique tapestry'. Rodin settled on the ground floor. The sale and subdivision of the garden were stopped thanks to a publicity campaign waged by Rodin's biographer Judith Cladel. Rodin agreed to leave his own work and collections to the nation and to restore the house, which in exchange would be converted into a museum. Thanks to these petitions, the nation acquired the house in 1911.

The wings built by the Duchesse de Maine and the Order of the Sacred Heart were destroyed in 1912. During World War I the minister Etienne Clémentel supported legislation, passed in 1916, accepting the donations offered by Rodin, who died in November 1917. By 1921 the Rodin Museum had welcomed 20,000 visitors. The garden was listed as a historical monument in 1926. However, the problem for the Musée d'Orsay was how to explain the history of sculpture without Rodin – although no one wanted to deplete the Rodin Museum. The solution was to leave *The Kiss, The Danaïd* and other works by Rodin from the Luxembourg at the Rodin Museum, and to transfer the marbles *Madame Vicuña* and *Thought* plus three bronzes to the Musée d'Orsay, along with four large plaster casts contributed by the Rodin Museum.

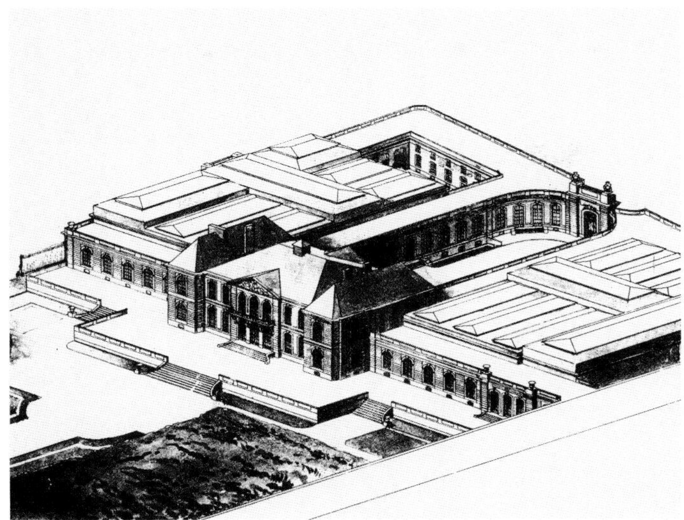

Henri Eustache (1861–1922). Prix de Rome, 1891. Proposal for a museum of contempory art to be erected on the site of the Rodin Museum (1917–20). French National Archives.

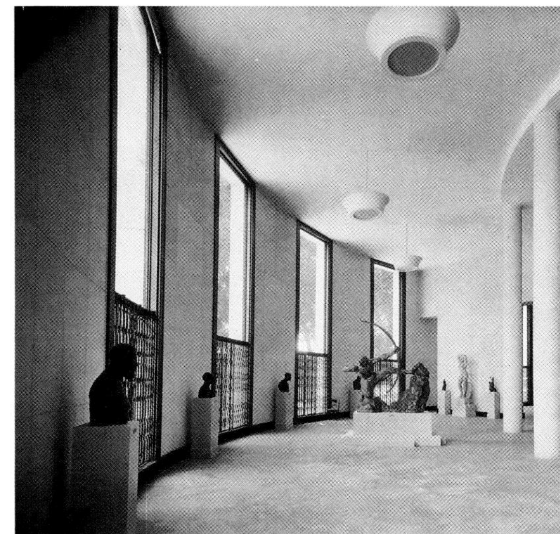

The Bourdelle Gallery with *Hercules the Archer.* Paris, Palais de Tokyo, National Museum of Modern Art, 1947.

Jeu de Paume, Museum of Foreign Art

Works by foreigners, eventually forming a separate group in their own right, which Bénédite displayed in turns, were also creamed off from the Luxembourg Museum. In 1922 the Museum of Foreign Art was opened at the Jeu de Paume in the Tuileries Gardens. Directed after Bénédite's death by André Dezarrois, this museum became autonomous in 1931 but was forced to close in 1940. Regrettably, and no doubt due to the war, this museum lost works by the English sculptors Alfred Drury and Alfred Gilbert, the Belgian Jules Van Biesbroeck, the Norwegian Stephen Sinding and the Czechoslovakian Joseph Vaclav Myslbek.

In 1927 the Luxembourg's print collection was transferred to the Bibliothèque Nationale by the museum's curator Louis Hautecoeur, who declared in the catalogue of 1931, 'The Luxembourg has neither space for them, nor staff to catalogue and inventory them, nor any way to exhibit them'.

Towards a new museum of modern art?

When the old Saint-Sulpice seminary was vacated due to the separation of Church and State, its premises were immediately coveted because of their proximity to the Luxembourg Museum. On 8 January 1907 the Conseil des Ministres approved a proposition to convert them into a museum, and Bénédite was already giving his Ecole du Louvre courses on 19th-century art there. In October 1911 a budget of 200,000 francs was approved for the project. M. de Ruaz, newly appointed official architect, drew up the blueprints: sculpture on the ground floor, in an inner courtyard to be glassed in as a winter garden; Rodin's *Gate to the Inferno* in the chapel. Like a latter-day Julius II commissioning the Sistine Chapel ceiling from Michelangelo, Dujardin-Beaumetz in 1910 commissioned frescoes from Rodin to complete the chapel's decor. However, the building ultimately went to the Minisitry of Finance – which still has it today.

Between 1917 and 1920, Henri Eustache came up with a new plan for a National Museum of Contemporary Art at the Rodin Museum, and Louis Bonnier suggested a rotunda in the gardens for Monet's *Water Lilies.* This would have brought together all the French and foreign collections from the Luxembourg Museum, but it was not to be.

Meanwhile, works of art continued to pile up at the Luxembourg. Of the 278 sculptures listed in the catalogue of 1914, some 120 were acquired after 1900.

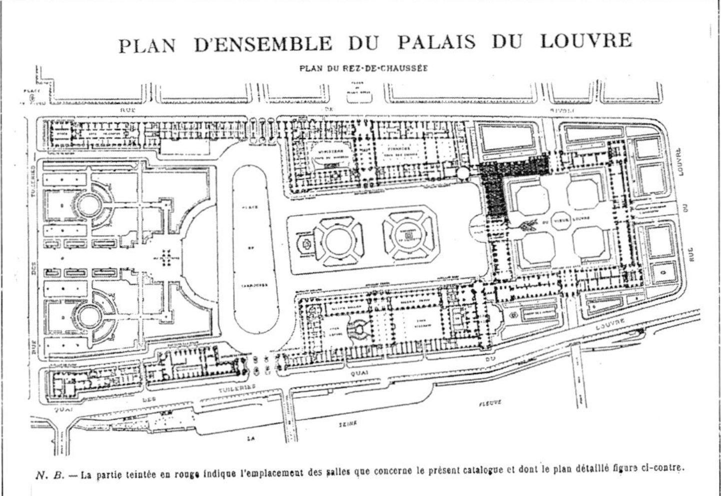

Location of modern sculpture on the north-west ground-floor corner of the Cour Carrée of the Louvre, 1922.

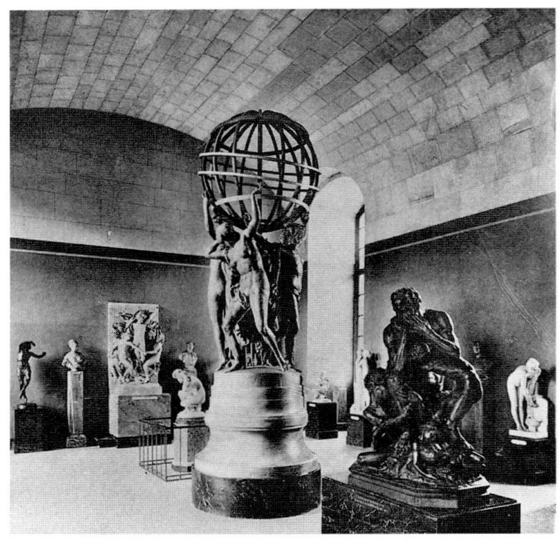

The Carpeaux Room on the north side of the Cour Carrée of the Louvre, c.1900.

The first Maillol, *The Cyclist*, was acquired in 1923, and seven works by Bourdelle were acquired by the museum during the latter's lifetime.

In 1929 Louis Hautecoeur and Pierre Ladoué refurbished the displays. Tapestries were returned to Les Gobelins, walls painted in light colours, sculptures cleaned. Some of the decidedly mixed reactions to this initiative were recorded in pencil in a catalogue of 1931 now in the Musée d'Orsay library, where they give a fair picture of contemporary tastes. Comments range from 'mediocre' (Georges Gardet, Landowski, Serruys, Sicard), to 'bad' (Bloch, Blondat, Alfred Boucher, Convers, Greber, Houdain, H. Lefebvre, C. Lefèvre, Monard, Rivoire, Roche, Sarrabezolles, Verhnes), to 'very bad' (Coutan, Dampt, Octobre, Puech), 'disastrous' (Gasq) and 'dreadful' (Dardé).

Henceforth all acquisitions had to be passed by a special commission created by government decree on 7 February 1929 (the idea had been first proposed in 1905). Collections were to be reviewed every three years: 'The Luxembourg Museum is a living museum. We cannot hold acquisitions in perpetuity', as Hautecoeur and Ladoué put it in the catalogue of 1931.

In 1934 the Commissariat General of the 1937 World's Fair sponsored a competition for a Museum of Modern Art in which Hautecoeur was not involved. The winner was the Palais de Tokyo, which in 1937 exhibited *Masterpieces of French Art*. A subsequent plan to place painting and sculpture in the west wing, belonging to the Nation, and decorative arts in the east wing, belonging to the City of Paris, was not pursued. The two separate Museums of Modern Art, one national and one municipal, both with large, high-ceilinged, well-lit galleries, stood facing each other. The Luxembourg Museum closed during World War II, but the National Museum of Modern Art was opened temporarily in 1942 by Ladoué, and permanently in 1945 by Jean Cassou, who had been ousted by the Vichy government. The most modern works remained in the Luxembourg. In the catalogue of 1947 by Jean Cassou, Bernard Dorival and Geneviève Homolle appeared reproductions of Bourdelle's *Hercules the Archer*, Maillol's *Desire* and Pompon's *Mighty Stag*.

The Impressionist Museum at the Jeu de Paume

However, the Palais de Tokyo on the avenue du Président Wilson was not the only home of modernity. In 1947 the Impressionist Museum in the Tuileries Gardens was inaugurated, and until 10 August 1986 it housed a partial but fascinating chronicle of modern art in which sculpture played only a minor role. The catalogue of 1947 listed only one work by Dalou, seven by Degas

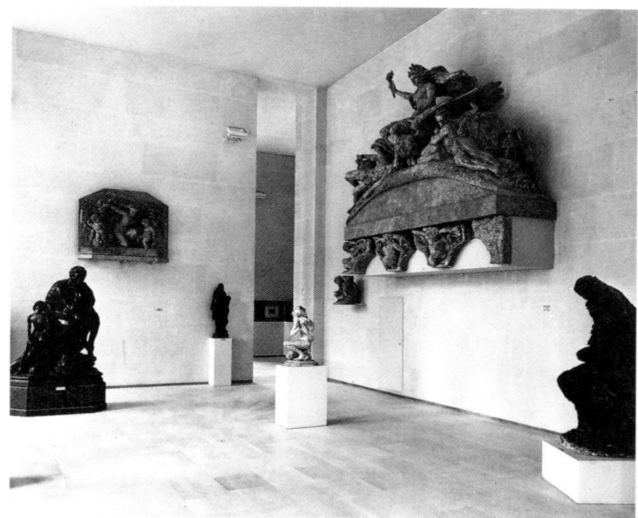

The Carpeaux Room in the Pavillon de Flore in 1970. Empty spaces predominate. The pedestals were wood, painted white, and the sculptures displayed as close to the ground as possible.

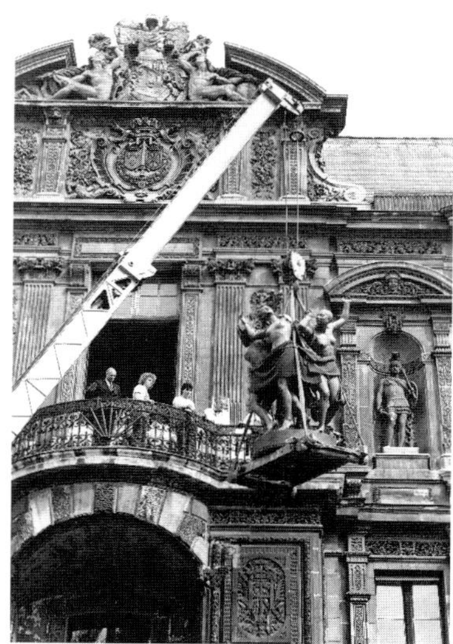

Removal of the model for Carpeaux's *Four Quarters of the World Bearing the Celestial Sphere* from the Grande Galerie of the Louvre in September 1986.

and five by Rodin – but even they did not remain there for long. Because of their painterly qualities, only the *Young Dancer of Fourteen* by Degas and the Gauguin sculptures were retained.

Thus, in a sort of atonement for the previous over-emphasis on official art, these museums exemplified the new credo: avant-garde on one side, Impressionists on the other. The fruits of the 'historical century' were roundly condemned and (if they were lucky) consigned for 50 years to cellars and attics.

The National Museum at the Château de Versailles

There are portrait galleries in England and the United States, but no single one in France, where portraits are almost hidden away in two separate places. Portraits on paper are kept in the print room of the Bibliothèque Nationale, and painted or sculpted portraits at the Château de Versailles, dedicated in 1837 by Louis-Philippe 'To all the glories of France'. Although most of the thousands of busts in the Château's holdings are in storage, they are now at least indirectly accessible thanks to Simone Hoog's and Roland Bossard's catalogue of 1993, which lists these sculptures alphabetically by subject.

The Louvre

The Louvre's modern sculpture collection was begun only in 1824, with the creation of the Galerie d'Angoulême on the western ground-floor side of the Cour Carrée. In 1875 the architect Hector Lefuel extended it northwards into the apartment formerly occupied by General Lepic. In the wake of Coysevox, Puget, the Coustous, Bouchardon and Houdon, a room of their own was given to Rude in 1880 and to Carpeaux in 1900 – a signal honour won by Chapu and Cavelier in 1908. Generous collectors vied with each other in largesse: the Thomy-Thiery room opened in 1906, the Chauchard collection was acquired in 1910, and the two Zoubaloff rooms devoted to Barye in 1913–14.

Paul Vitry, named curator of sculpture in 1920 after having served as André Michel's assistant since 1905, published the catalogue that bears his name in 1922. On the diagram, 19th-century sculpture extends to the Marengo archway. Because medieval and Renaissance works on the south side of the Cour Carrée were separated from modern ones, plans were formed to move everything and to unite the collections in a new exhibition area. After the major renovations of 1931, sculpture was moved to the ground-floor gallery on the

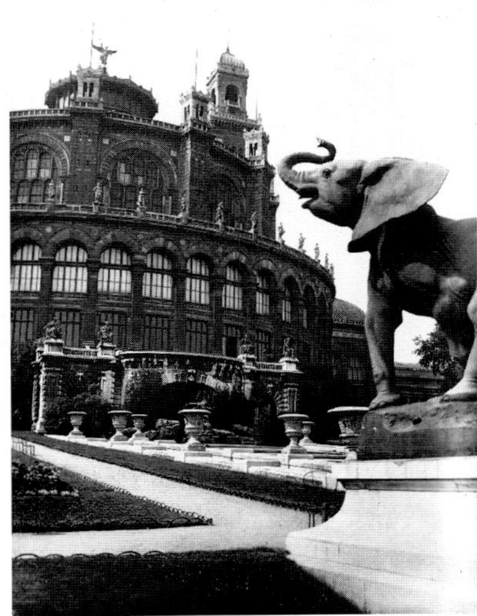

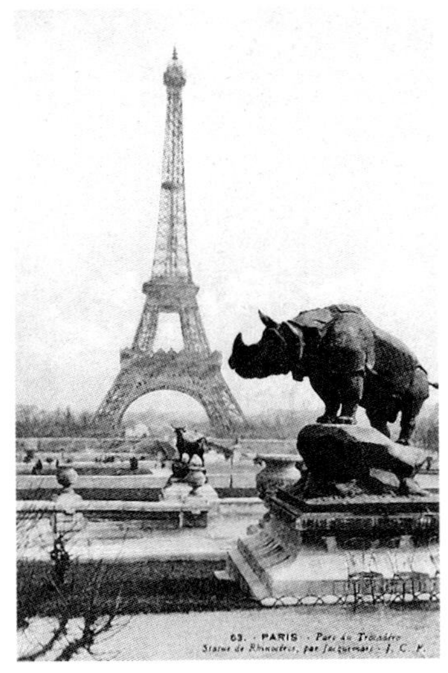

The Trocadéro Palace in 1878. In the foreground, Fremiet's *Young Elephant Caught in a Trap*. Behind, on the balcony, the six *Continents*: *Europe* (Schoenewerk); *Asia* (Falguière); *Africa* (Delaplanche); *North America* (Hiolle); *Oceania* (Mathurin Moreau, left); *South America* (Millet, right).

Jacquemart's *Rhinoceros* below the Trocadero waterfall in 1878; opposite the Eiffel Tower in 1889. Successive World's Fairs account for its transfer to the opposite bank of the Seine.

river side, with a special entrance at the Porte de la Tremoïlle under the Carrousel archways. Medieval and Renaissance sculpture was magnificently exhibited, reflecting meticulous research by Léon de Laborde, Louis Courajod, and Paul Vitry. Twentieth-century sculpture remained in storage, waiting until the Louvre could recover the Pavillon de Flore. An initial attempt to do so was made on 19 September 1910, but the National Lottery was 'temporarily' occupying the premises. It was not until the second attempt, spearheaded by André Malraux on 13 November 1961, that the Ministry of Finance finally relinquished it. It had taken 51 years.

The Pavillon de Flore was inaugurated in 1969, but its exhibition of 19th-century works was notable for the dearth of works representing the second half of the century. Carpeaux reigned supreme, amid two works by Chapu – a bust of *Bonnat* and a study for *Youth*; two by Falguière – *Tarcisius* and *Winner of the Cockfight*; one by Fremiet – *Saint George*; and a few studies.

The Musée d'Orsay

Plans to convert the Gare d'Orsay into a museum were drawn up at the Louvre in 1972. First, because the Impressionists had outgrown the Jeu de Paume, and because the National Museum of Modern Art (scheduled to open in 1976 at the Centre Georges Pompidou) needed to weed out some of its older works; and, second, the huge disaffected railway station just seemed too good to let go. 'This station looks like a Palace of Fine Arts', wrote the painter Detaille in 1900, and time was to prove his words prophetic. Politics were also involved. Georges Pompidou had given his name to the National Centre of Art and Culture at the Beaubourg, and now Valéry Giscard d'Estaing wanted a monument – but this time for the 19th century. His proposal of October 1977 was approved in 1978 by a legislative bill for museum planning. A strict budget of 363,000,000 francs was allocated, but due to revisions of the original plan under the next president, it was increased three-fold (to 1,340,000,000 francs) and the period covered by the museum reduced to 1848–1914. This was because it would be impossible to exhibit romantic paintings – particularly the larger works by Delacroix – in a railway station with limited hanging possibilities. Inclusion was based on the artists' date of birth. Works by artists born before 1820 would go to the Louvre; between 1820–70, to the Musée d'Orsay; and after 1870, to the National Museum of Modern Art. A few exceptions were made to reduce the arbitrary nature of the criterion, which would have eliminated precursors and followers. To the Musée d'Orsay, for example, went Clésinger, Courbet, Daumier and

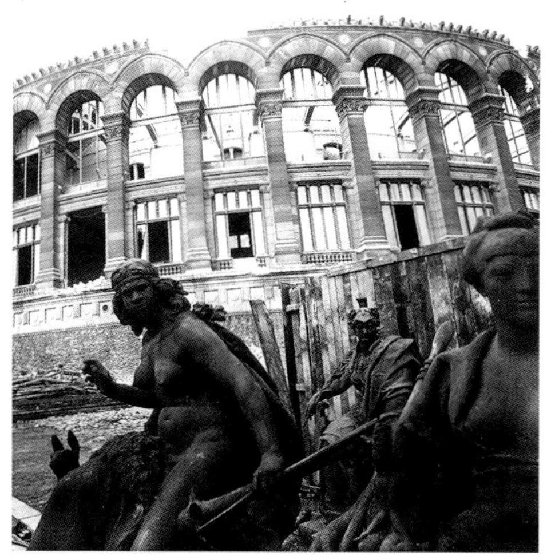

Destruction of the central portion of the Trocadéro in 1878 and modernization of the wings for the World's Fair of 1937. The *Continents* were placed in storage in 1935 and then sent to the City of Nantes.

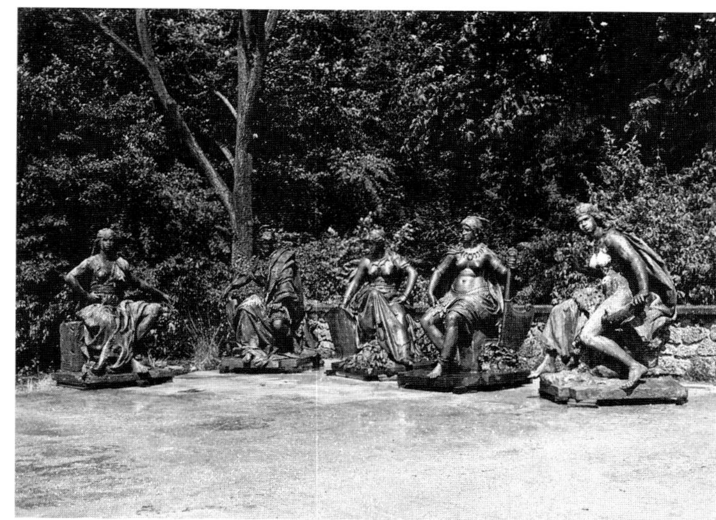

Rediscovered in 1977 in the public dump where they had lain since 1963 (because sculpture interferes with road traffic), the *Continents* were restored in 1985 by the Musée d'Orsay, which sought to reconstruct the 1878 decor of the Trocadéro Palace.

Meissonier – all born before 1820; while Matisse (born in 1869) assumed his proper place in the Pompidou Centre.

The Gare d'Orsay was like a great empty vessel. How to fill it? The placing of the Impressionist collection was a key issue in the deliberations, but Victor Laloux's vaulted space was also recognized as a work of art in its own right. The six architects invited to participate in the competition of 1978 were told that the vault had to remain visible. But what could be exhibited beneath it? This is where sculpture came in. Only sculpture could resist the sun pouring through the skylight, the shifting light, the crowds of visitors. However, the collection would have to be a substantial one. Where to find it? There were the works displayed in the Louvre, whose number (103) we had augmented, and the even greater number (790) in storage. There were the works (184) returned by the National Museum of Modern Art in 1977 and 1983. We borrowed from the Museum of African and Oceanic Art (6), the Museum of Decorative Arts (4), the Rodin Museum (9), the National Museum of Versailles (10), the Architecture Division of the Paris Opera (28), the Thiers Library (3), the National Trust (1), the Department of Historic Monuments (1) and the Senate (2). The most daunting task was scouring the storage areas to which sculptures had been relegated over the past 100 years because they took up too much space. This task involved field work and research. Field work, to find the sculptures in the hideaways where they had languished for so long, to select the best ones, measure and photograph them. And research in order to create our archives, which had to be done from scratch. Without this pre-catalogue, as it were, we would not have been able to get very far. Through our detective work we reclaimed 20 sculptures from the old Luxembourg Museum, and transferred to the Musée d'Orsay 51 sculptures that had been sent to the provinces by the Department of Artistic Creation. The list of works needing restoration grew by leaps and bounds. Two-way traffic was heavy.

Through an exchange agreement the Musée d'Orsay won Cabanel's large canvas *Paolo and Francesca* in return for Dalou's terra-cotta group *Reading* and Carpeaux's *Woodland Laughter*, which joined the extensive sculpture collection in the Amiens Museum. Marseille had listed Préault's *Ophelia* for return to the National Depository, but we signalled the importance of the work we would thus be recovering by exchanging it for Signac's *Entrance to the Port of Marseille*. The Lyon Museum, on the other hand, was reluctant to hand over Rodin's *Man Walking*. We were obliged to offer two paintings, Cézanne's *The Bathers* and Camille Pissarro's *Kew Gardens*, to obtain it – and to bring it indoors. It had been exposed to wind and weather ever since its initial installation in the courtyard of the Palazzo Farnese in Rome in 1911. *Nature Revealed*

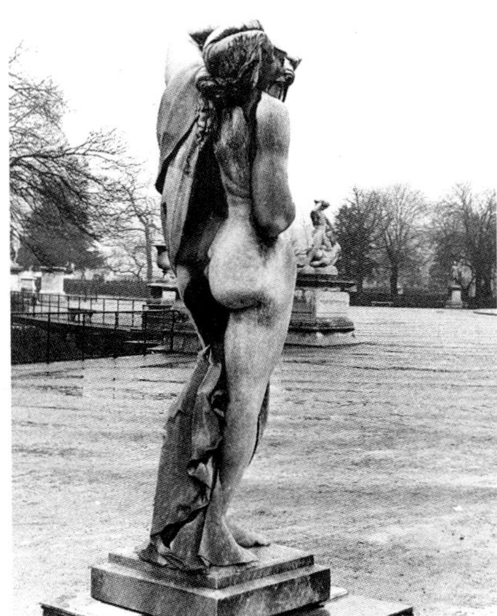

Ernest Christophe's *Human Comedy* (1859–76), which inspired canto XX of Baudelaire's *Fleurs du mal* was removed from the Tuileries Gardens in 1982 for restoration before being exhibited in the controlled environment of the Musée d'Orsay.

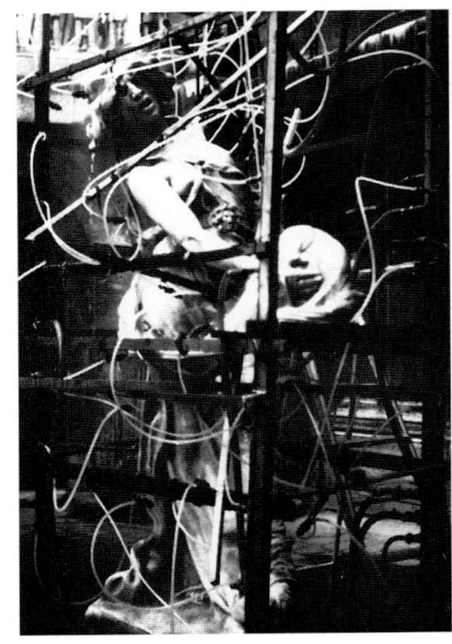

The sound but filthy marble of Victor Ségoffin's *Sacred Dance* (1905), from the National Depository, was sprayed with a fine mist of water for an entire month by the Louvre's marble specialists, in order to uncover its original whiteness.

to Science by Barrias, from a staircase at the Conservatoire des Arts et Métiers, was replaced with a copy.

It was easier to obtain works that were not publicly displayed. These included *Goethe* by David d'Angers, a gift from the sculptor to the City of Saumur where it languished in the turret of a château, visited only by pigeons; the large models by Barrias and Coutan for the museum, relegated to a disaffected gallery of the Ecole Nationale des Arts et Industries Textiles in Roubaix; Gérôme's *Gladiators* at the Fort du Mont-Valérien; Bartholomé's *Monument to Jean-Jacques Rousseau* in the municipal transport garage in Le Mans; and Schoenewerk's *Young Tarentine* in the old kitchens of the Château de Compiègne.

We found *The Continents* from the Trocadero Palace (1878) at the public dump where they had been discarded in 1963, but made the mistake of seeking authorization from the Nantes mayor's office. Interest breeds interest, and we had to offer Sisley's painting *Rainy Spring* to the Nantes Museum of Fine Arts in exchange for our find. We also, of course, had to pay for having the rusted, pock-marked casts restored, which was done by the Coubertin Foundry. This was also a wonderful opportunity to bring the most important sculptures in the Tuileries Gardens indoors, and to visit the cellars of the National Depository (then located on rue de la Manutention), where works had been stored because they were damaged.

One especially rewarding aspect of our work has been meeting the descendants of the 19th-century artists, and thus forging links with them spanning only one or two generations. The Musée d'Orsay owes the acquisition of many new sculptures to the generosity of the artists' families. Below we list donors' names, with the artist's name in parentheses if it differs from that of the donor:

1974: Françoise Du Castel (Paul Dubois); Catherine J. Tudor Hart.

1975: L'Ebé Bugatti, again in 1976 and 1979; the Carvin heirs.

1979: Widow of Pierre Schommer (Carpeaux); Mme Morel-Izambard (Gumery); Blanche Fauré-Fremiet; the Messrs Hugues.

1980: Mireille Godet; André Lwoff; Pierre Vidal; Cécile Armagnac (Bonnassieux); Jacques Thomas (Monard); Jean Bernard.

1981: Françoise Cachin (Alexandre Charpentier), again in 1988; Jean-Marie Desbordes (R. Bugatti); Mme Pajot-Villerelle (Cavelier); M. and Mme Ruprich-Robert.

1982: François Bonnassieux; Eiffel heirs; Dubufe heirs; Pierre Fix-Masseau.

1983: Mme Testard-Reclus (Bourdelle); Dr Ulmann (Hannaux).

1984: Jean du Pasquier (Meissonier).

1985: Mme Cointreau and Olivier Lefuel (Guillaume); Yvonne Prins.

1986: Mmes Guillaumin, Debaecker and Micheaux (Paulin); Dina Vierny (Maillol), again in 1992 and 1994; Mme G. Lomon-Hawkins (A. Charpentier).

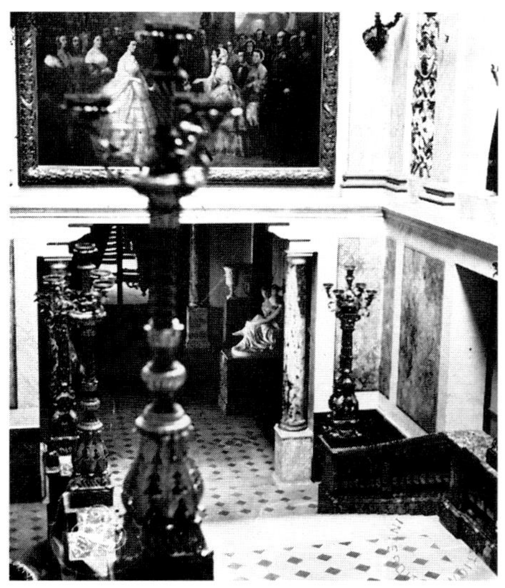

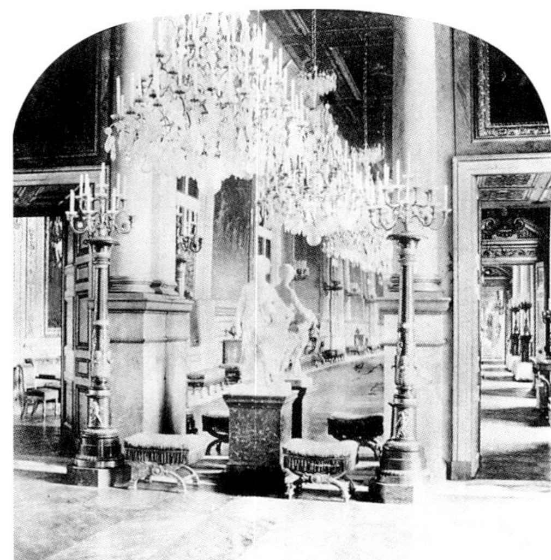

Pradier's *Sappho* (1852) was placed by Napoleon III at the entrance to the Palace of Saint-Cloud. Charles-Louis Müller's sycophantic painting of the *Meeting between the Empress Eugénie and Queen Victoria*, above it, was destroyed in 1871.

Carpeaux's *The Imperial Prince and his Dog* (1865), photographed between 1867 and the fire of May 1871 in the Galerie de Diane of the Tuileries Palace.

1987: Mme Barrez (Zoegger).
1988: Mme des Ylouses et Carnot (Marquet de Vasselot).
1989: Jeanne René-Demeurisse and Anne Demeurisse (Pompon).
1991: Philippe Amyot d'Inville (Maillard).
1992: Louis-Antoine Prat (Del'Bo); Gérard Thomann and Francine Libert (Gardet).
1993: Alain Sourdille (Richer).
1994: Agathe Rouart and François Valéry (Paul Valéry).

There are also donors who are unrelated to either the artists or the figures depicted:

1974: Mme René Martin; Mme Claude Grange; Le Masle bequest.
1975: M. Sokolowski.
1977: Ulysse Moussali.
1978: Charles Kunstler bequest.
1979: Marcel Beurdeley bequest; Mme Lacaze-Serre and M. Tournadre; Bruno Foucart.
1982: Michel Laclotte; M. Fetrot; Annie Caubet; Mme Schlumberger; André Lemaire, again in 1988 and 1990; Emmanuel Bréon.
1983: Jacques and Elisabeth Foucart.
1984: Patrice Bellanger.
1985: Les Amis du Musée d'Orsay (whose generosity has been renewed almost annually); Pasteur bequest; Marie Geneviève de la Coste Messelière; Pierre Rosenberg; Pomme de Mirimonde bequest.
1986: Raisa Gorbacheva; Mme Cabanel.
1987: Barlach and Laurence Heuer; Christian Reiss; Mme Damiens.
1990: Georges Poisson.
1992: Paul Mellon and the Foundation for French Museums, Inc., in memory of Emmanuel de Margerie.
1994: Georges-Guillaume Cassan.

Between 1972 and 1994 the museum received 302 gifts to help defray expenses for particularly costly acquisitions. Among the most famous works in this category are Gauguin's polychrome woodcarving *Be Mysterious* (1978); Daumier's *The Parliamentarians* (1980), thanks to Michel David-Weill and the Lutèce Foundation; Camille Claudel's *Maturity* and Lacombe's *Isis* (1982); the fifth and final panel of Gauguin's hut *The House of Pleasure* (1990). We regret that Chapu's *Tomb of the Duchesse de Nemours*, acquired at auction in London in 1993, did not receive an exit visa from England, forcing us to retire in favour of the Walker Art Gallery in Liverpool.

Over 650 of the 1,200 sculptures collected for the opening of the Musée d'Orsay are currently on display. However, another 1,200 works that once formed part of the national collections are dispersed, sometimes in precarious circumstances.

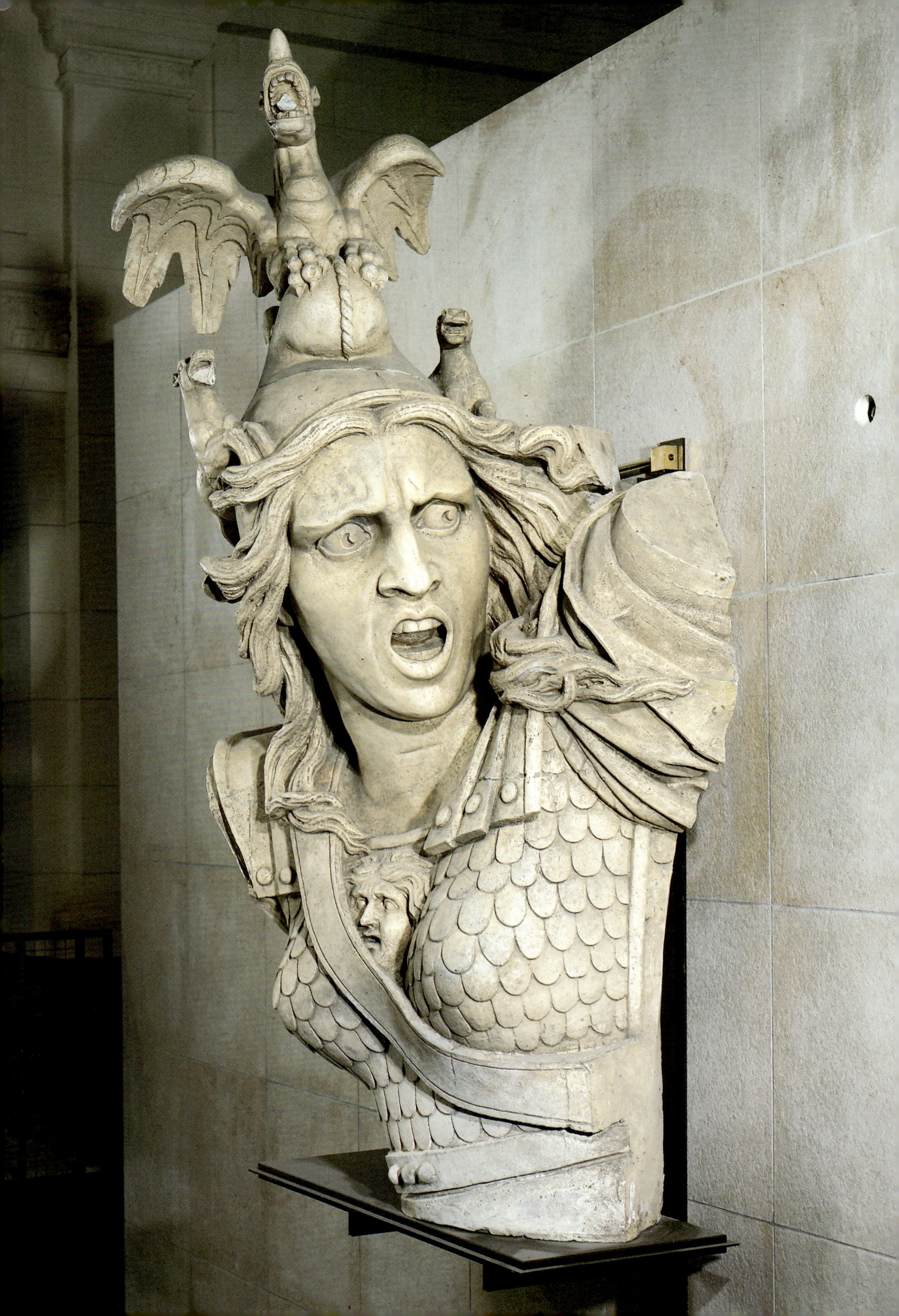

Romanticism in the Second Half of the 19th Century

The preference for feeling over reason gave birth to the kind of romanticism that characterizes periods of youthful uncertainty and historic upheaval. Is sculpture a fertile ground for the expression of this anguish? As icons of stability, statues would seem as ill-fitted to the expression of transitory passion as to the romantic aesthetic avowed by the sculptor Préault: 'I am for the infinite, not the finished'; and yet Préault was able to deliver a complicated message through subterfuges of matter and manner, bronze and relief.

Lagging far behind the sister arts of painting and literature, romantic sculpture reached its apogée in the 1830s, although masterpieces were still being produced under the Second Empire. Romantic values lived on, expressed through the torments of sensitive heroes, nostalgia for the Middle Ages, and the supremacy of literature. However, as a tribute to the 1830s, the Musée d'Orsay chose as its standard-bearer Rude's *Spirit of the Motherland*, a work familiar to the people of France as *Marseillaise*. In order to endow the work with energy, Rude altered the form: 'I believe I have succeeded this time because there is something in it that makes my own soul go hot and cold.'

Rude and David d'Angers, who both died in the 1850s, are prominently displayed at the Musée d'Orsay in order to underscore their role as masters – although much of their work is housed in the Louvre, at Dijon and at Angers. The aim of David d'Angers was to embody the genius of men he admired in sculpted portraits. As he wrote in one of his notebooks: 'The task of sculpture ... is to express ... the poetry, the apotheosis of a noble soul.' This was an allusion to his visit to Weimar in 1829, where he modeled a colossal head of *Goethe* featuring the broad brow of a universal sage and 'neck muscles that become auxiliaries of the brain'.

The 19th century has been called the historical century, the century of retrospective consideration. This backward glance was often accompanied and sometimes stimulated by the arts. The Museum of National Antiquities opened in Saint-Germain-en-Laye, and Napoleon III wrote a book about Caesar and expressed interest in the latter's Gallic adversary, Vercingétorix; although he paid for Aimé Millet's statue of the Gallic chieftain shown meditating at Alésia on the eve of battle, the emperor did not live long enough to have this monument to the victor of Gergovia erected. While Bartholdi can be considered a historical realist, there is an obviously romantic quality in the gigantism of some of his works, and in the spirit of his *Vercingétorix* astride a winged steed – a group that was to measure some 35 metres in length. The visionary Préault, who dreamed of taking on an Auvergne volcano, was even more ambitious.

Literature was a fertile source of inspiration for romantic sculpture, and Préault's *Ophelia* offers a consummate example of the reaction to neoclassicism. The subject is Shakespearean rather than mythological, despair has replaced self-discipline, and formal equilibrium is destroyed by the drift of the figure's hair in the eddying water and the drapery swirling around the curve of the drowning body. A fleeting moment of drama has become more important than eternal verities.

François Rude
Dijon 1784–
Paris 1855
Spirit of the Motherland
Plaster haut-relief.
2.24 x 1.96 x 0.90 m
Mould taken for the City of Dijon from *Departure of the Volunteers in 1792* on the Arc de Triomphe at the Etoile, 1898;
Dijon Musée des Beaux-Arts
Depository to Orsay, 1985.
DO 1985-2

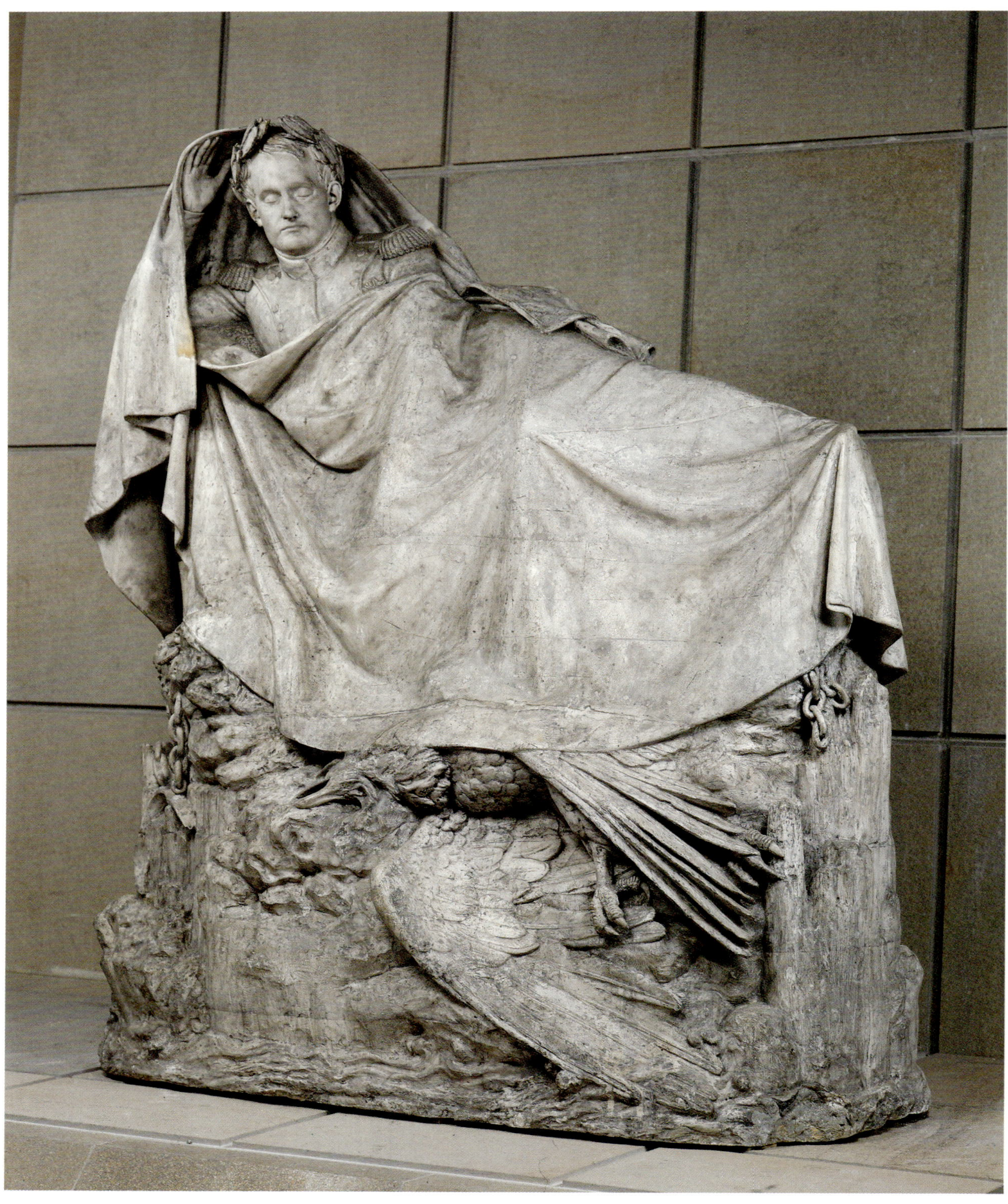

François Rude
Dijon 1784 – Paris 1855
Napoleon Awakening to Immortality, 1846
Original plaster model. 2.15 x 1.95 x 0.96 m
Commission from Noisot, who had been Captain of the Grenadiers on the Island of Elba, for the grounds of his estate at Fixin (Côte d'Or).
Model acquired from M. Montagny, 1892; Louvre, 1892;
Orsay Depository, 1986.
RF 904

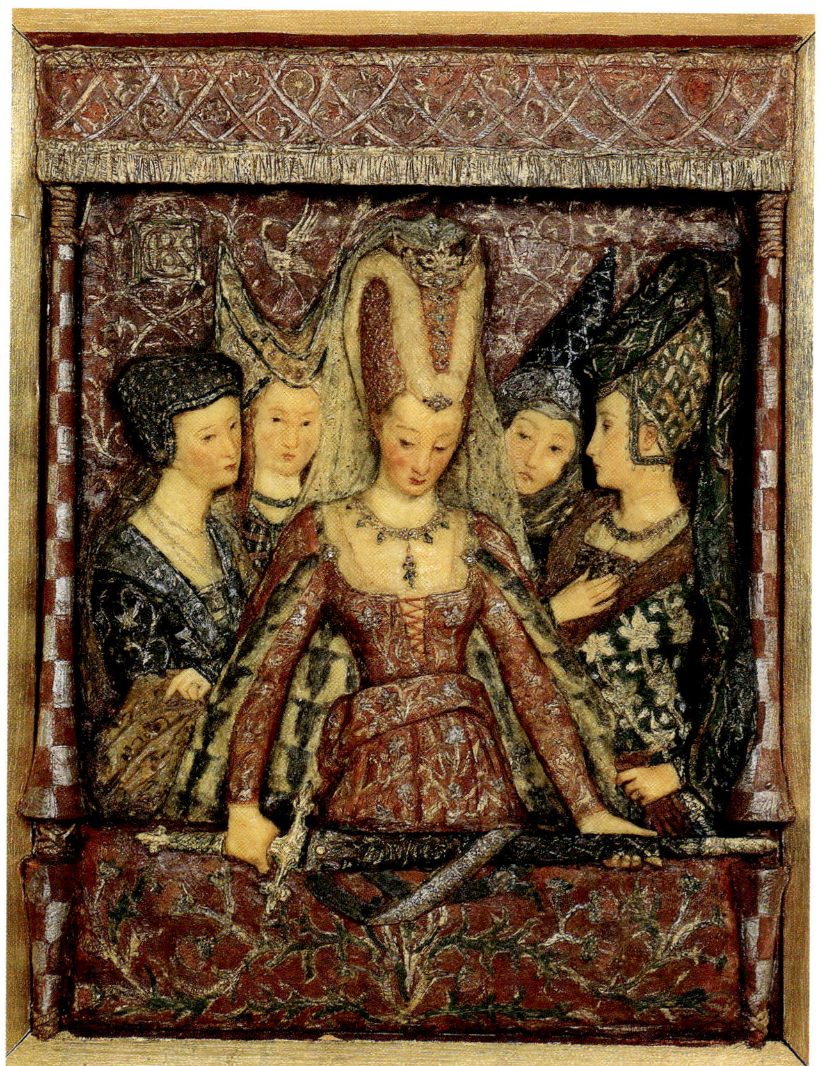

Henry Cros
Narbonne 1840 – Sèvres 1907
The Tournament Prize, 1873
Polychrome wax and pearl bas-relief.
1.25 x 1.095 x 0.20 m
Acquired by the Nation from the 1873 Salon;
Avignon Calvet Museum, 1873; Orsay, 1981.
REF 3661

Frédéric-August Bartholdi
Colmar 1834 – Paris 1904
Vercingétorix, 1870
Plaster study. 0.18 x 0.21 x 0.06 m
Gift from Osiris to Malmaison, 1906;
Orsay, 1982.
A 4 meters bronze was erected
in the Place de Jaude
in Clermont-Ferrand in 1903.
MDO 51

The eagle has expired on the sea-battered rocks of St Helena, but his chain is severed. In epaulettes and laurel wreath, the emperor emerges from his shroud in a strange pose reminiscent of the prone figures propped on their elbows we associate with the Renaissance.

The Second Empire was so obsessed with the Middle Ages that the Château of Pierrefonds was actually rebuilt. Although Henry Cros has been claimed by the symbolists as one of their own, his *Tournament Prize* is as reminiscent of an illuminated medieval manuscript as it is of the Restoration's troubadour style.

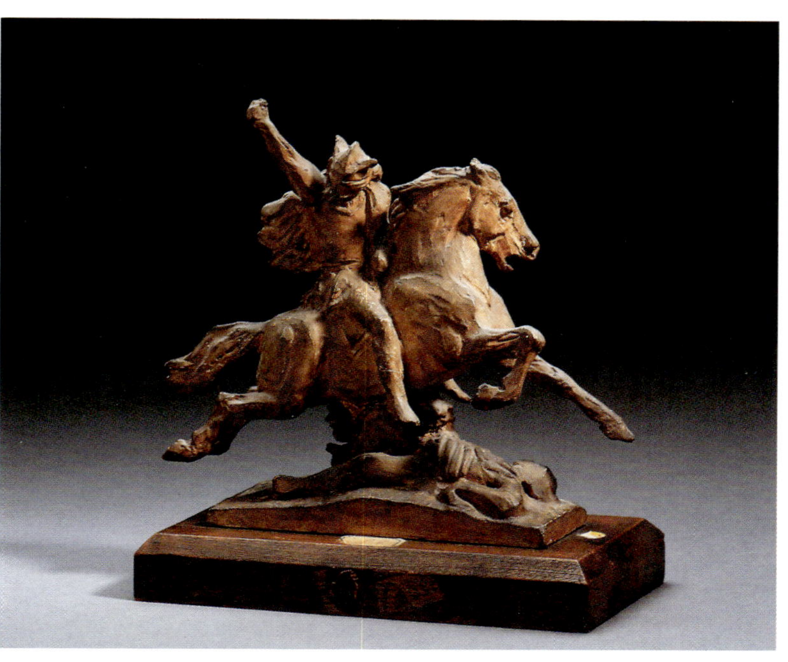

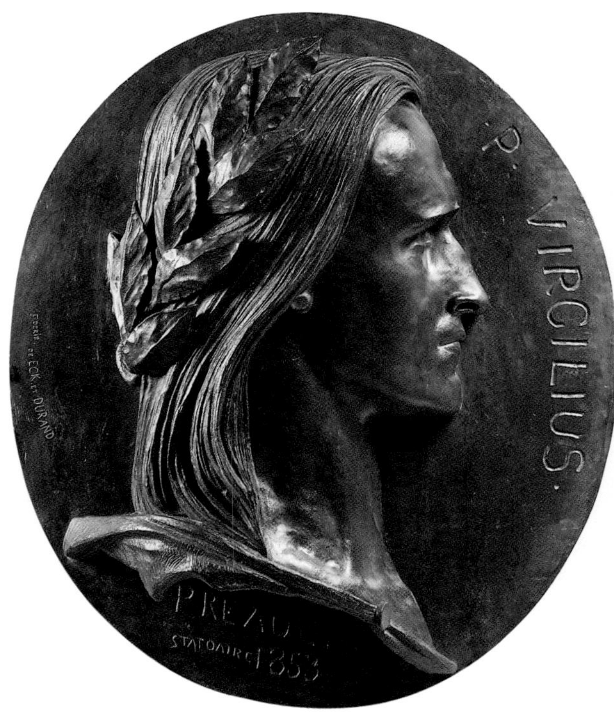

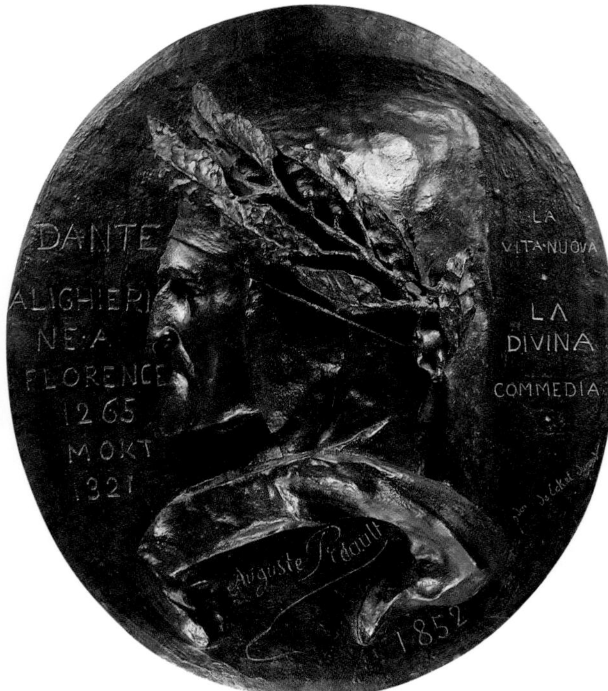

Auguste Préault
Paris 1809 – Paris 1879
Dante, 1852; *Virgil*, 1853.
Bronze medallions cast by Eck & Durand. 0.95 x 0.855 x 0.23 m
Acquired by Napoleon III from the 1853 Salon; guardhouse of the Louvre; Orsay, 1986.
RF 2, RF 3

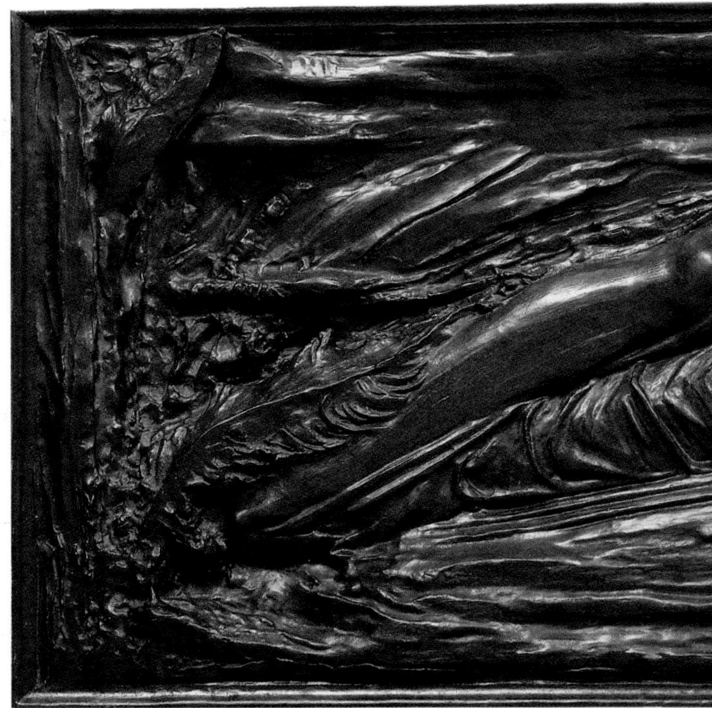

Auguste Préault
Paris 1809 – Paris 1879
Ophelia, 1842–76
Bronze bas-relief cast by Thiébaut & fils. 0.75 x 2 x 0.20 m
Commission from the Nation, 1876; 1876 Salon; Marseille Museum, 1878; Orsay, 1982.
RF 3641

Dante exerted a strong influence on 19th-century artists. Those French who could not read Italian turned to an old 18th-century translation by Rivarol. Contemporary imaginations were inflamed by the graphic details of the *Inferno*, with Carpeaux and Rodin both falling under its spell. It is therefore fitting that when visitors embark on their journey through the Musée d'Orsay, they are greeted by the two protagonists of the *Divine Comedy*, classical poet *Virgil* and modern poet *Dante*.
In his treatise *Le Génie du Christianisme* Chateaubriand created the character Velléda, a Druid priestess who dies of love for Eudorus the Christian. In Maindron's statue (1839) of her in the Luxembourg gardens (replica of 1871 in the Louvre) she is shown contemplating her beloved's home.

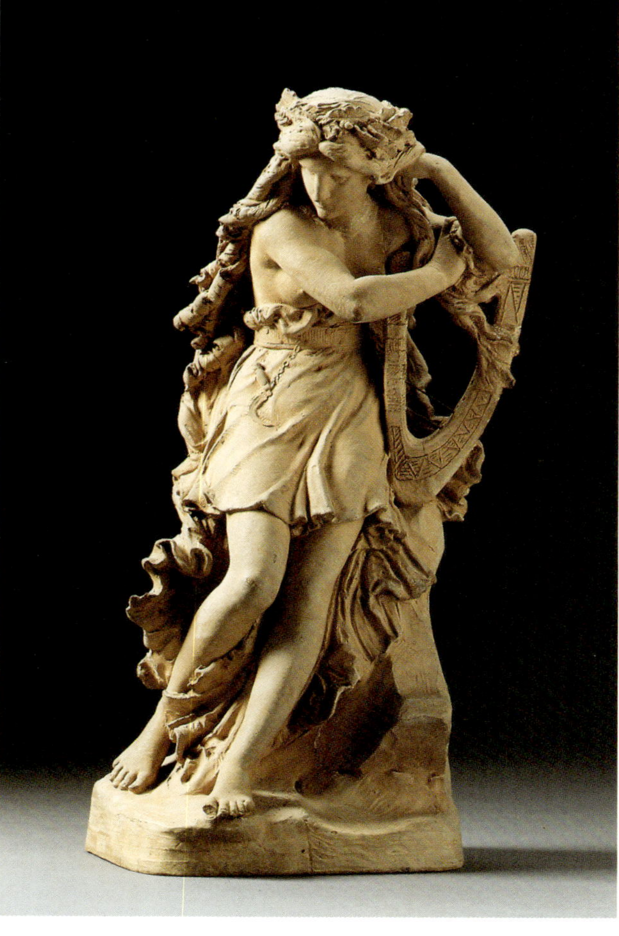

François Lepère
Paris 1824 – ? 1871
Velléda, c.1860
Terra-cotta study. 0.50 x 0.262 x 0.19 m
Acquired in 1976;
Louvre, 1976; Orsay, 1986.
RF 3087

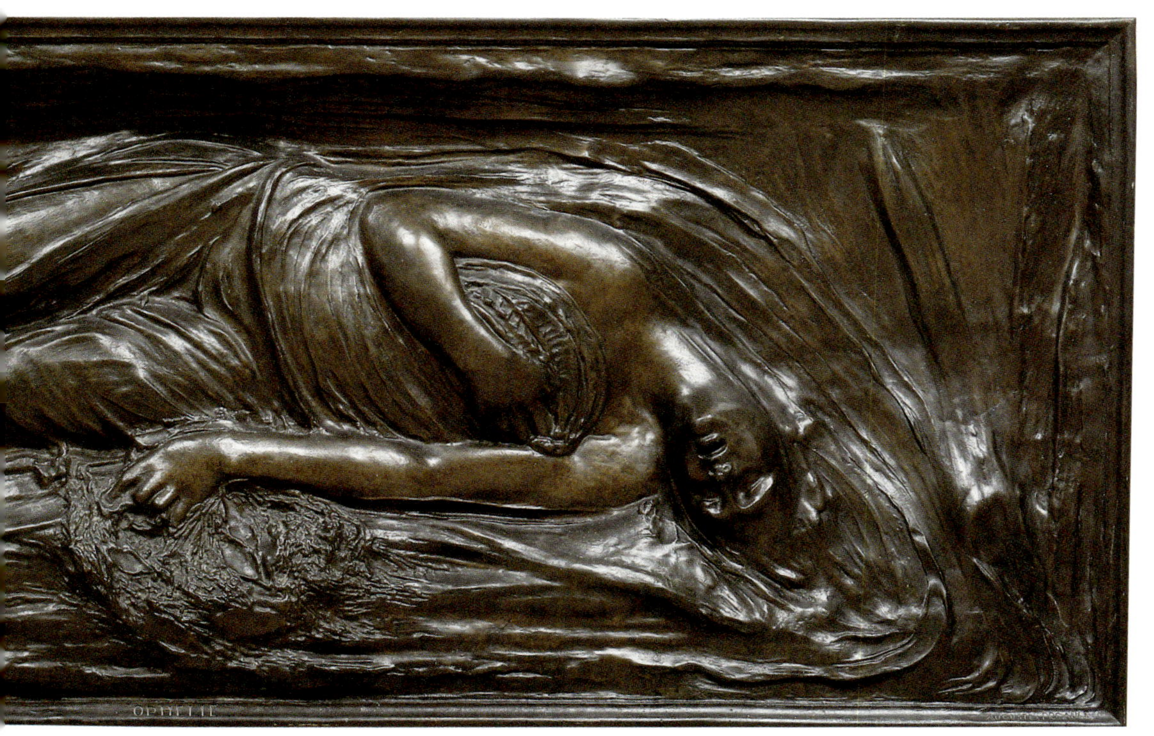

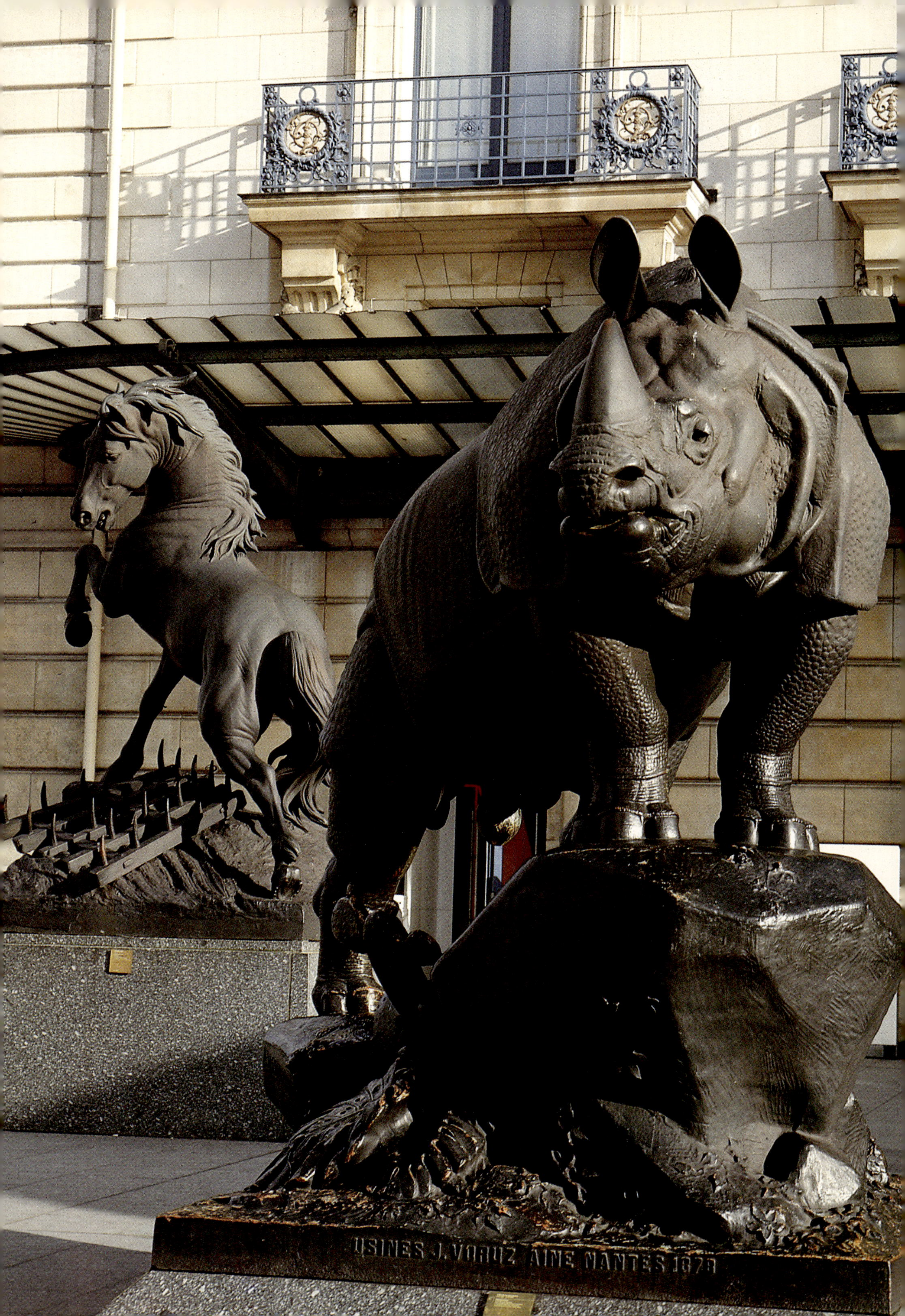
USINES J. VORUZ AINE NANTES

Animal Sculpture in the Musée d'Orsay

Although romantics sometimes devoted as much attention to animals as they did to human beings, not all animal sculptors were romantics. For example, Fremiet's realistic study of a prosaic *Wounded Dog* (1850) stands in sharp contrast to the savage violence of the unsurpassed master in the genre, Barye. Although Antoine-Louis Barye was born in 1796, he belongs in the Musée d'Orsay both because his life extended to 1875 and because under the Second Empire he produced the finest portions of the decor for the new Louvre, the man and child with animal group in the Cour Napoléon. The studies and models for this work are displayed at the Musée d'Orsay. The plaster cast of Barye's *Crouching Lion* also serves to remind us that a single national collection is split between the Louvre and the Musée d'Orsay. Each has a lion to symbolize the links uniting them. The bronze commissioned by King Louis-Philippe in 1846 was cast in 1847, removed from the Tuileries Gardens under Napoleon III, and then re-erected as a pair with a newly cast replica at the south gate of the Tuileries, where it still stands today.

The forecourt of the Musée d'Orsay partially re-creates the apolitical decor of the World's Fair Trocadero Palace (1878), an allusion to a period in the nation's history when doubt still remained as to which would prevail, the monarchy or the republic. To three out of four painted cast-iron animals which once adorned the Trocadero fountain have been joined the six *Continents*. The latter were stored at Nantes in 1937, during restoration work on the Trocadero Palace before the final World's Fair Paris was ever to hold, and in 1963 they were summarily discarded into a public dump where they languished for fifteen years with their emblematic familiars (tortoise for *Africa*; kangaroo for *Oceania*, etc.). Although Fremiet's *Trapped Elephant*, Jacquemart's *Rhinoceros* and Rouillard's *Horse and Harrow* are romantic in size, they are realistic in detail – a factor which led the government to send the fourth animal, Cain's *Bull*, to Nîmes, in commemoration of that city's bullring.

Much closer to Barye's work are the groups by Cain, and the latter's wax studies for *Lion and Lioness Struggling over a Wild Boar* and *Rhinoceros Attacked by Tigers* are displayed with the small Barye bronzes from the Chauchard collection.

The date of Rembrandt Bugatti's birth should logically place him in the Pompidou Centre. However, a proposed donation from Ebé Bugatti, daughter of the car-maker and aunt of the sculptor, was refused by the National Museum of Modern Art, and so the Musée d'Orsay received the contents of his studio, expanded in 1980 by the donation from Jean-Marie Desbordes, Ebé's godson and heir. In any case, Rembrandt Bugatti's untimely suicide in 1916 brought his work within the Musée d'Orsay's chronological limits. Thus the analytical animal studies made by R. Bugatti at the Anvers zoo have joined the comprehensive ones done by François Pompon at the Jardin des Plantes in Paris.

Our plans for an Animal Gallery were not implemented for the opening of the Musée d'Orsay in 1986, although this would have been the ideal way to demonstrate the 19th century's obsession with animal sculpture, while paintings concentrated on landscape.

Alfred Jacquemart
Paris 1824 – Paris 1896
Rhinoceros, 1878
Iron statues cast in Nantes by J. Voruz the elder.
2.86 x 2.29 x 3.78 m
Commissioned in 1877 for the Trocadero fountain (1878 World's Fair); Porte de Saint-Cloud, 1935; Orsay, 1985. Restored by the Coubertin Foundry.
RF 3753

Pierre Rouillard
Paris 1820 – Paris 1881
Horse with Harrow, 1878
Iron statue cast in Sommervoire by A. Durenne.
3.50 x 2.23 x 2.20 m
Provenance as above.
RF 3754

Barye, 'the Michelangelo of the menagerie', according to Théophile Gautier, was perhaps alluding with his *Lion with Snake* and *Crouching Lion* to the July monarchy's astrological sign.

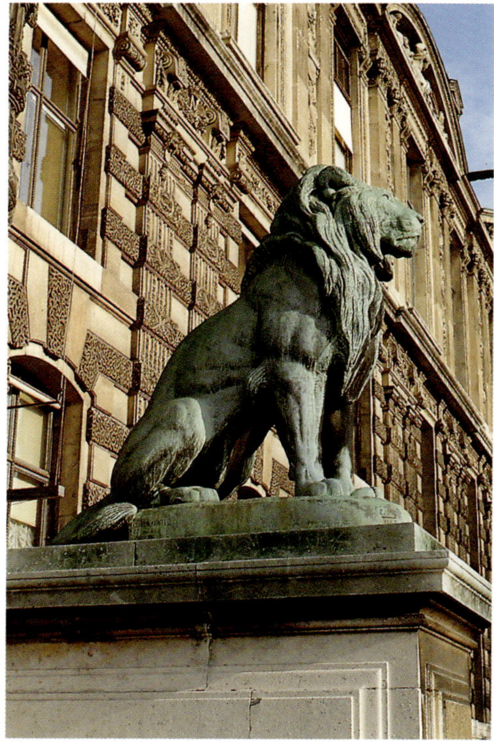

Emmanuel Fremiet
Paris 1824 – 1910
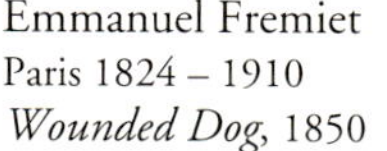
Wounded Dog, 1850
Bronze statue cast by Eugène Gonon. 0.69 x 0.69 x 0.425 m
Commissioned by the Nation, 1849; 1850 Salon;
Luxembourg Museum, 1851;
Louvre, 1927; Orsay, 1986.
RF 177

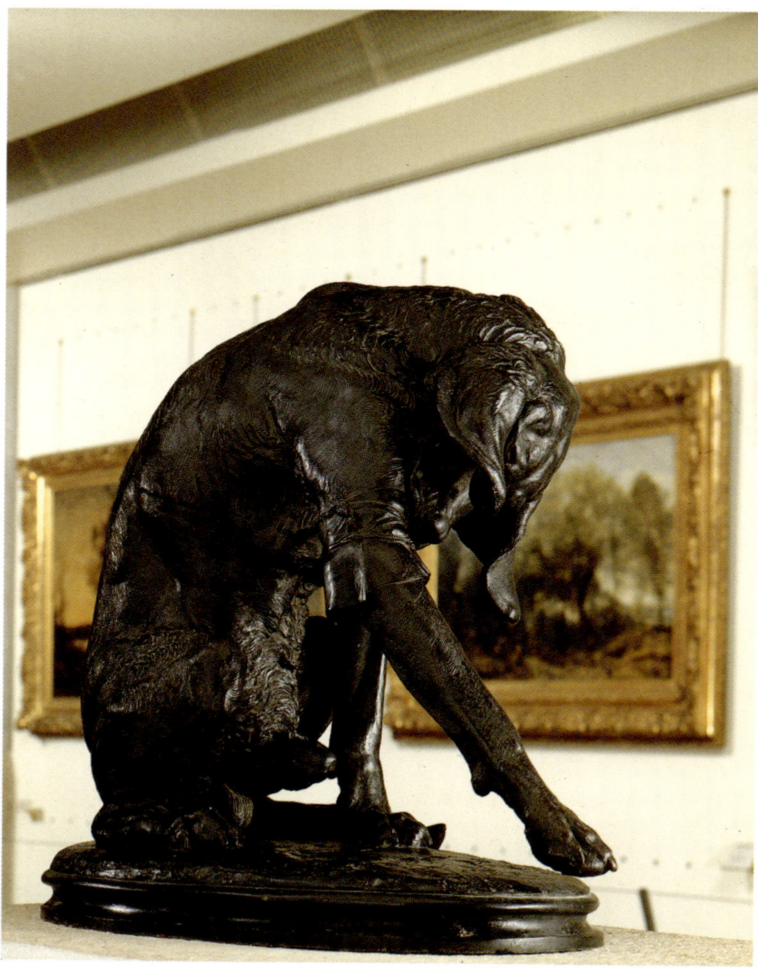

Antoine-Louis Barye
Paris 1795 – Paris 1875
Crouching Lion, 1847
Bronze cast by Lebeau.
2 x 1.86 x 0.85 m
Tuileries Gardens, 1847; south gate of Tuileries Gardens, 1858.
Replica cast for purposes of symmetry
has Barye's signature on the back.

Antoine-Louis Barye ▷
Paris 1795 – Paris 1875
Crouching Lion, 1847
Original patinated plaster model. 2 x 1.86 x 0.85 m
Gift of Jacques Zoubaloff, 1914;
Louvre, 1914; Orsay, 1986.
RF 1599

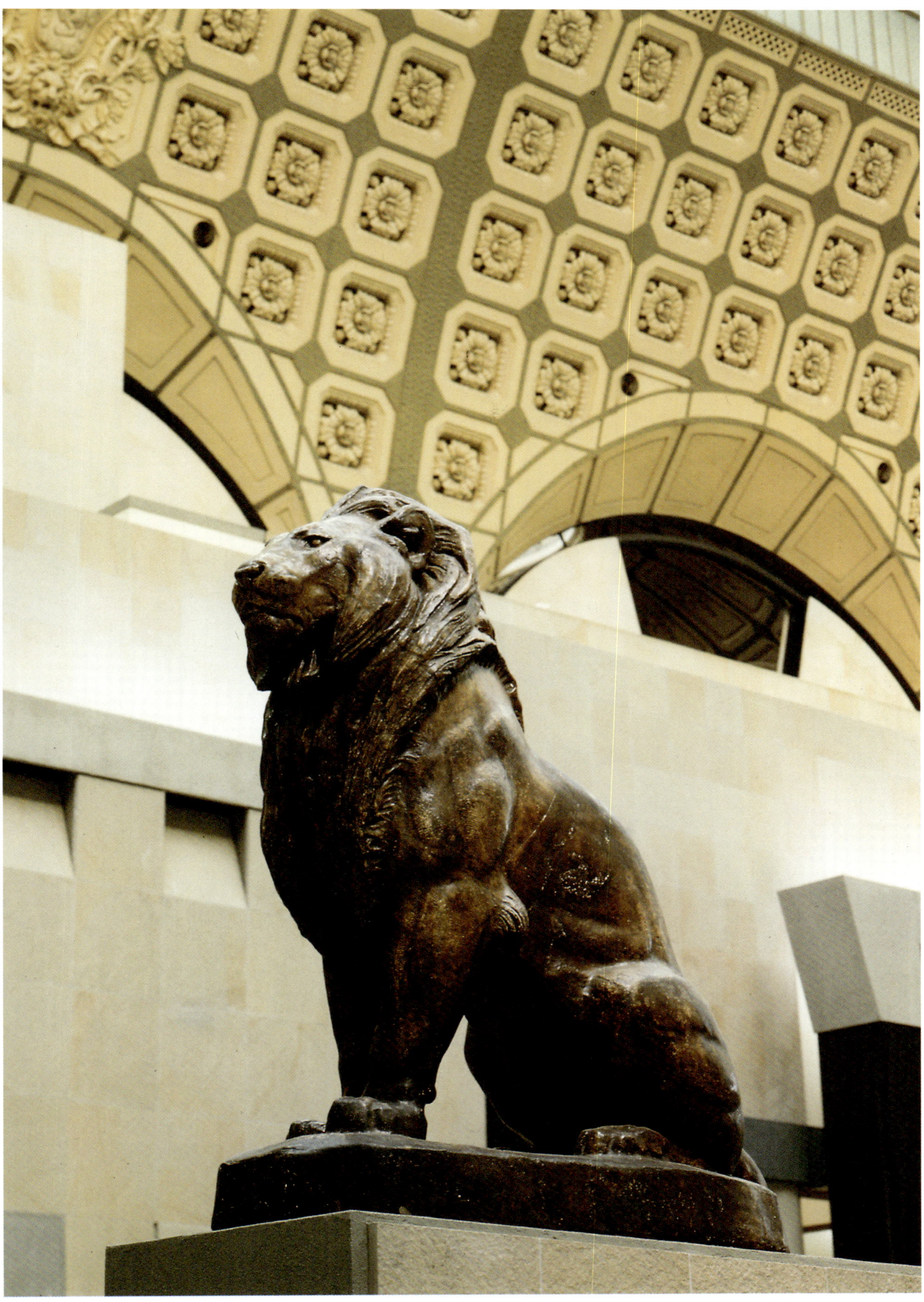

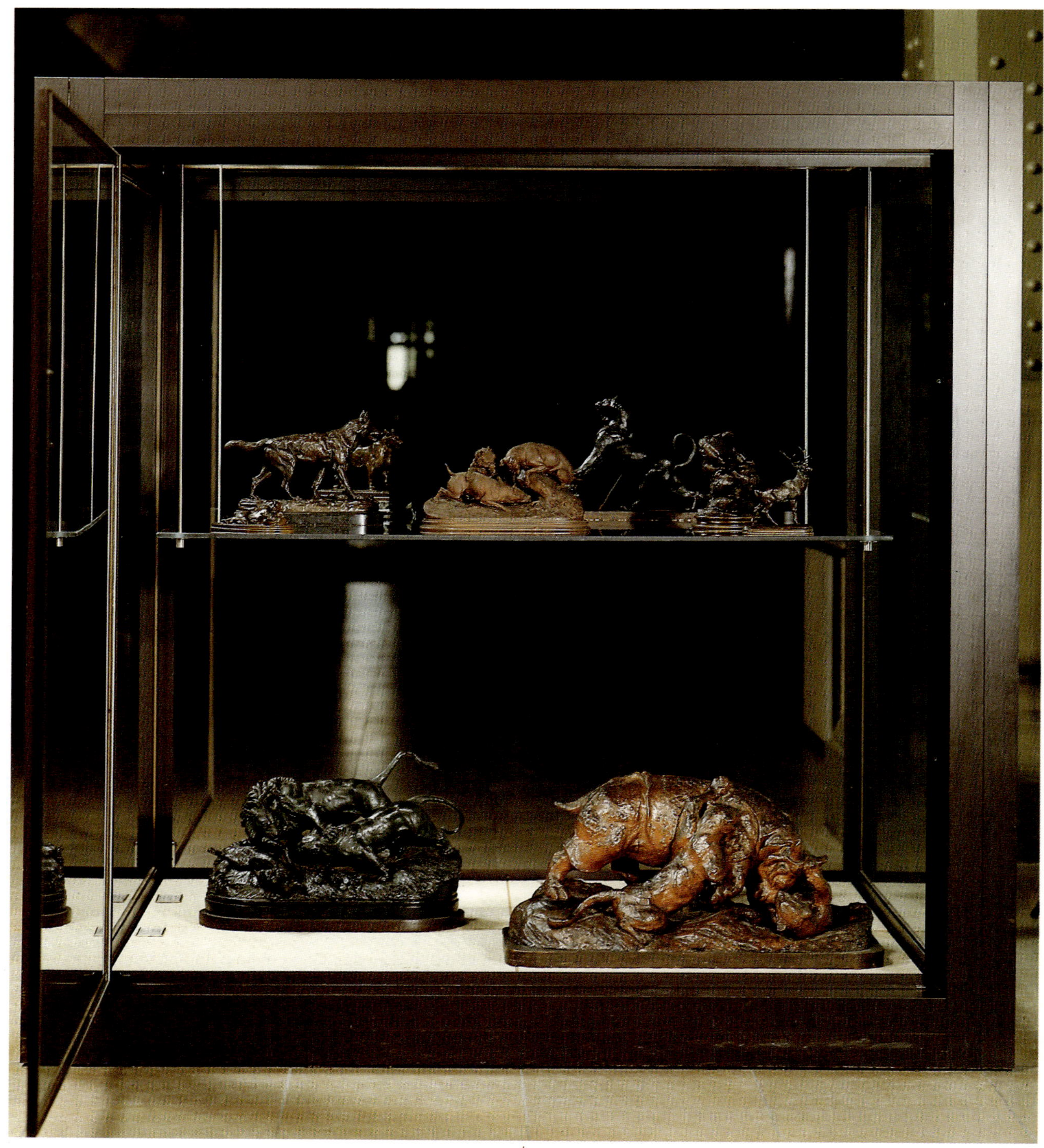

Auguste-Nicolas Cain
Paris 1821–1894
Lion and Lioness Struggling over Wild Boar, 1875
Rhinoceros Attacked by Tigers, 1882
Wax models. 0.415 x 0.62 x 0.422 m; 0.39 x 0.83 x 0.45 m
Gift from Georges and Henri Cain, 1927; Louvre, 1927; Orsay 1986.
RF 1905, RF 1904
The full-scale bronzes graced the Castiglione entrance to the Tuileries Gardens from 1883 onwards.

In this cube-shaped display case designed by Gae Aulenti are exhibited: (below) Cain wax models for the large bronzes in the Tuileries Gardens. Note the north-south *Rhinoceros* axis leading from Cain's at the Tuileries Castiglione entrance to Jacquemart's on the forecourt of the Musée d'Orsay; (above) small Barye bronzes from the Chauchard collection, which was transferred to the Musée d'Orsay.

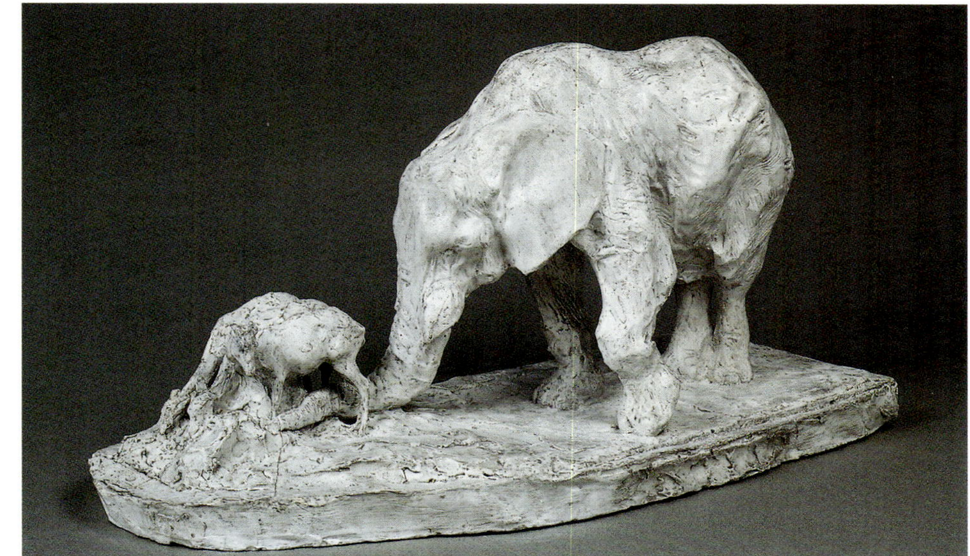

Rembrandt Bugatti
Milan 1884 – Paris 1916
Elephant and Three Gazelles, 1905
Plaster model. 0.33 x 0.63 x 0.31 m
Gift of Jean-Marie Desbordes, godson of Ebé Bugatti (the sculptor's niece and car-maker's daughter), 1980; Louvre, 1980; Orsay, 1986.
RF 3560

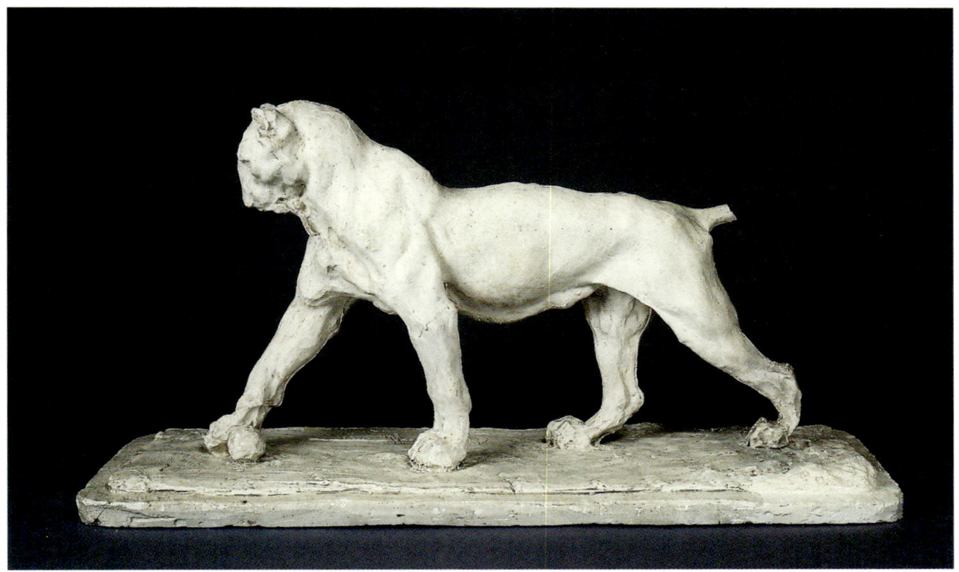

Rembrandt Bugatti
Milan 1884 – Paris 1916
Lion and Ball, 1903
Plaster model. 0.363 x 0.77 x 0.254
RF 3570
Provenance as above.

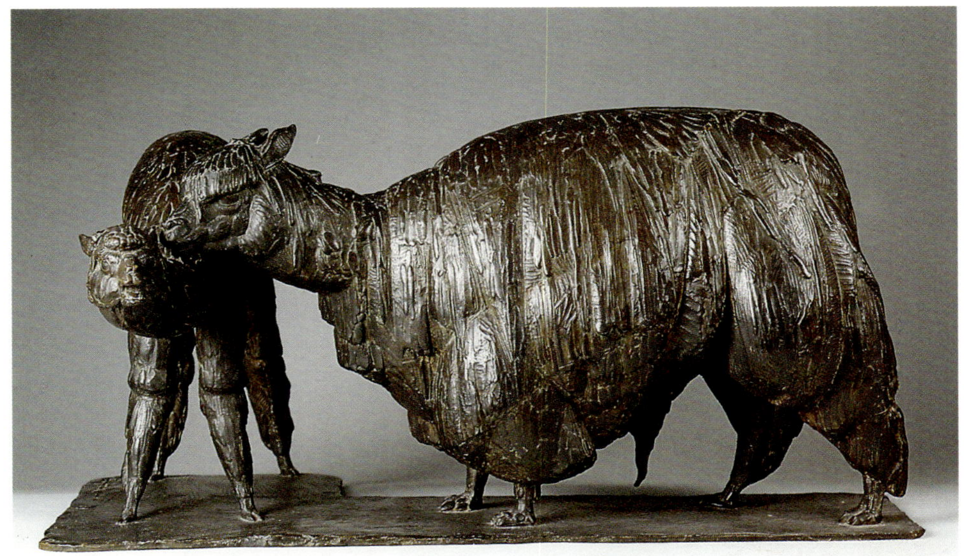

Rembrandt Bugatti
Milan 1884 – Paris 1916
Two Llamas, 1911
Bronze group cast by A.A. Hébrard; proof (1). 0.35 x 0.33 x 0.725 m
Gift of Ebé Bugatti, 1975; Louvre, 1977; Orsay, 1986.
RF 3060

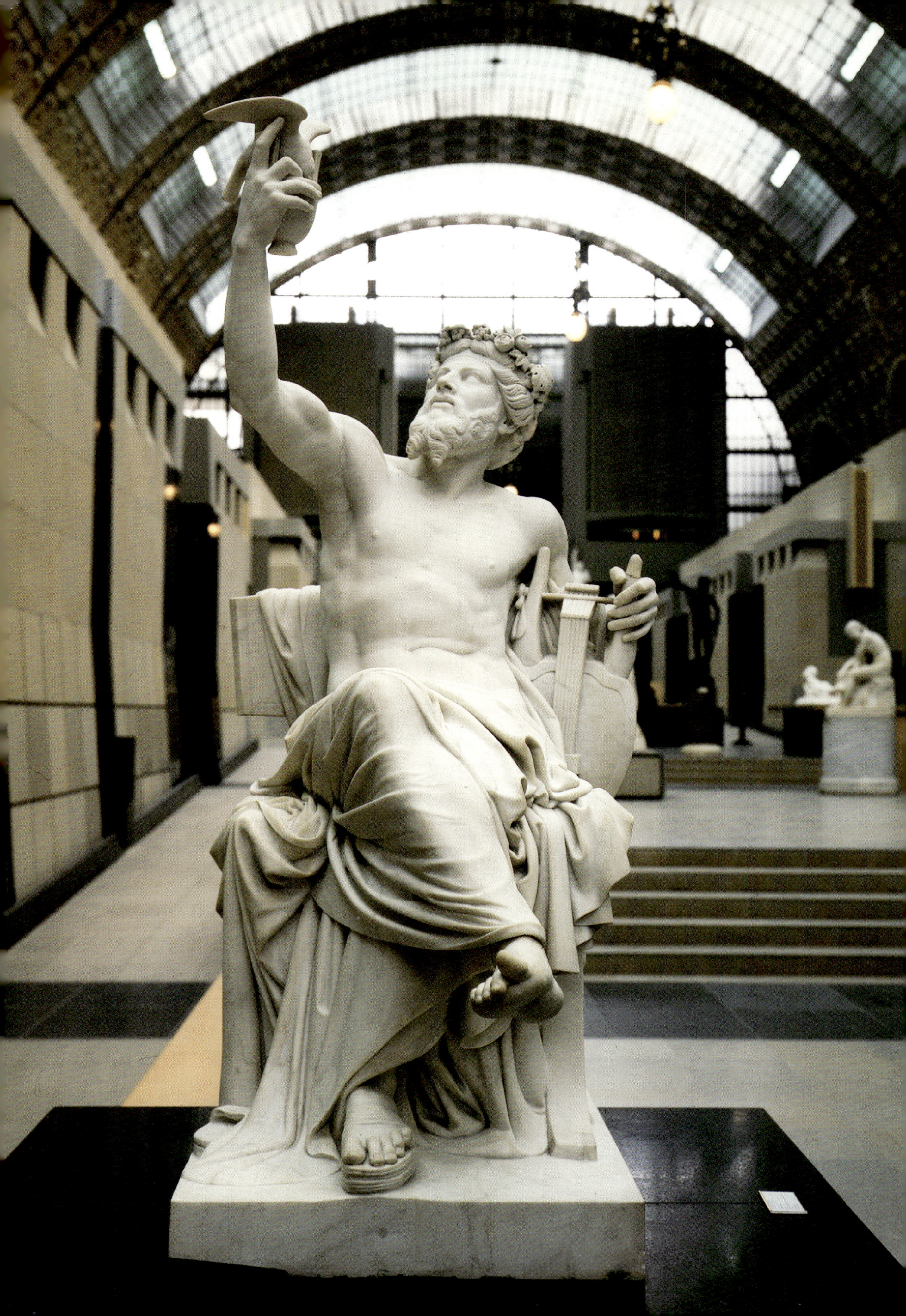

Neoclassicism: the Imperial style

As a genre capable of surviving the passage of time, sculpture is one of the rare material links we have with the ancient world. This very solidity, however, can paralyse succeeding artists, hypnotized by the weight of a venerated past that they may feel incapable of equalling.

Napoleon Bonaparte built up his collection of classical sculpture at the Louvre with marbles plundered from Italy in 1798, such as the *Apollo* and torso of the *Belvedere*, and the *Adonis* and *Venus* from the Capitol. Their triumphant transferral to Paris was intended to impress the French populace, which it definitely did; meanwhile, the classical style was already impelling giants such as Canova the Venetian and Thorvaldsen the Dane towards emulation.

At the same time, a public dominated by the rising bourgeoisie was seeking ways to distinguish itself. Already highly educated in the classics, this group used the ancient world as a benchmark against which to measure their own artistic taste. The figures of Anacreon, Sappho, Cornelia and Virgil were already familiar to them. It is therefore not surprising that Charles-Louis Müller's *The Allegory of Taste* at the Louvre, painted at the Salon Denon (1864-5), is shown grasping the *Venus de Milo*.

This was a significant trend under the Second Empire. Furthermore, use of the classical style, with its references to the glories of imperial Rome, was an indirect way of flattering the regime in France. Inaugurated at the Academy by Petitot, Dumont, Jaley, Jouffroy, Guillaume and later G.J. Thomas, this emulation of ideal models not found in nature – this 'grand style' for depicting moral virtue – often lacked real power. A case in point was Pradier, who 'left every morning for Athens and returned home at night to the modest Breda quarter of Paris' (Préault). Eugène Guillaume's gaze was resolutely fixed on Antiquity, a conscious choice which, combined with his affable personality, earned him exceptional popularity during his lifetime and utter oblivion after his death. A poem by the Greek poet Anacreon appears to have inspired his statue: 'As I twined a garland of roses, I found love among them; seizing it by the wings, I plunged it into wine, and drank; and now, a prisoner in my breast, it moves me with the trembling of its wings.' Pierre-Jules Cavelier managed more gracefully. To gain some idea of the reverence enjoyed by the classical style, we have only to remember, for example, that Gabriel-Jules Thomas – whose academicism fell somewhere between that of Guillaume and Cavelier – executed a *Virgil* for the Cour Carrée of the Louvre which contemporaries deemed too fine for mere decoration: it was sent first to the Paris World's Fair (1867) and then to the Vienna World's Fair (1873), before being consigned definitively to the Luxembourg Museum. A replica of the work was also made, to adorn the opulent Rothschild château in Ferrières.

Neoclassical works were not always executed in marble. Guillaume's *The Reaper* and Salmson's *The Spinner* show that the malleability of bronze was not exploited solely by the romantics. *The Reaper* was modelled on the Borghese *Gladiator* (with the addition of a scythe), and *The Spinner* was an awakened version of Cavelier's *Penelope* (1849), shown sleeping at the foot of the Château de Dampierre staircase.

Eugène Guillaume
Montbard 1822 – Rome 1905
Anacreon, 1851
Marble statue.
1.85 x 0.80 x 1.22 m
Plaster executed in Rome, 1849; marble acquired by the Nation from the 1852 Salon; Luxembourg Museum, 1856; Louvre, 1923; Orsay, 1986.
RF 179

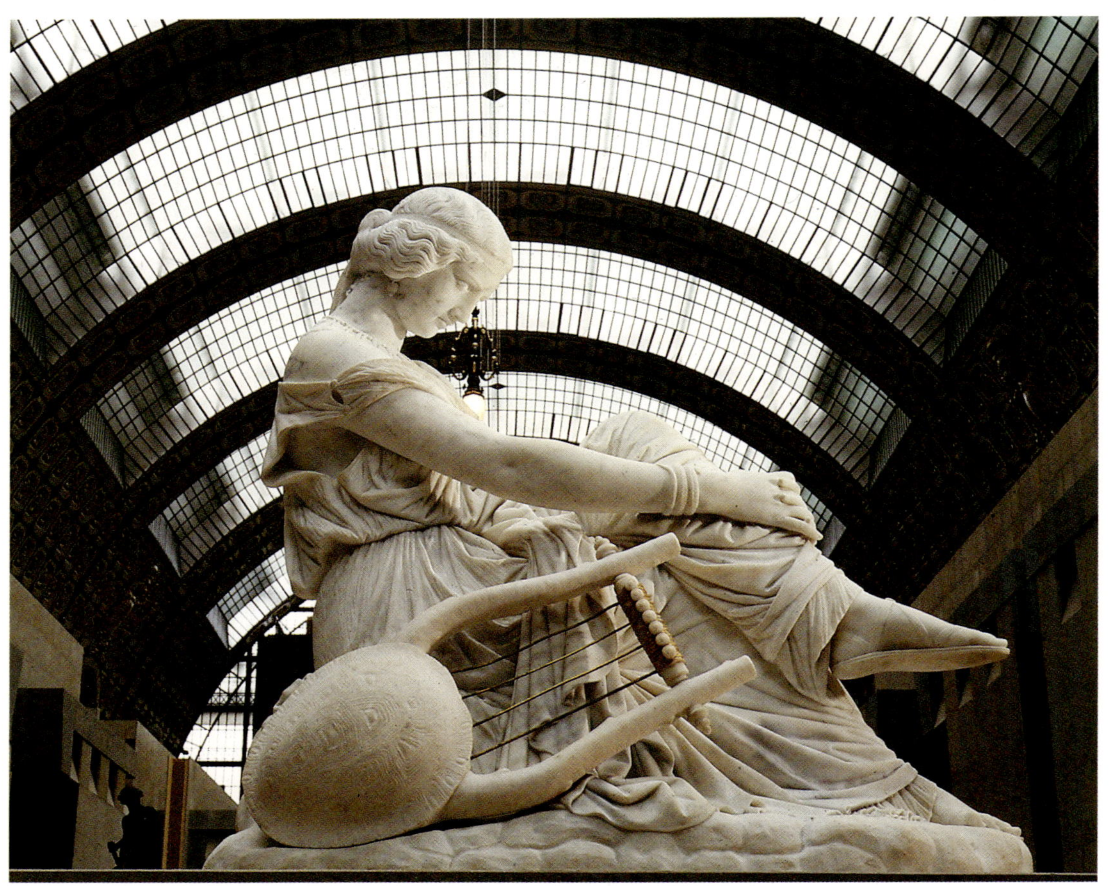

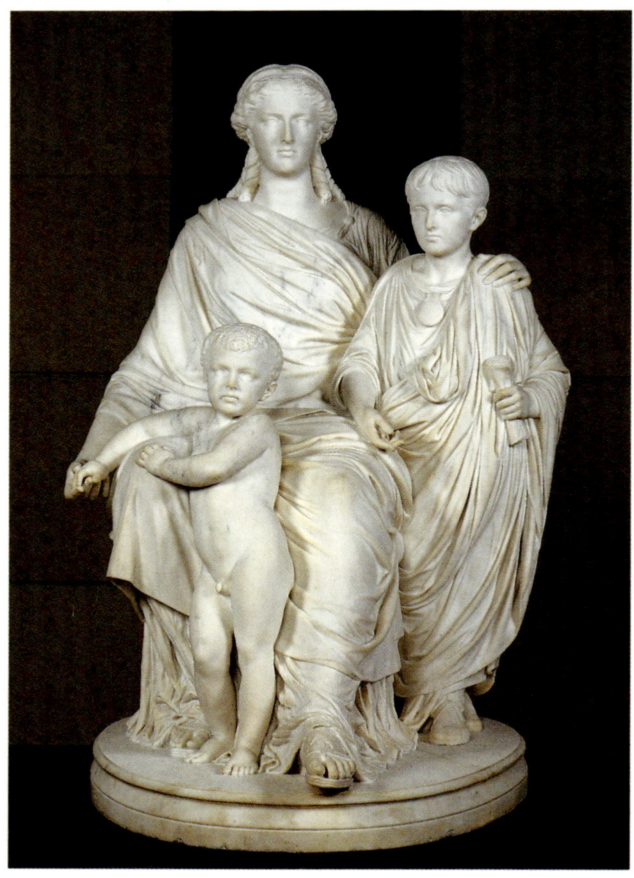

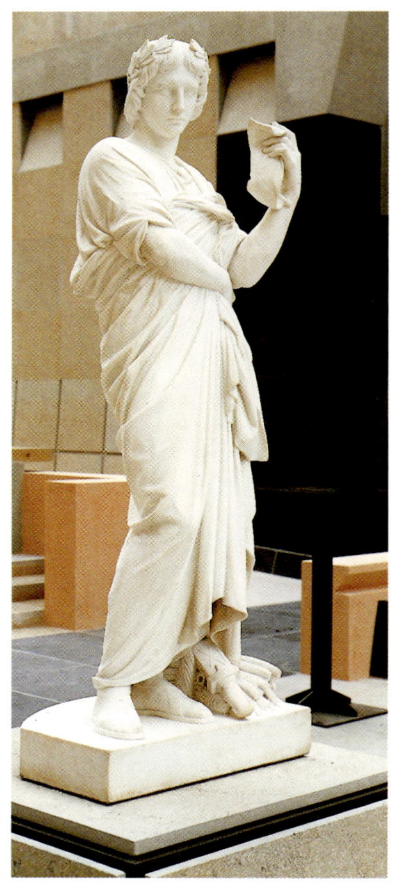

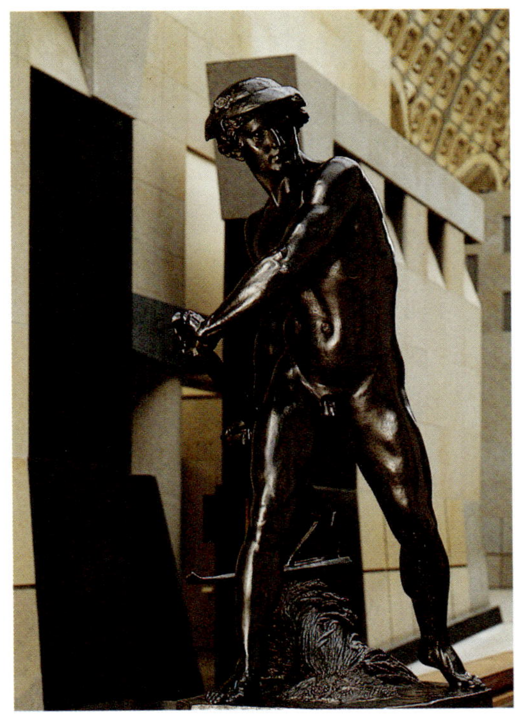

Eugène Guillaume
Montbard 1822 – Rome 1905
The Reaper, 1849
Bronze statue cast by Eck & Durand. 1.68 x 0.78 x 0.95 m
Plaster executed in Rome (1848–9); bronze purchased by Napoleon III from the 1855 World's Fair; Château de Fontainebleau after 1856; Luxembourg Museum, 1876; Louvre, 1916; Orsay, 1986.
RF 3990

Jean-Jules Salmson
Paris 1823 – Coupvray 1902
The Spinner, 1863
Bronze statue. 1.20 x 0.684 x 0.94 m
Acquired from the 1863 Salon (3rd-place medal); Luxembourg Museum before 1867; Louvre, 1926; Orsay, 1986.
RF 193

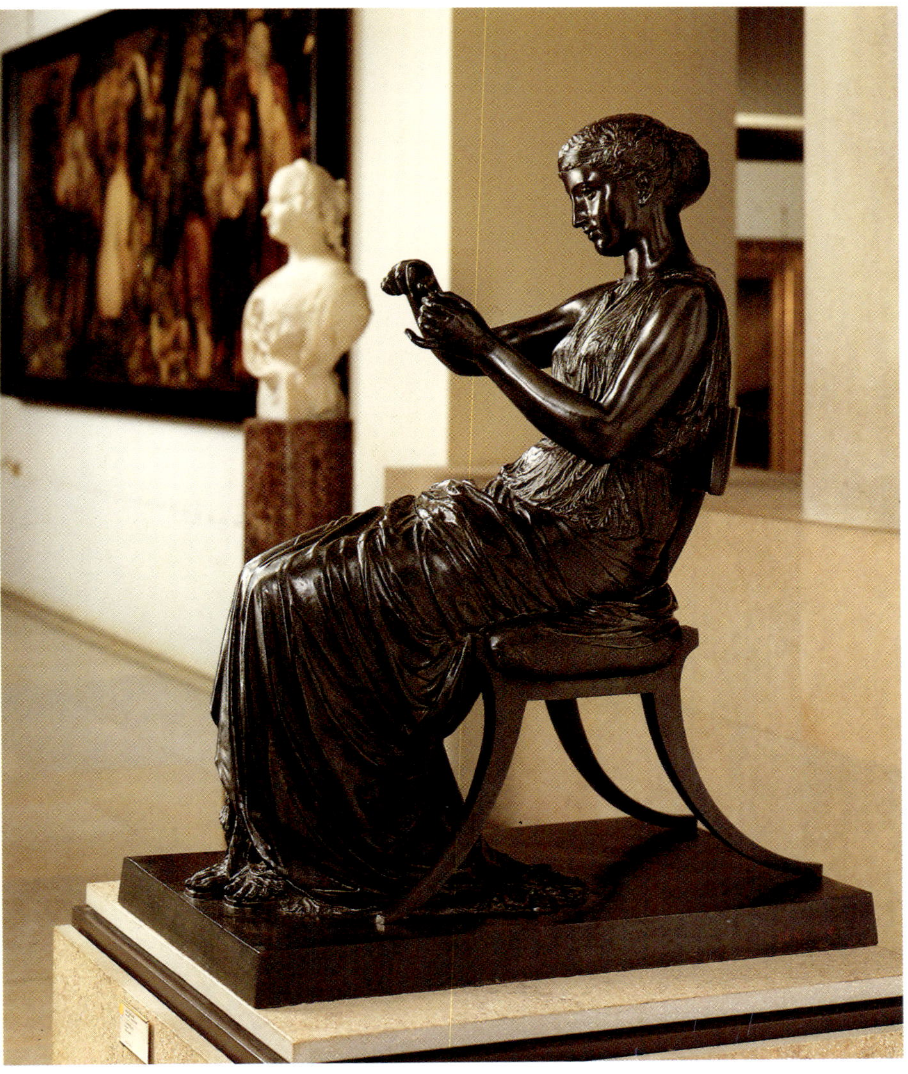

◁ James Pradier
Geneva 1790 – Bougival 1852
Sappho, 1852
Marble statue. 1.18 x 0.70 x 1.20 m
Enlargement of a small model popular in 1848; purchased by Napoleon III from the 1852 Salon (Medal of Honour); Palace of Saint-Cloud, 1852; Louvre, 1870; Orsay Depository, 1986.
RF 2990

◁ Pierre-Jules Cavelier
Paris 1814 – Paris 1894
Cornelia, Mother of the Gracchi, 1861
Marble group. 1.71 x 1.21 x 1.27 m
Acquired by the Nation from the 1861 Salon; Luxembourg Museum before 1867; Louvre, 1903; Orsay, 1986.
RF 164

◁ Gabriel-Jules Thomas
Paris 1824 – Paris 1905
Virgil, 1861
Marble statue. 1.83 x 0.72 x 0.56 m
Plaster commissioned in 1859 for the Cour Carrée of the Louvre.
Marble Salon, 1861 (1st-Prize medal);
Luxembourg Museum, 1874; Louvre, 1923; Orsay, 1986.
RF 2224

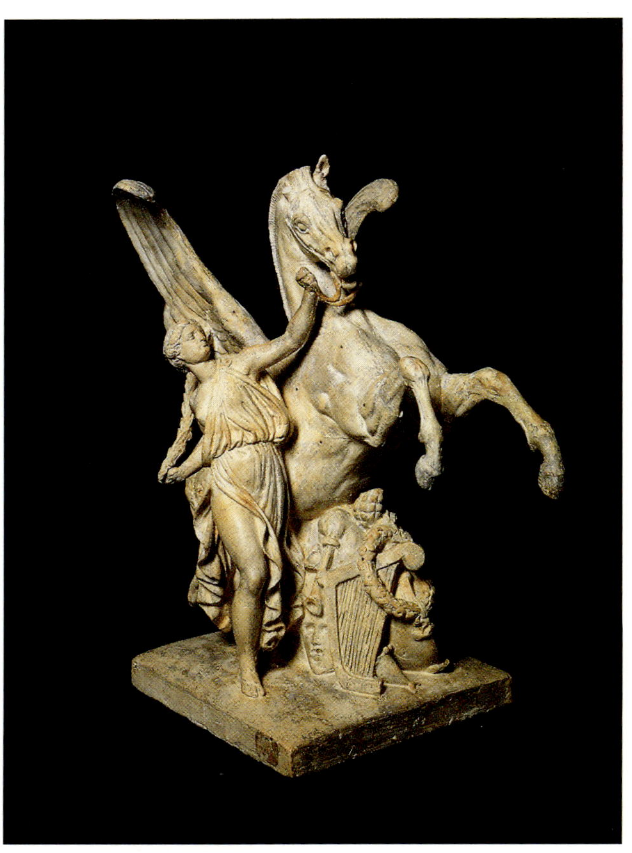

Eugène Lequesne
Paris 1815 – Paris 1887
Fame Restraining Pegasus, 1865
Plaster study. 0.628 x 0.44 x 0.575 m
For the acroteria of the Opera stage, in galvanoplasty.
Paris Opera Architectural Agency; Orsay Depository, 1983.
DO 1983 – 203

The neoclassical style was *de rigueur* for official buildings, especially courthouses. Temples of the law were expected to be in a style as eternal as justice and immutable as virtue. Although it is relatively surprising to find neoclassical groups on Charles Garnier's Opera House, the triumph of eclecticism also called for a touch of the serious style, with antique drapery used to emphasize the motion of the body.

Aimé Millet ▷
Paris 1819 – Paris 1891
Apollo between Dance and Music, 1866
Plaster study. 0.752 x 0.50 x 0.198 m
For the bronze group on a gable of the stage
at the Charles Garnier Opera House.
Paris Opera Architectural Agency; Orsay Depository, 1983.
DO 1983 – 205

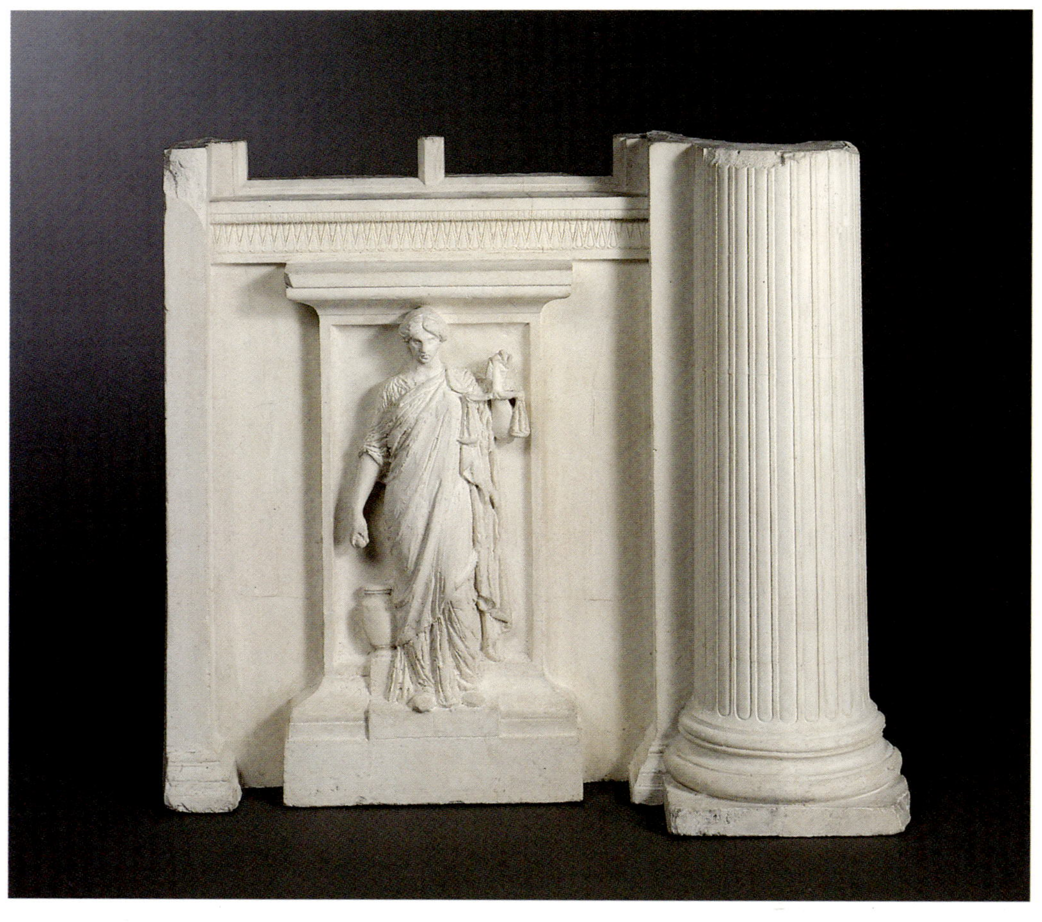

Nicolas Jaley
Paris 1802 – Neuilly 1866
Impartiality, 1859–65
Plaster haut-relief.
0.567 x 0.632 x 0.19 m
Model for the Paris Palais de Justice (courthouse), rue de Harley façade by Louis Duc. Acquired in 1989.
RF 4277

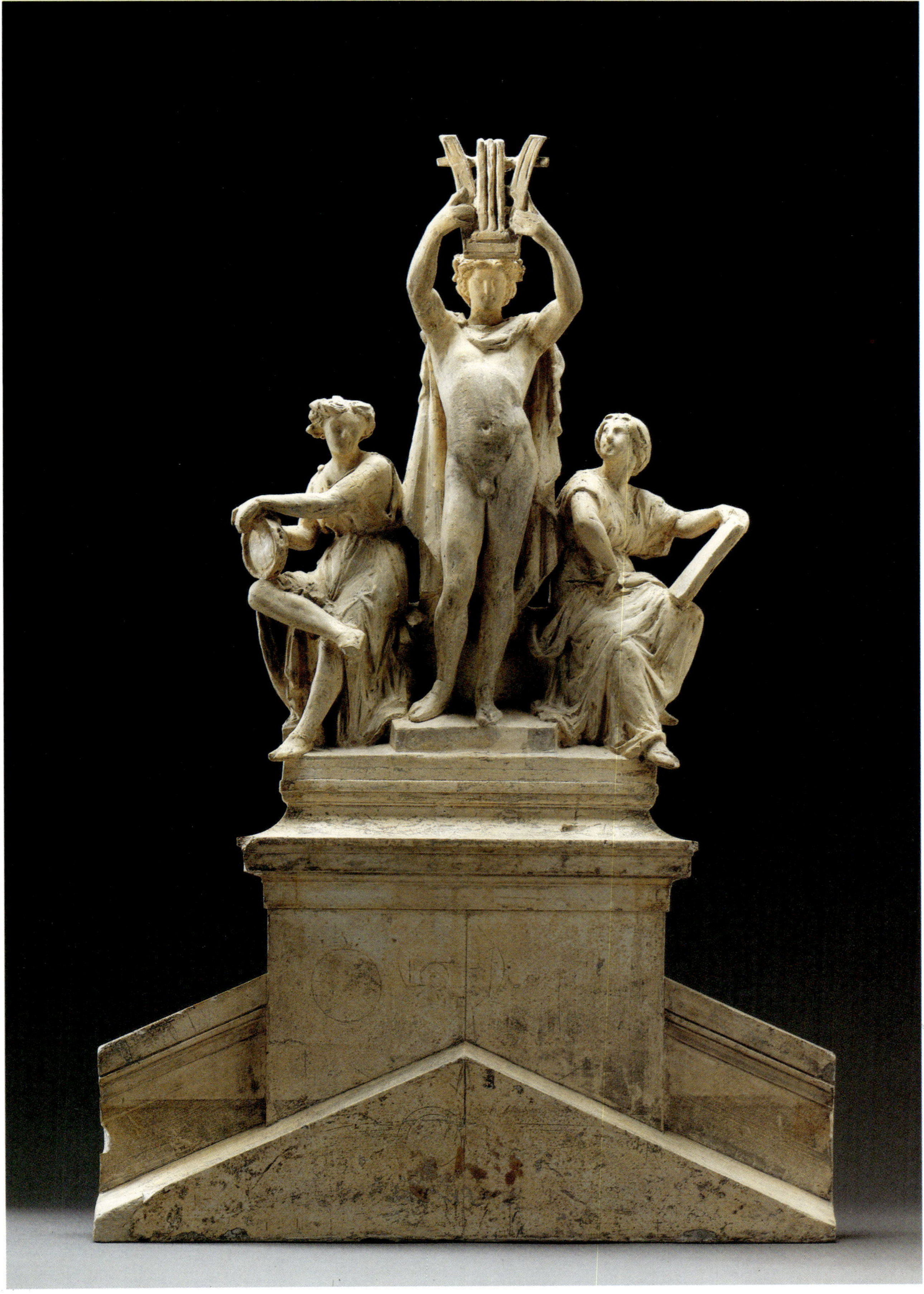

Antoine-Louis Barye
Paris 1795 – Paris 1875
Victory Distributing Laurel Wreaths, 1865
Plaster study retouched with wax. 0.195 x 0.107 x 0.153 m
Study for the globe borne by *Napoleon I* in Ajaccio.
Barye Sale, 1876; gift of Jacques Zoubaloff to the Louvre, 1914; Orsay Depository, 1986.
RF 1593

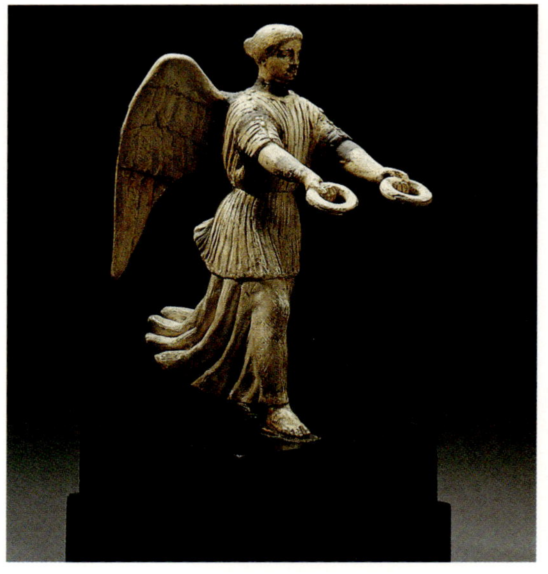

Antoine-Louis Barye
Paris 1795 – Paris 1875
Napoleon I as Roman Emperor
For the *Monument to Napoleon and his Brothers* in Ajaccio, 1865.
Plaster model. 1.35 x 1.18 x 0.55 m
Acquired by Barbedienne at the 1876 Barye Sale; gift of Jacques Zoubaloff to the Louvre, 1912; Orsay Depository, 1986.
RF 1562

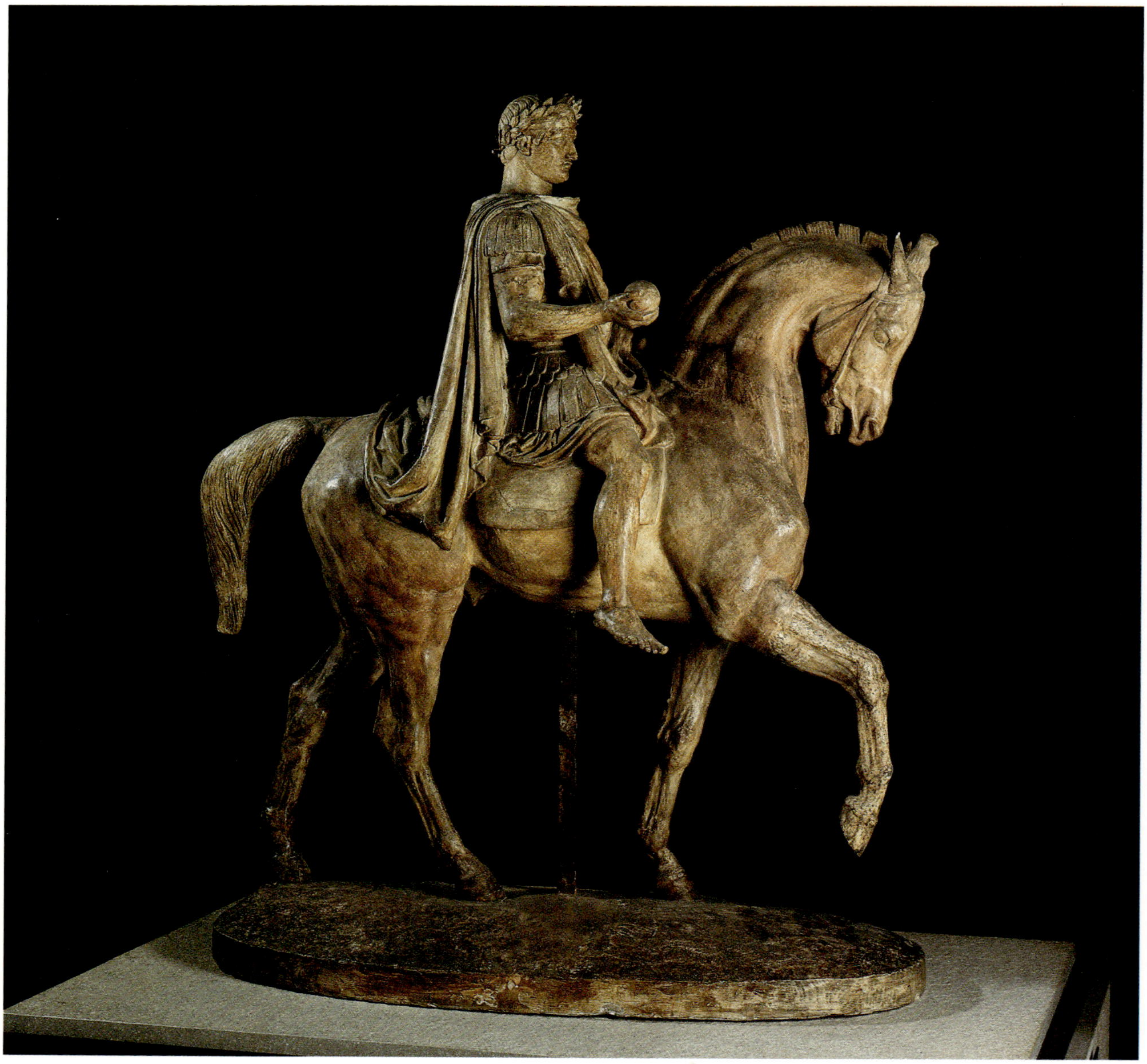

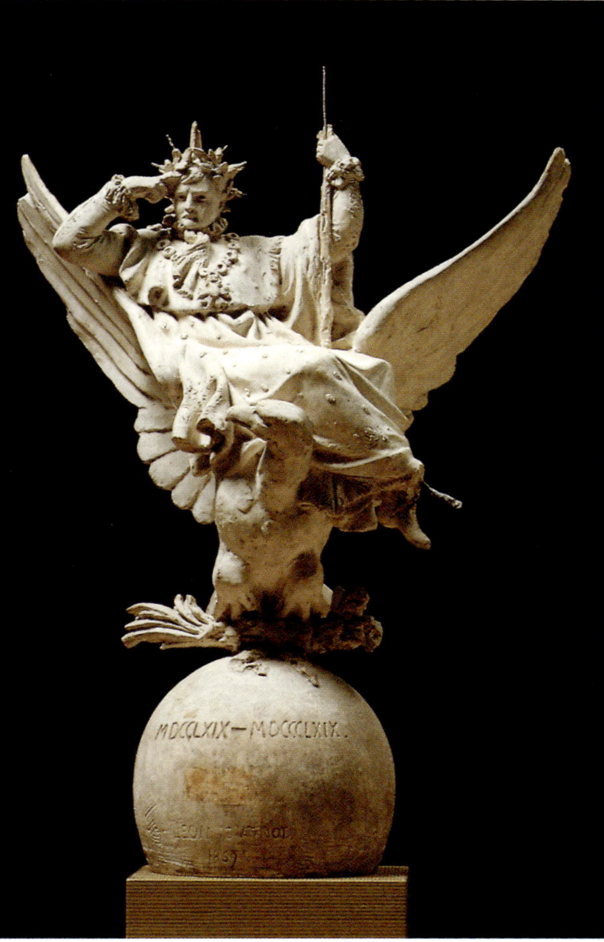

Costume played a major role in projecting power. We know that considerations of costume were behind a change at the top of the Vendôme column: Louis-Philippe had in 1833 erected Emile Seurre's effigy of *Napoleon I as 'Little Corporal'*, replacing the white flag that itself had replaced the destroyed Chaudet statue (1810). In 1863 Napoleon III had the *'Little Corporal'* taken down (after many vicissitudes it now rests in the courtyard of Les Invalides), replacing it with a *Napoleon I as Roman Emperor* by Augustin Dumont. Guillaume proposed the same versions in his sketches of equestrian statues for the Cour Napoléon of the Louvre, where Pei's pyramid stands today.

Louis-Léon Cugnot
Paris 1835 – Paris 1894
Napoleon I Seated on an Eagle Resting on a Globe, 1869
Plaster study. 0.585 x 0.405 x 0.275 m
Institut de France Depository, Dosne Foundation; Orsay, 1983.
DO 1983–77

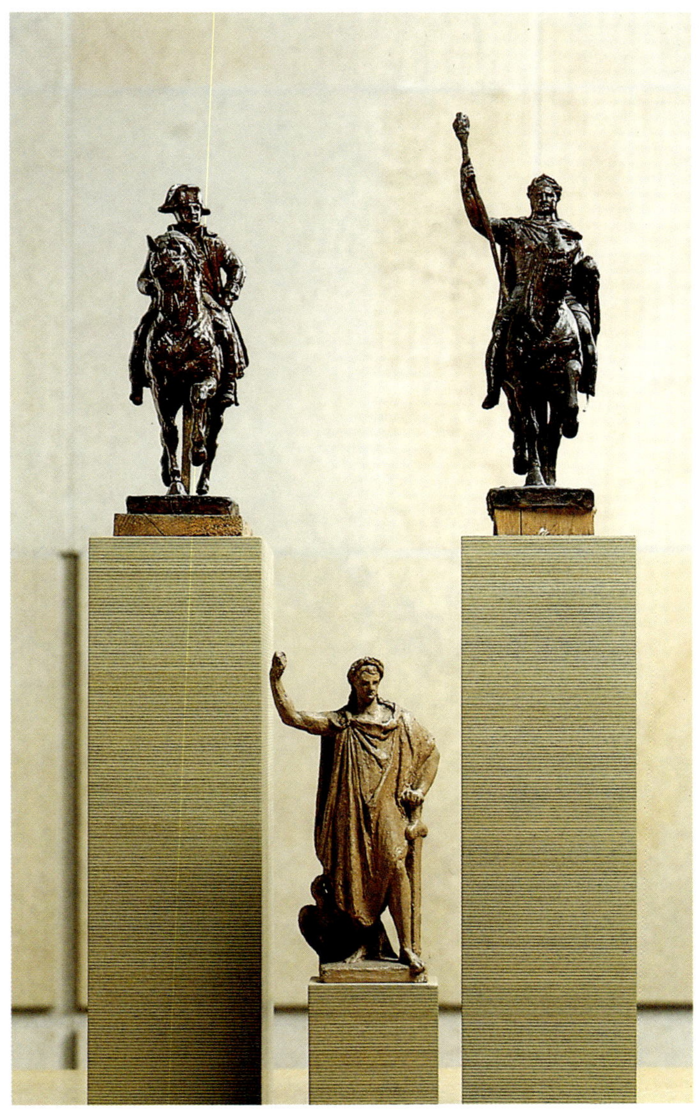

Eugène Guillaume
Montbard 1822 – Rome 1905
Napoleon I as Roman Emperor, 1859
Patinated plaster study. 0.257 x 0.138 x 0.085 m
The marble statue displayed in the Prince Napoleon 'Pompeian House', Avenue Montaigne, Paris, is today in the Château de Prangins (Switzerland).

Napoleon I on Horseback, in Military Uniform, 1862
Wax. 0.31 x 0.253 x 0.104 m

Napoleon I on Horseback, in Roman Costume, 1862
Wax. 0.362 x 0.268 x 0.123 m
Studies (never cast) for the Cour Napoléon of the Louvre, showing indecision as to the final costume. Gift of Thérèse Lefuel (daughter of the sculptor and daughter-in-law of the Louvre architect), 1921; Orsay, 1986.
RF 1733, RF 1731, RF 1732

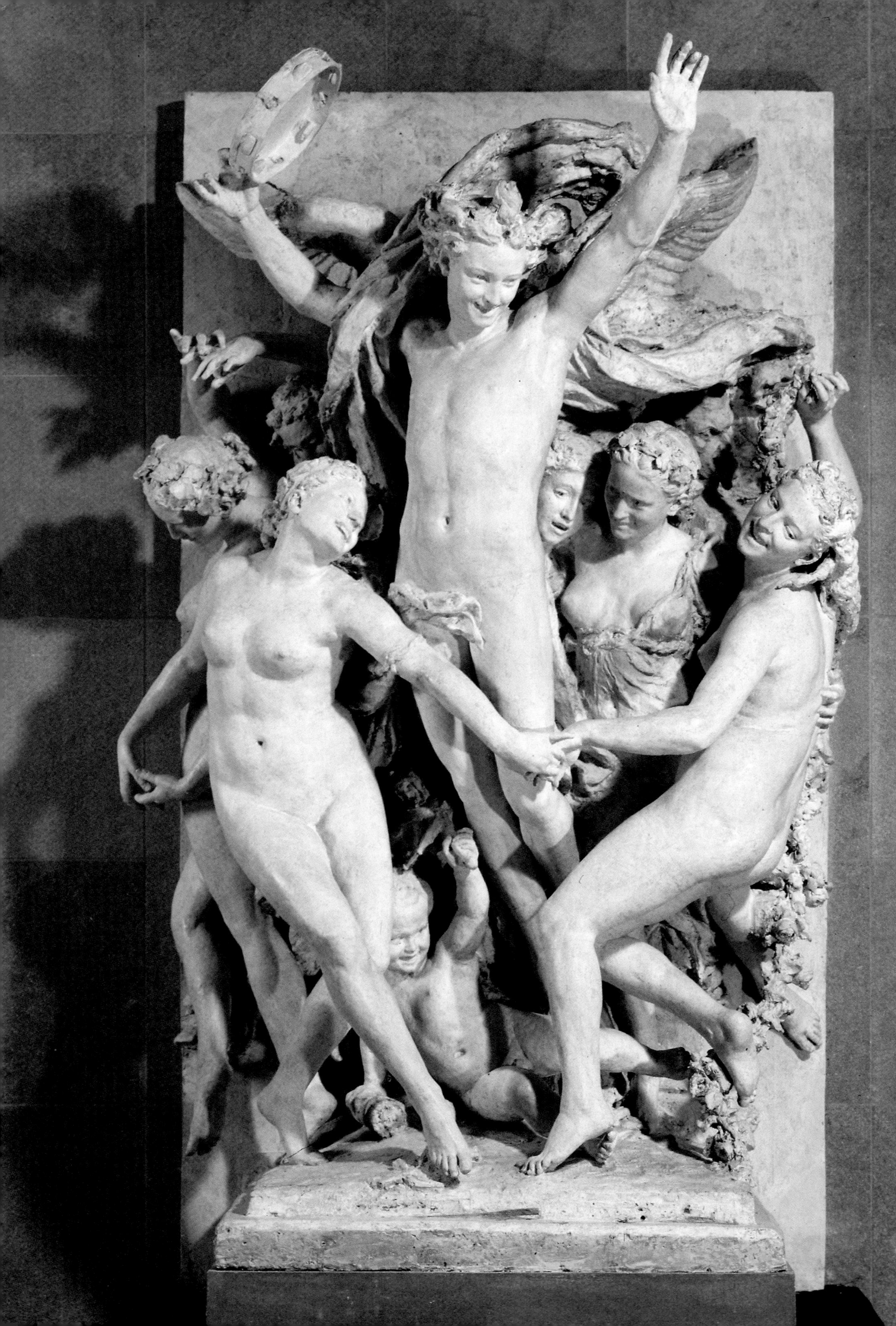

Jean-Baptiste Carpeaux

Son of a stonemason and a lace-maker, this notable participant in the 'imperial fête' was born, like most sculptors, into a poor family. He perhaps owed his vocation to his birthplace, Valenciennes. This city customarily honoured its Prix de Rome winners (22, including those who won second prize) in great style, which no doubt had its effect on the town's admiring youngsters. Carpeaux eked out a meagre living making models for foundries and teaching at the Petite Ecole (forerunner of the Ecole des Arts Décoratifs) with subsidies granted by the city and the department. It took him ten years to win his own first prize, in 1854. During his belated stay at the Villa Medici he produced two masterpieces, the *Fisherman with Shell* (1858), a tribute to the *Neapolitan Fisherman* (1831–3, Louvre) by his master Rude, and *Ugolin.* His sketches for the latter show that his aim was to create a work on the Dantesque theme capable of rivalling the Hellenist *Laocoön*, Michelangelo's *Moses* and Géricault's *Raft of the Medusa.* This tactic of drawing on the past in order to surpass it was a common one among 19th-century artists.

When Carpeaux returned to France from Rome, he received numerous official commissions. The City of Paris ordered *Temperance* (1863–6) for the Trinité church; and the national government decorations for the south side of the Pavillon de Flore restored by Hector Lefuel. The government also ordered a group for the Opera House: *The Dance*, commissioned by Garnier in 1863, for which Carpeaux's aim was to surpass Rude's sculptures on the Arc de Triomphe. However, the realism of the finished work shocked viewers at the unveiling in 1869. The figures are real nude women, and they are clearly intoxicated. The architect was ordered to remove the offending group and commission a more decorous one, which was then executed by Charles Gumery. However, the events of 1870 and Carpeaux's subsequent death transformed outrage into reverence, and *The Dance* was allowed to remain at the Opera. It was removed from the Opera façade in 1964 to protect it from pollution, and was sent first to the Louvre and then to the Musée d'Orsay. The study for this group, with its female *Genius of the Dance*, and the half-scale plaster model (both at the Musée d'Orsay), even more than the stone version seems to reverberate with the sculptor's intense passion. On the museum's central aisle is the shellacked plaster model for *The Four Quarters of the World Bearing the Celestial Sphere*, which adorns the fountain of architect Davioud's 1867 Observatory; the model was exhibited at the Salon of 1872. By placing the foot of the allegorical figure for *America* firmly on the chain binding *Africa*, Carpeaux expressed his support for the Northern side in the American War of Secession. Carpeaux did not live long enough to finish his *Watteau Fountain* (1860–70) for the city of Valenciennes, and it was completed by the sculptor Ernest Hiolle in 1876.

In addition to his portraits, Carpeaux used two faces alternately in his works: the happy face of *Anna Foucart* (1860), sister of his friend from Valenciennes; and the sad face of *La Palombella* (1864), who died in 1861 during his stay in Rome and who lent her features to *Imperial France.*

Carpeaux's keen sensitivity and burning nervous energy are apparent in his letters, drawings and 'slap-dash' paintings. In the unyielding materials of sculpture they found an adversary worthy of their power.

Jean-Baptiste Carpeaux
Valenciennes 1827 – Courbevoie 1875
The Dance, 1868
Plaster model.
2.32 x 1.48 x 1.15 m
Commissioned by Charles Garnier for the façade of the Opera House; acquired from the sculptor's widow at the 1889 World's Fair; Louvre, 1890; Opera House, 1972; Louvre, 1977; Orsay, 1986.
RF 818

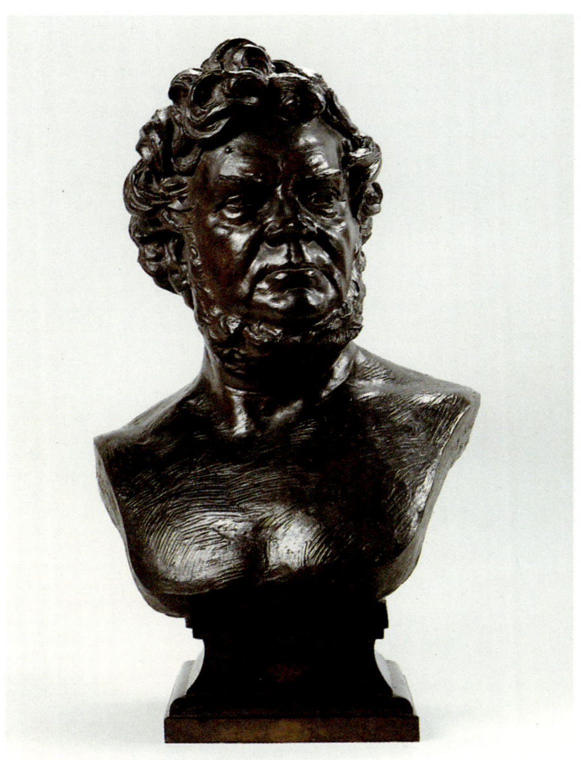

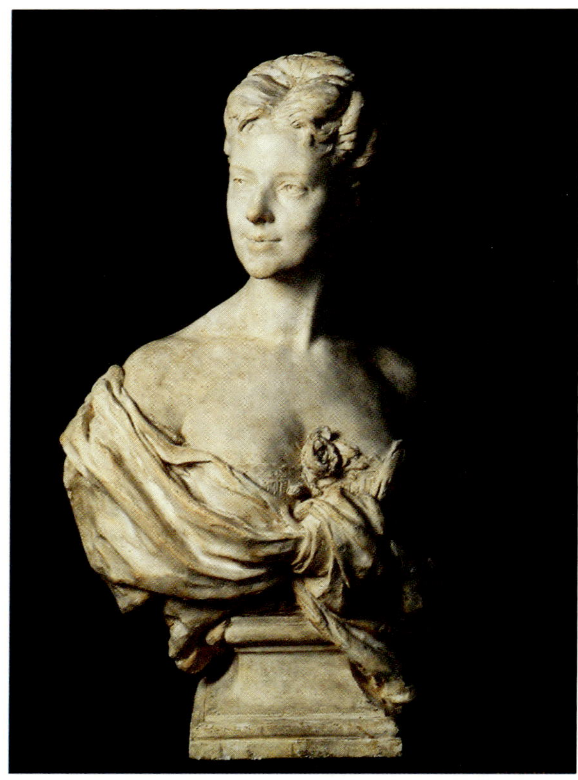

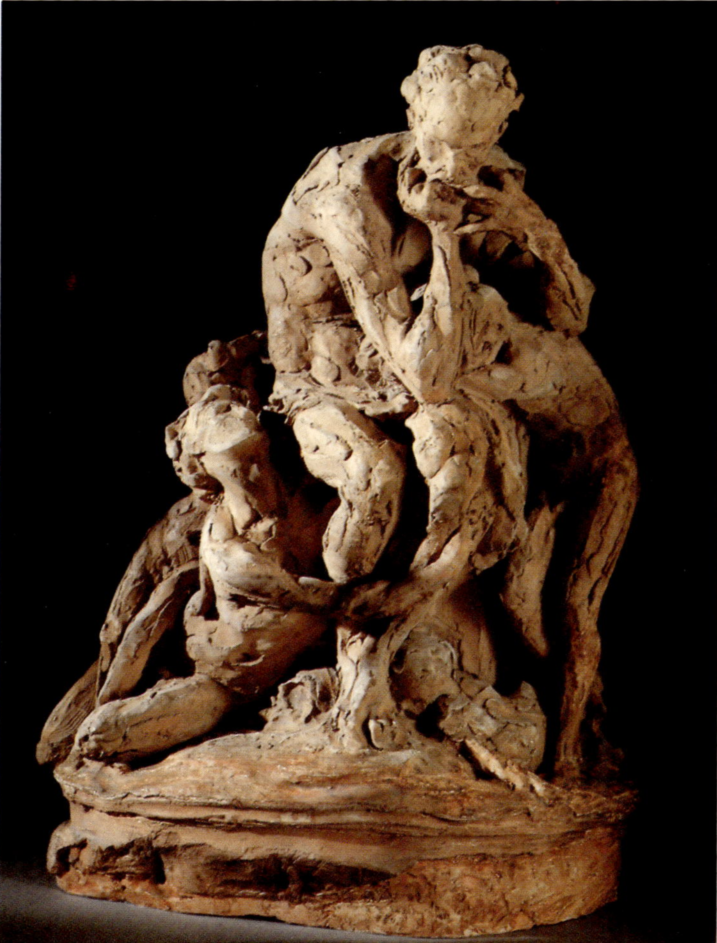

Jean-Baptiste Carpeaux
Valenciennes 1827 – Courbevoie 1875
Eugénie Fiocre (1845–1908), 1869
Plaster bust. 0.83 x 0.51 x 0.37 m
Opera ballerina sponsored by the Duc de Morny; painted by Degas in the ballet *The Spring*; the Goncourts described her as a 'sweet, saucy little thing, slender and pretty, whose cleavage line has a touch of the whole bust's *amoroso* about it'. Acquired from the sculptor's widow, 1892; Louvre, 1892; Orsay, 1986.
RF 930

Jean-Baptiste Carpeaux
Valenciennes 1827 – Courbevoie 1875
Louis Maximilien Beauvois (1796–?), 1862
Bronze bust cast by Victor Thiébaut. 0.654 x 0.389 x 0.327 m
Carpeaux transformed his compatriot into a 'Vitellius of the Legal Fraternity' (Goncourt).
Beauvois Sale, 1879; gift of Jean-Baptiste Foucart to the Louvre, 1884; Orsay, 1986.
RF 645

Jean-Baptiste Carpeaux
Valenciennes 1827 – Courbevoie 1875
Ugolin, 1860
Terra-cotta study. 0.56 x 0.415 x 0.284 m
Acquired from M. Lévy, 1891; Louvre, 1891; Orsay, 1986.
RF 2995

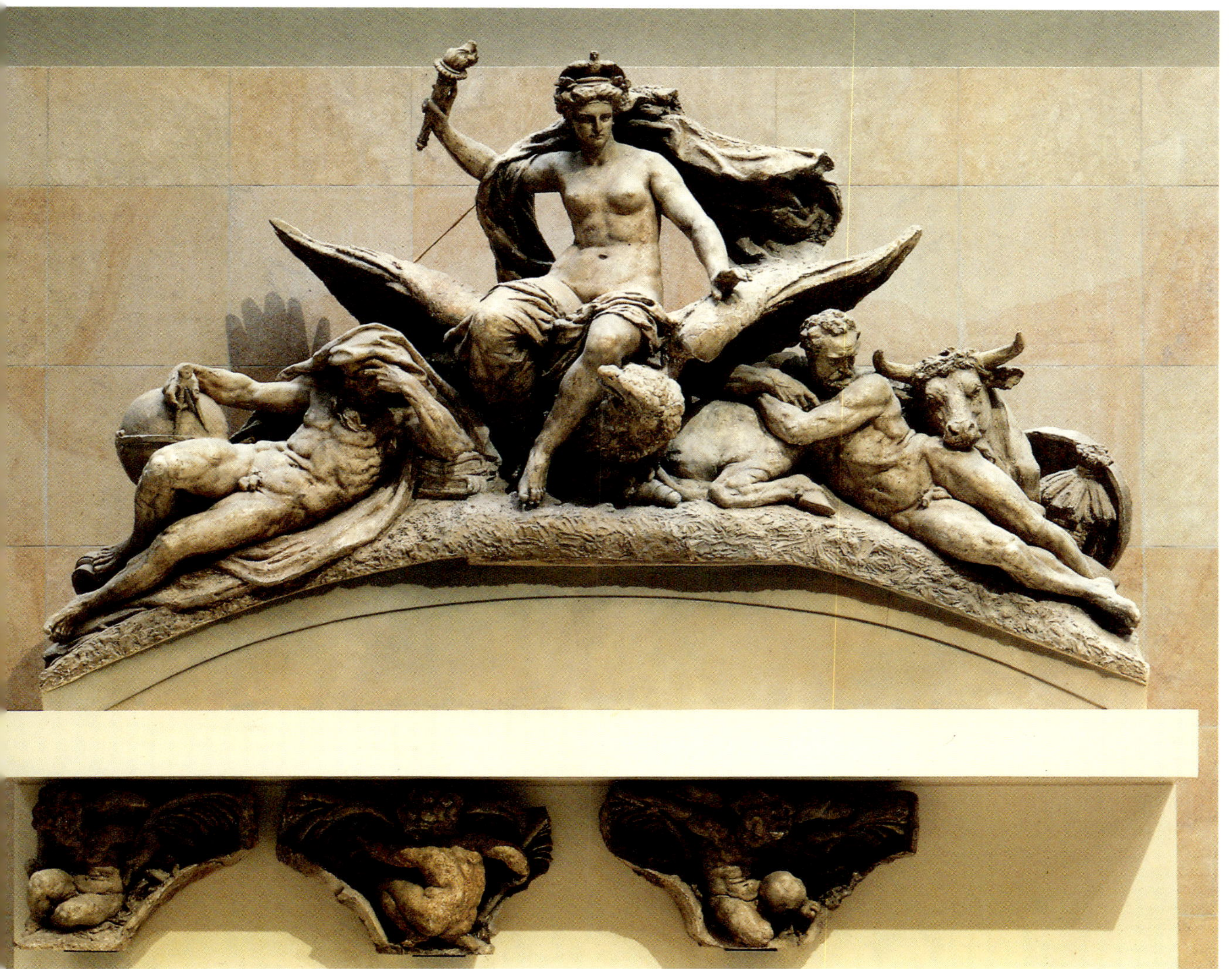

Jean-Baptiste Carpeaux
Valenciennes 1827 – Courbevoie 1875
Imperial France Bringing Light to the World and Protecting Agriculture and Science, 1863–6
Patinated plaster model. 2.68 x 4.27 x 1.62 m
Commission from Hector Lefuel for the top of the Pavillon de Flore of the Louvre;
1866 Salon; acquired from the sculptor's widow, 1892; Museum of Comparative Sculpture, 1892;
Louvre, 1927; Museum of French Monuments, 1949; Louvre, 1964; Orsay, 1986.
RF 1948–50

Despite its southern exposure, few passers-by are aware of the fine piece of propaganda for Napoleon III which crowns the Pavillon de Flore. Its shape has been distorted by the stone's deterioration, which is why the model at the Musée d'Orsay is both an original work, and a reference to the damaged one. This grandiloquent scene borrows its supine poses for the allegories from Michelangelo's San Lorenzo chapel in Florence.
The *Ugolin* study is as powerful as Michelangelo's *Moses* and shows the fourth child, thus completing Carpeaux's rondo of death.

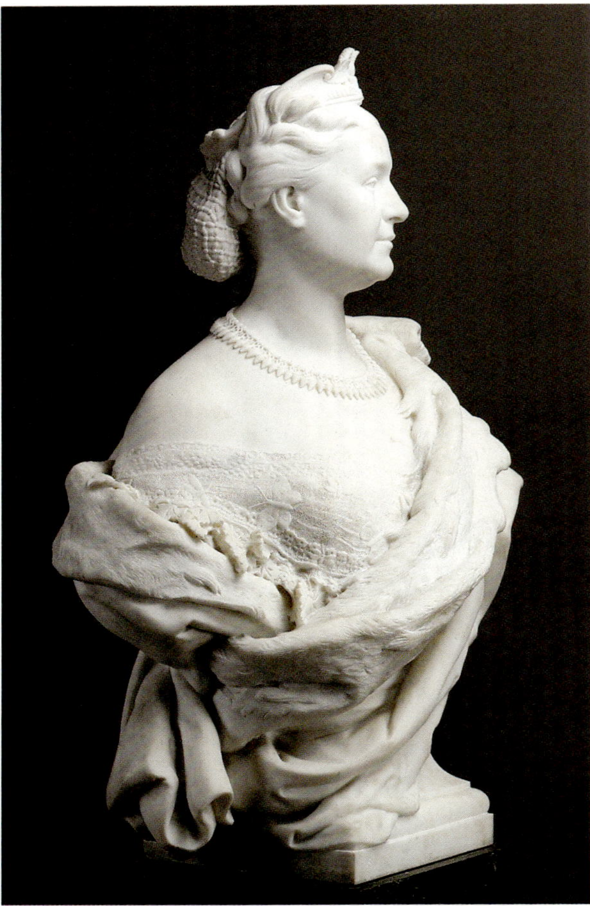

Worthy of Coysevox is Carpeaux's *Princess Mathilde*, an elaborate bust on which the ermine, the bees embroidered on the lace and the eagle on the tiara proclaim the model's rank and function. This marble was bequeathed to the Louvre by the princess, and has therefore had only two owners. The ball gown worn by *Mme Lefebvre* must have been a reminder during her exile in London (1871) of the brilliance of France's last Court.
Carpeaux was named drawing master to the prince imperial in 1864, and was commissioned to execute his young pupil's portrait as a bust, and also full-length. Could the sculptor possibly have sensed that this nine-year-old heir to the throne had no future ahead of him?

Jean-Baptiste Carpeaux
Valenciennes 1827 – Courbevoie 1875
Princess Mathilde (1820–1904), 1862
Marble bust. 0.953 x 0.704 x 0.437 m
Commissioned by the model (daughter of Jérôme Bonaparte, King of Westphalia, and of Catherine de Wurttemberg) and executed on her Saint Gratien estate. Bequest to the Louvre, 1905; Orsay, 1986.
RF 1387

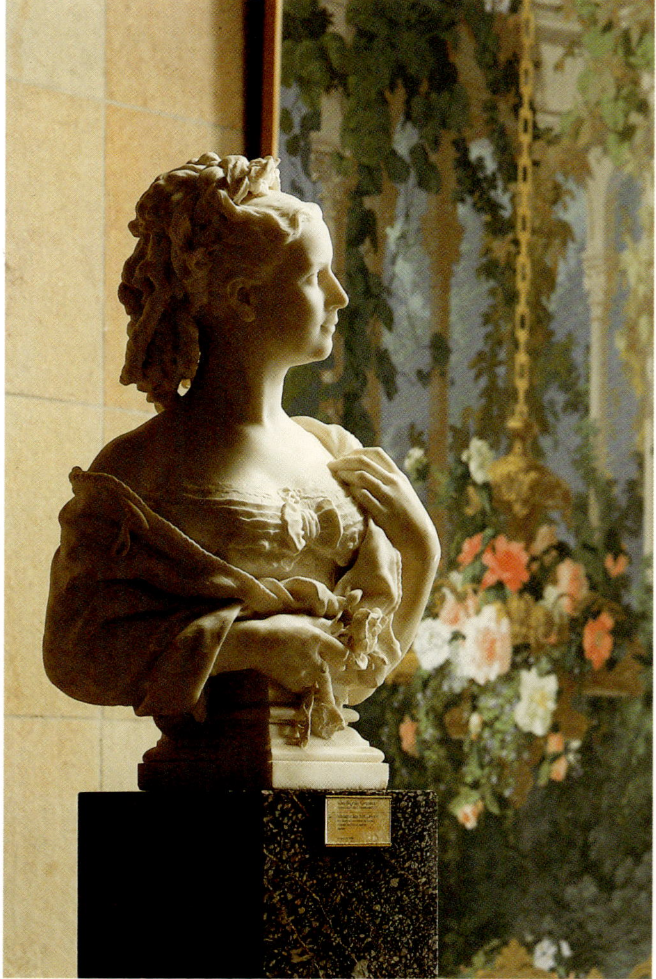

Jean-Baptiste Carpeaux
Valenciennes 1827 – Courbevoie 1875
Mme Joachim Lefebvre, née Marie d'Escoubleau de Sourdis, 1871
Marble bust. 0.82 x 0.538 x 0.353 m
Executed in London; acquired in 1936; Louvre, 1936; Orsay, 1986.
RF 2399

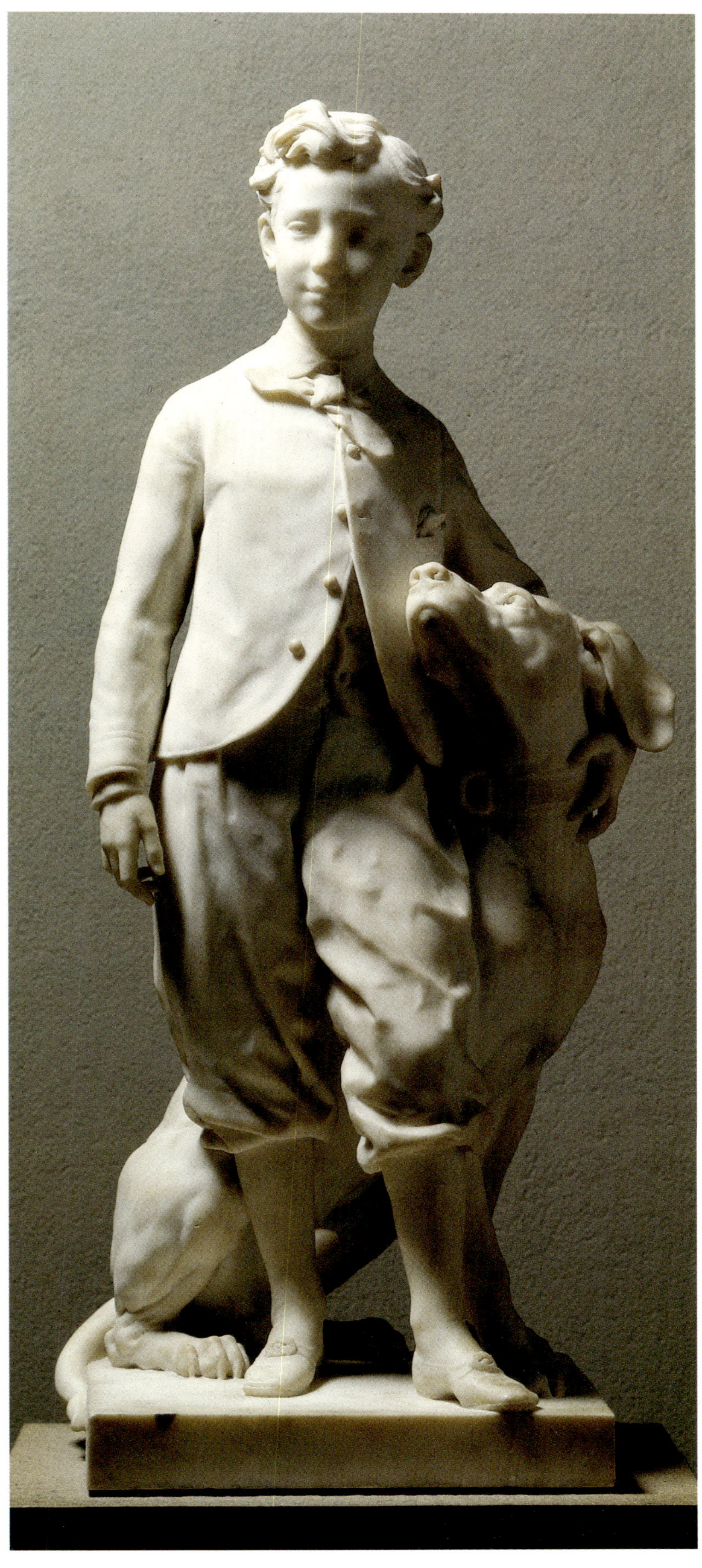

Jean-Baptiste Carpeaux
Valenciennes 1827 – Courbevoie 1875
The Prince Imperial (1856–1879)
and his Dog, 1865
Marble group. 1.40 x 0.654 x 0.615 m
Executed in the Orangerie of the Tuileries; Tuileries Palace (Galerie de Diane), 1867; after 1870, Farnborough, England; acquired by the Fabius family at the empress's 1927 sale; donated to the Nation by Mme Deutsch de la Meurthe, 1930; Palais de Compiègne, 1956; Louvre, 1969; Orsay, 1986.
RF 2042

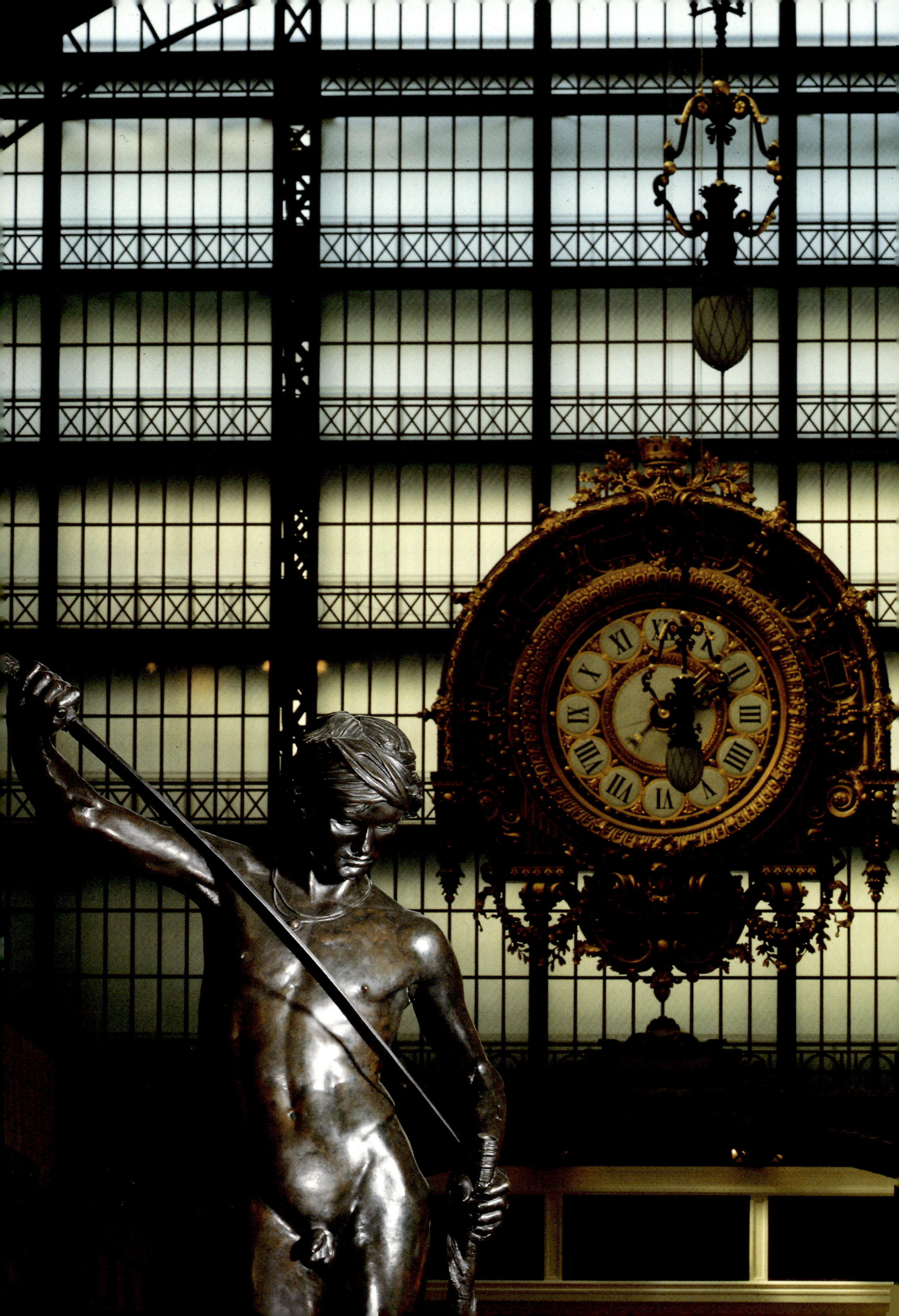

The Eclecticism of the Second Empire

The backward-looking 'historical' 19th century produced that strange mixture known as eclecticism. This new a aesthetic language created out of bits and pieces from the past led to a sort of intoxication with learning among people eager to appropriate both past and future for themselves. Was the French Ecole des Beaux-Arts and its training to blame? It is true that pupils were taught to copy Old Masters. All 19th-century artists were copyists, but this has never been held against Degas or Cézanne, both of whom spent many hours at the Louvre. However, the 20th century has indeed been harsh on those who seemed unable to surpass their sources. This is unfair. There is always something of the period and something of the individual artist in 19th-century works. For example, the exuberant youths of Falguière (Prix de Rome, 1859) and of Moulin, shown together at the Salon of 1864 as we show them at the Musée d'Orsay, may be reminiscent of Giambologna's *Mercury* or the Hellenist *Faun* at the Villa of the Faun in Pompeii, but they are still recognizably Second Empire. Paul Dubois went to Italy at his parents' expense and settled in Florence – a move that left an indelible mark on all of his subsequent sculpture. This enduring influence accounts for the three Medals of Honour won by Dubois (1865, 1876 and 1878), who served first as Assistant Curator of the Luxembourg Museum (1873) and then for 27 years as director of the Ecole des Beaux-Arts. Antonin Mercié, a sculptor who in his youth enjoyed a success denied Rodin, five years his elder, extended the Florentine tradition. After a series of youths à la Donatello came women à la Michelangelo. However, the first woman of the kind was not from this group: Clésinger's *Woman Bitten by a Snake*, a *succès de scandale* that ensured its creator's notoriety at the Salon of 1847. The scandal surrounding the work was orchestrated by Théophile Gautier, who spread a rumour that the cast for the statue had been taken from life. The model was Apollonie Sabatier, called 'camp-follower of the fauns' by the Goncourt brothers, but by Baudelaire 'the beautiful, the good, darling', 'a guardian angel, muse, Madonna' and 'girl who laughs too much'. This notorious work exerted a lasting influence. Sculptors began making the female body more curvaceous and languishing, but omitted the cellulite rippling above Mme Sabatier's thighs that had lent credence to the live-casting rumour. 'A daguerreotype in sculpture', wrote Delacroix, in his journal for 7 May 1847. However, the tide of realism was arrested by subsequent titles for nudes. They were called *Sleeping Hebe* (Carrier-Belleuse), *Eve after the Fall* (Delaplanche) and *Young Tarentine* (Schoenewerk). Mathurin Moreau's *Bacchante* continued this series late into the century.
Another aspect of 19th-century eclecticism was curiosity about other civilizations. Charles Cordier set out to record for posterity the 'various human types that are on the brink of blending into a single, undifferentiated people' and obtained a subsidy from the government to do so. He artfully exploited the beauty of native onyx quarried in Algeria, and returned to the polychromatic style characteristic of wealthy civilizations but rejected by the neoclassical school, which believed that contemporary statues should be as white as excavated antique ones.

Antonin Mercié
Toulouse 1845 – Paris 1916
David, 1871
Bronze statue cast by Victor Thiébaut & Fils. 1.84 x 0.76 x 0.83 m
Plaster executed in Rome (1869–70); bronze commissioned by the Nation, 1872; Luxembourg Museum, 1874; Louvre, 1927; Orsay, 1986.
RF 186

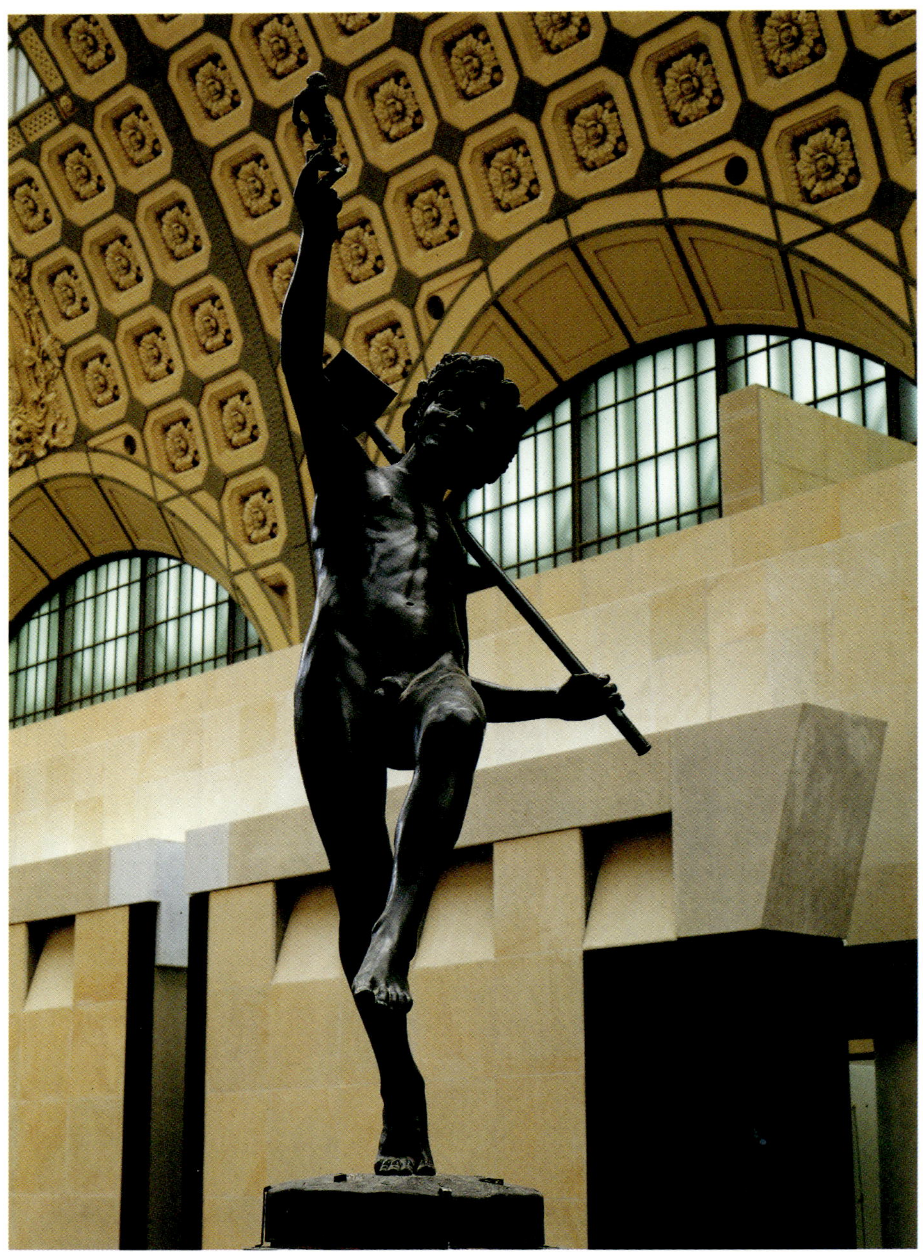

Hippolyte Moulin
Paris 1832 – Charenton 1884
A Find at Pompeii, 1863
Bronze statue cast by Jacquier. 1.87 x 0.64 x 1.055 m
Acquired by the Nation from the 1864 Salon;
Luxembourg Museum before 1866; Louvre, 1931; Orsay, 1986.
RF 190

Duret's *Young Fisherman Dancing the Tarantella* (1833, Louvre) was the first in a promising series. The bronze medium fostered a sense of movement anchored to a single point considered excessive by the critic Castagnary. Although classical and Renaissance models were still in evidence, they later yielded ground to the picturesque, as the title of these two bronzes by Moulin and Falguière attests. The subject of Baujault's even later marble, taken from the Tuileries Gardens, places it in the series of Gauls so prevalent in the second half of the 19th century.

Alexandre Falguière
Toulouse 1831 – Paris 1900
Winner of the Cockfight, 1864
Bronze statue cast by Victor Thiébaut. 1.74 x 1 x 0.82 m
Acquired by the Nation from the 1864 Salon; Tuileries Gardens, 1872; Luxembourg Museum, 1878; Louvre, 1923; Orsay, 1986.
RF 144

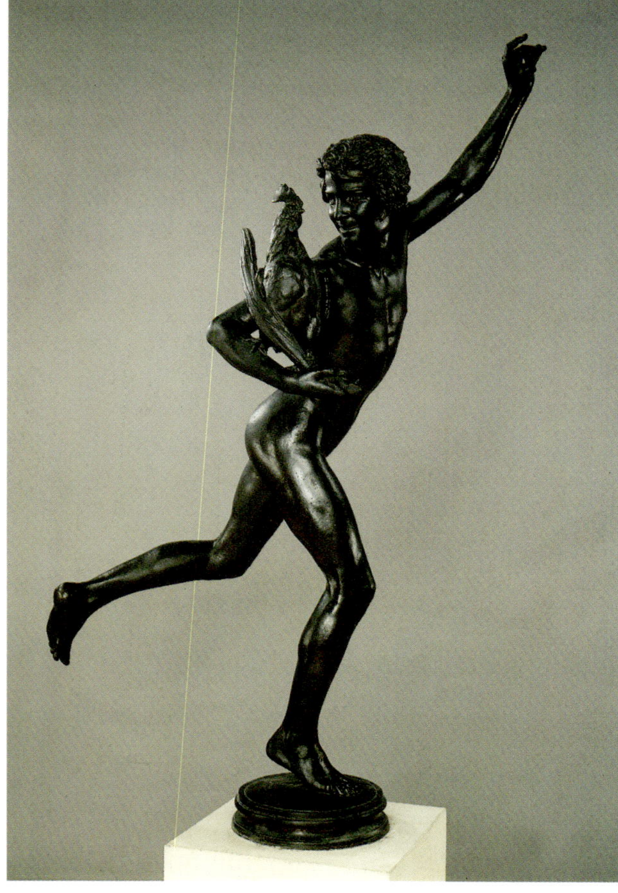

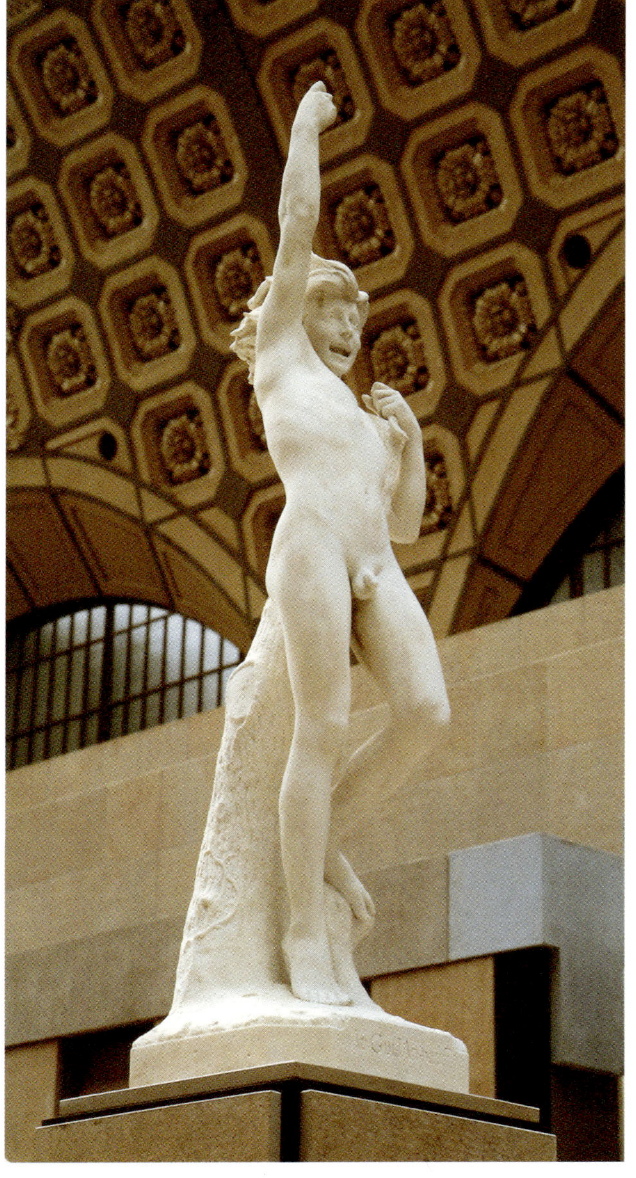

Jean-Baptiste Baujault
La Crêche 1828 – La Crêche 1899
Young Gaul or 'New Year's Mistletoe!', 1870–75
Marble statue. 2.42 x 0.53 x 0.55 m
Acquired by the Nation, 1875; Tuileries Gardens, 1878; Louvre, 1979; Orsay, 1986.
(The mistletoe has disappeared before 1979.)
RF 207

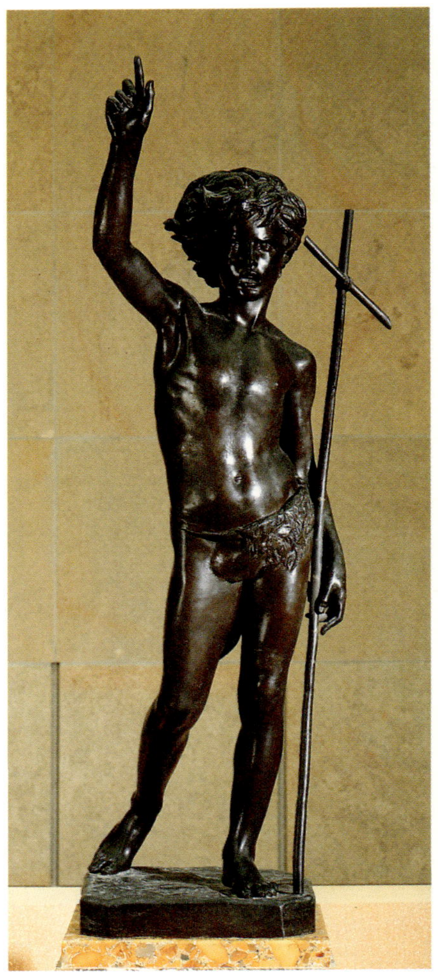

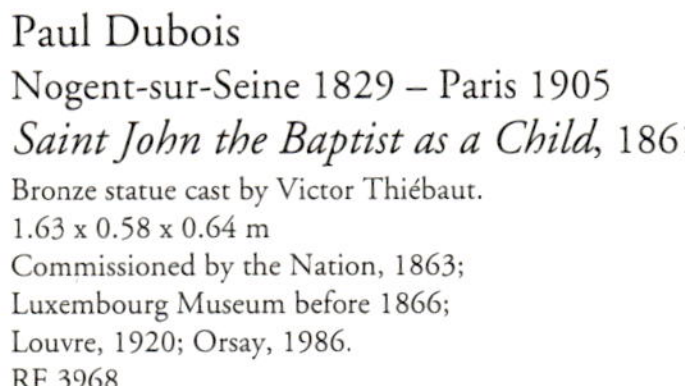

Paul Dubois
Nogent-sur-Seine 1829 – Paris 1905
Saint John the Baptist as a Child, 1861
Bronze statue cast by Victor Thiébaut.
1.63 x 0.58 x 0.64 m
Commissioned by the Nation, 1863;
Luxembourg Museum before 1866;
Louvre, 1920; Orsay, 1986.
RF 3968

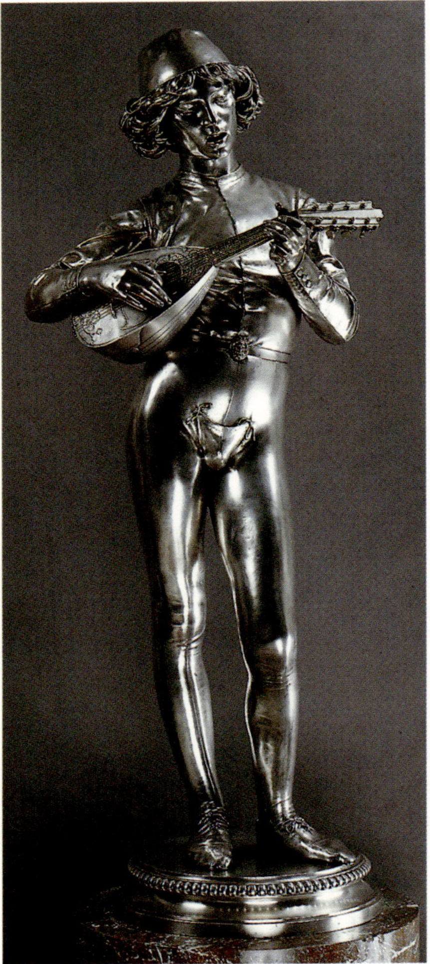

Paul Dubois
Nogent-sur-Seine 1829 – Paris 1905
15th-Century Florentine Singer, 1865
Silver-plated bronze statue cast by F. Barbedienne.
1.55 x 0.58 x 0.50 m
Ordered after the 1865 Salon (Medal of Honour);
Superintendent Nieuwerkerke's apartment at the Louvre, 1866;
Luxembourg Museum, 1871; Louvre, 1920; Orsay, 1986.
RF 2998

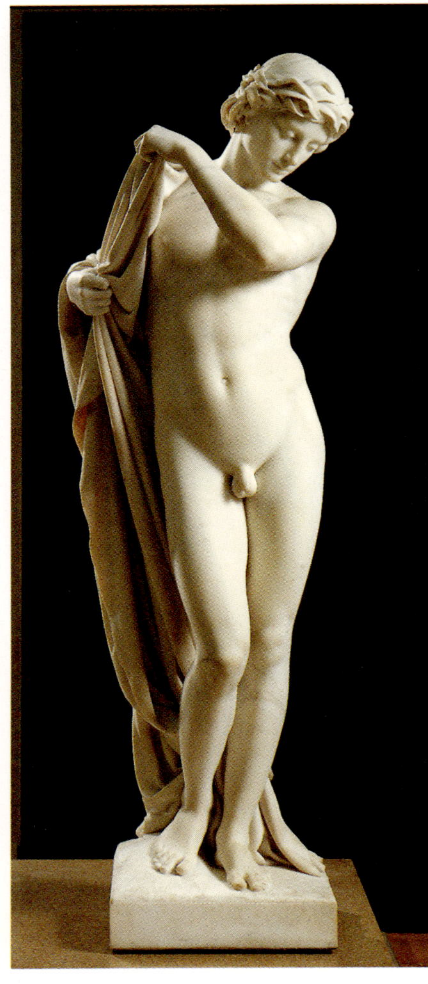

Paul Dubois
Nogent-sur-Seine 1829 – Paris 1905
Narcissus, 1862–7
Marble statue. 1.852 x 0.67 x 0.62 m
First marble placed in the Cour Carrée of the Louvre, 1866;
replica made for the 1867 World's Fair;
Luxembourg Museum, 1878;
Louvre, 1923; Orsay, 1986.
RF 2221

Here we see the elegance of Paul Dubois, whether the subject is religious, picturesque or mythological. Dubois modelled his drawing on 14th-century frescoes, which was a novelty at the time and gave his figures a delicate grace. Miniature replicas abounded.

The virtuoso decorative artist Carrier-Belleuse is represented here by a monumental group executed with astonishing grandeur. Jupiter's eagle is a benevolent allusion to the Empire.

Albert-Ernest Carrier-Belleuse ▷
Anisy-le-Château 1824 – Sèvres 1887
Sleeping Hebe, 1869
Marble group. 2.07 x 1.46 x 0.85 m
Commissioned by the Nation, 1868;
Luxembourg Museum before 1872; Louvre, 1904;
Orsay, 1986.
RF 163

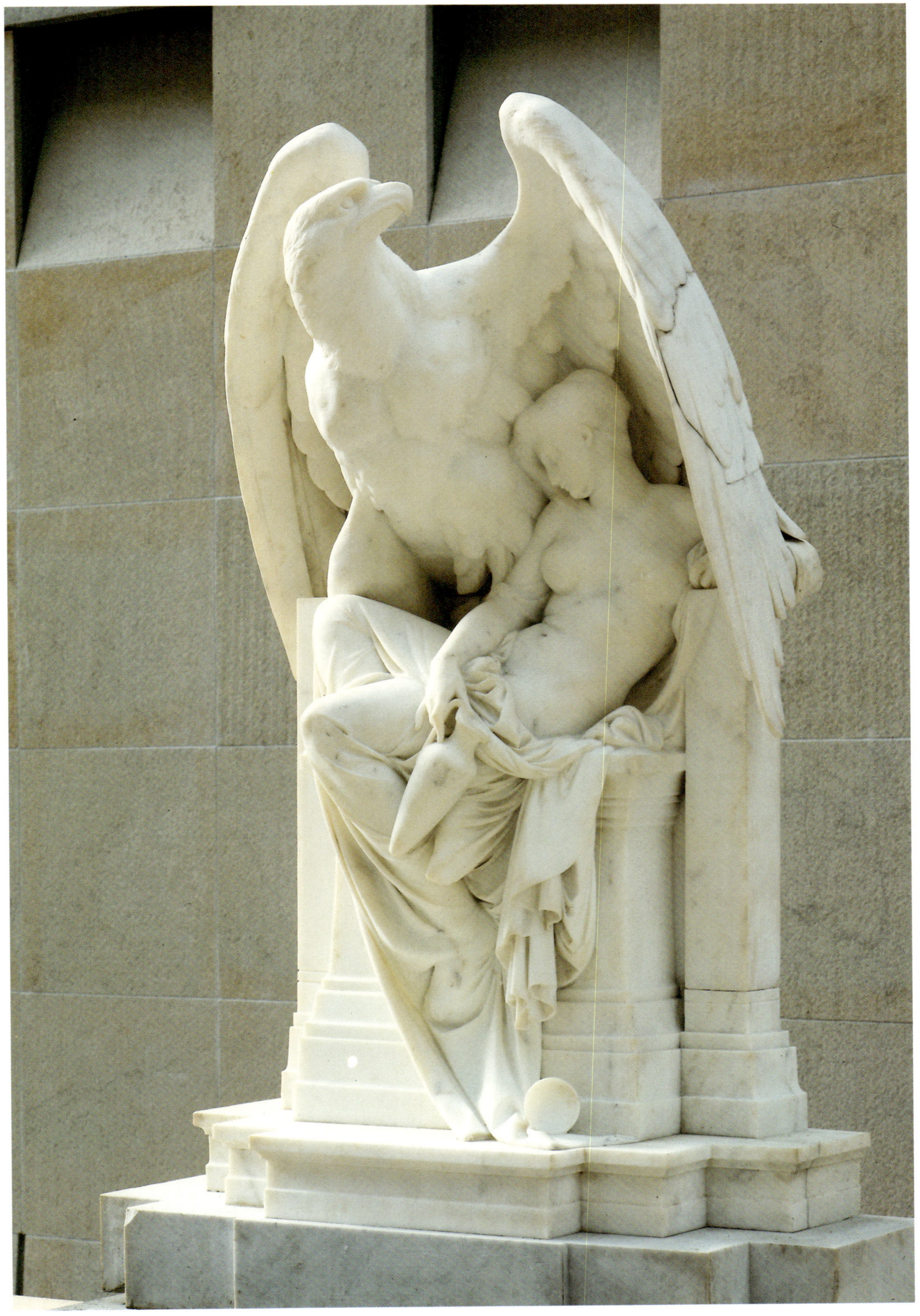

Jean-Joseph Perraud
Monay 1819 – Paris 1876
Despair, 1869
Marble statue. 1.08 x 0.68 x 1.18 m
Acquired by the Nation from the 1869 Salon (Medal of Honour); Luxembourg Museum; Lons-le-Saunier Museum, 1902; exchanged for Perraud's *The Childhood of Bacchus* (1863); Orsay, 1986.
RF 197

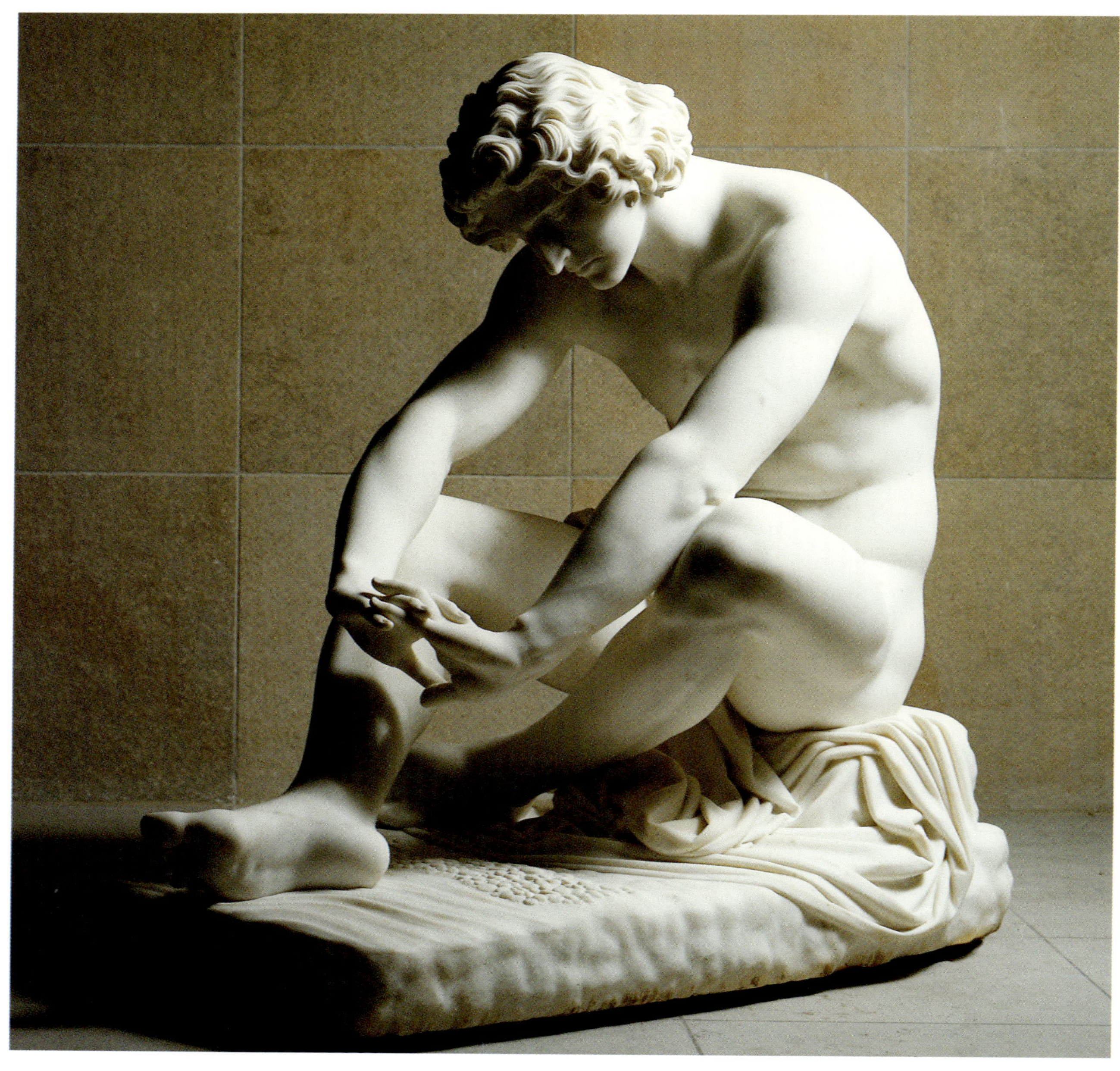

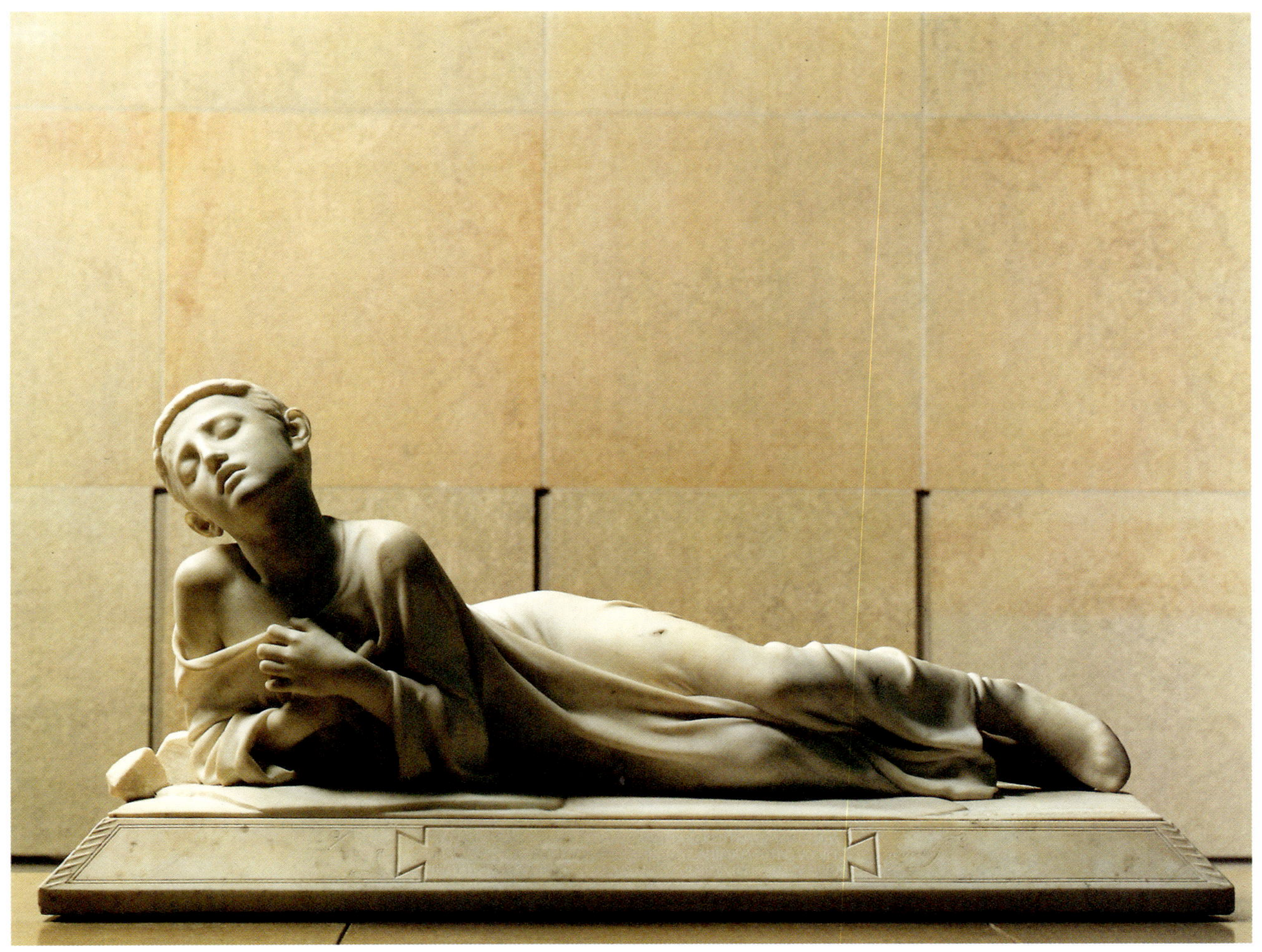

Alexandre Falguière
Toulouse 1831 – Paris 1900
Tarcisius, 1868
Marble statue. 0.645 x 1.40 x 0.60 m
Commissioned by the Nation in 1867; 1868 Salon (Medal of Honour);
Luxembourg Museum, 1871; Louvre, 1926; Orsay, 1986.
RF 174

These two marbles were each, in succeeding years, awarded the Salon's Medal of Honour. *Tarcisius*, drawn from Cardinal Wieseman's famous novel *Fabiola* (1854), depicted the 'contagious passion ... for emaciated little children' denounced by the critic Théophile Thoré in his *Salon de 1868*, and the religiosity of the Second Empire, which re-established the ties between throne and altar. Perraud's *Despair*, a romantic subject with neoclassical muscles, would be a masterpiece if it were not for the head – as noted in 1869 by another critic, Jules Antoine Castagnary.

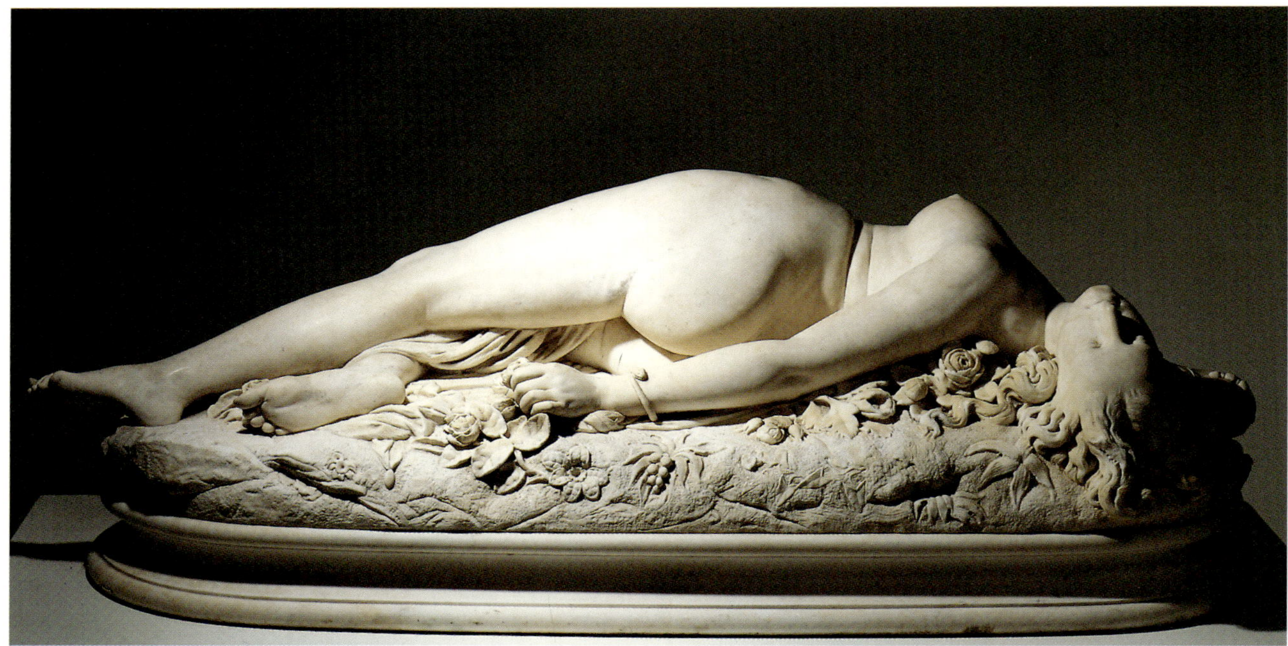

Auguste (Jean-Baptiste) Clésinger
Besançon 1814 – Paris 1883
Woman Bitten by a Snake, 1847
Marble haut-relief. 0.565 x 1.80 x 0.70 m
1847 Salon (2nd-place medal); acquired from the Princess Galitzine in 1931 despite the Committee's objections to its 'indecency'; Louvre, 1931; Orsay, 1986.
RF 2053

Alexandre Schoenewerk
Paris 1820 – Paris 1885
Young Tarentine, 1871
Marble statue. 0.74 x 1.71 x 0.68 m
Acquired by the Nation from the 1872 Salon; Luxembourg Museum, 1874; Louvre, 1876; Château de Compiègne, 1881; Orsay, 1986.
RF 215

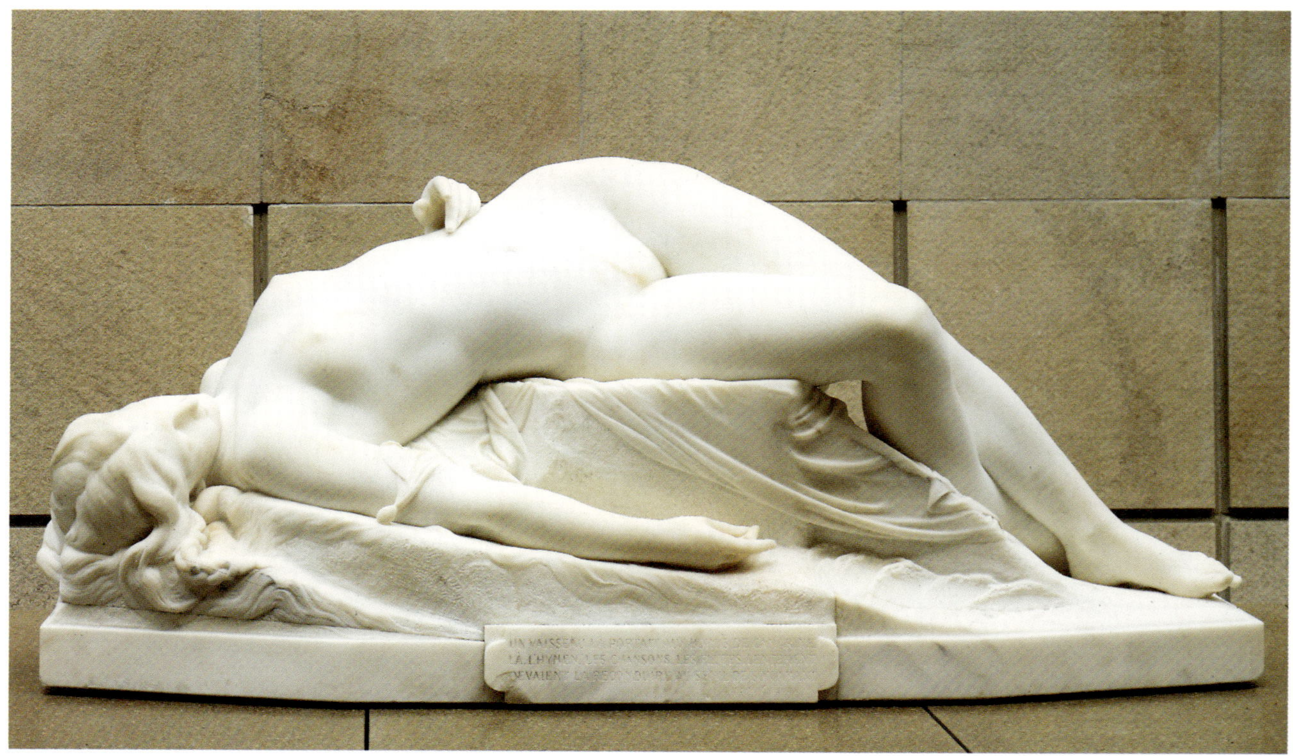

Eugène Delaplanche
Belleville 1836 – Paris 1891
Eve after the Fall, 1869
Marble statue. 1.45 x 0.92 x 0.74 m
Final-year submission from Rome;
acquired by the Nation from the 1870 Salon;
Luxembourg Gardens, Luxembourg Museum, 1874;
Tuileries Gardens, 1893; Lécuyer Museum,
Saint Quentin, 1935; Orsay, 1982.
RF 196

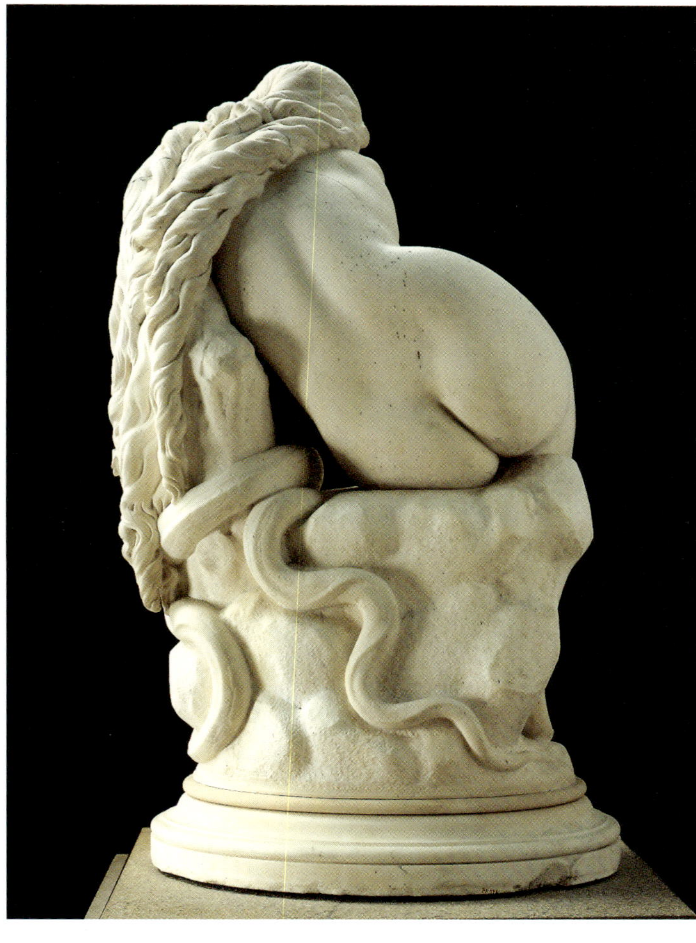

Its lush forms recalling Michelangelo and its unruly tresses Baudelaire, Delaplanche's *Eve after the Fall* is the only Second Empire work whose true place is here.

Augustin-Jean Moreau-Vauthier
Paris 1831 – Paris 1893
Reclining Bacchante, 1892
Marble haut-relief. 0.58 x 1.86 x 0.74 m
SAF Salon, 1892; gift of the artist's heirs, 1895;
Luxembourg Museum, 1896; Louvre, 1929;
Orsay, 1986.
RF 2225

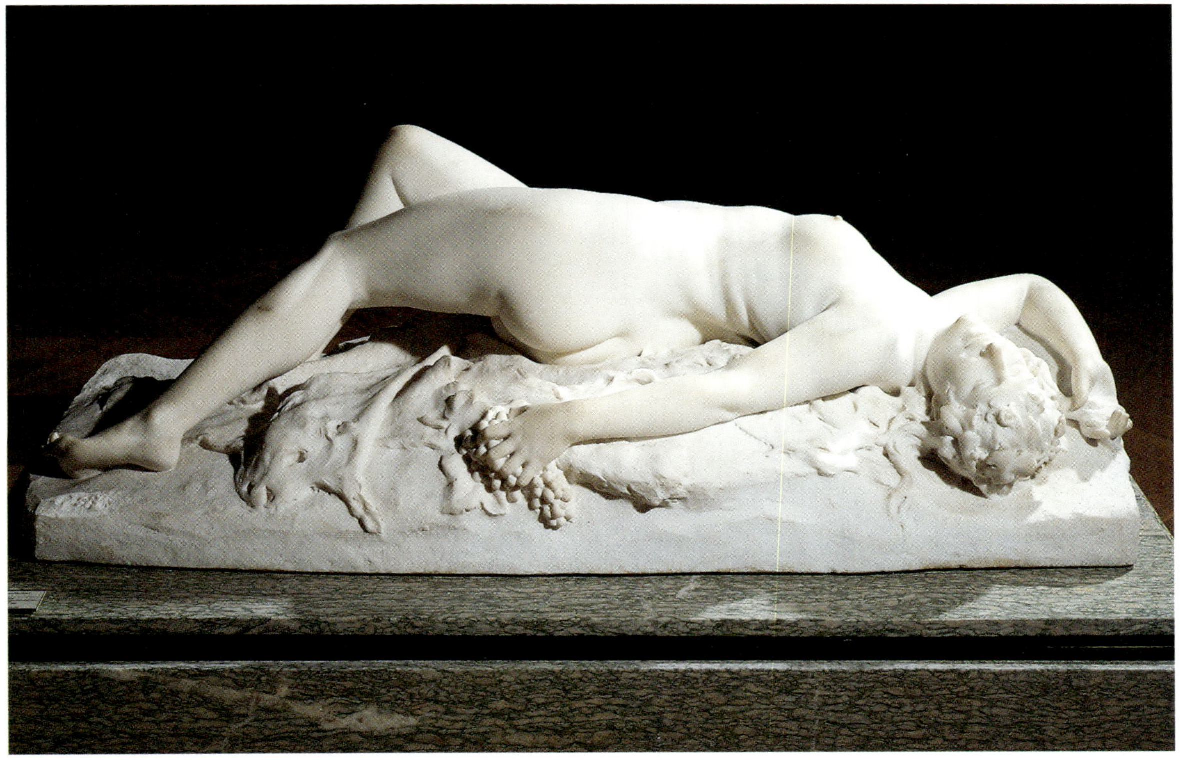

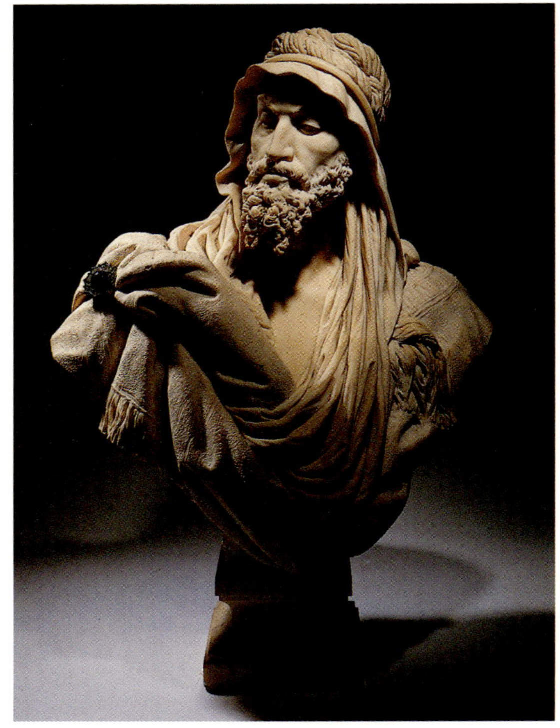

Marcello (pseud.)(Adèle d'Affry, Duchess of Castiglione-Colonna)
Givisiez, Switzerland 1836 – Castellamare, Italy (Papal States) 1879
Abyssinian Chieftain, 1870
Bust in marble, bronze and lapis-lazuli.
1.06 x 0.76 x 0.51 m
Acquired by the Nation in 1871;
Luxembourg Museum, 1873;
Lyon Musée des Beaux-Arts, 1886; National Depository, 1951; Orsay, 1984.
RF 3685

Charles Cordier
Cambrai 1827 – Algiers 1905
Negro of the Sudan, 1857
Bust in Algerian onyx, Vosges porphyry and bronze. 0.96 x 0.66 x 0.36 m
Acquired by Napoleon III from the 1857 Salon;
Luxembourg Museum, 1872; Louvre, 1920; Orsay,1986.
RF 2997

Charles Cordier
Cambrai 1827 – Algiers 1905
Cape Colony Woman, 1861
Bust in Algerian onyx, Vosges porphyry and gilded bronze. 0.96 x 0.54 x 0.28 m
Acquired by the Nation from the 1861 Salon;
Luxembourg Museum, 1870; Louvre, 1920; Orsay, 1986.
RF 2996

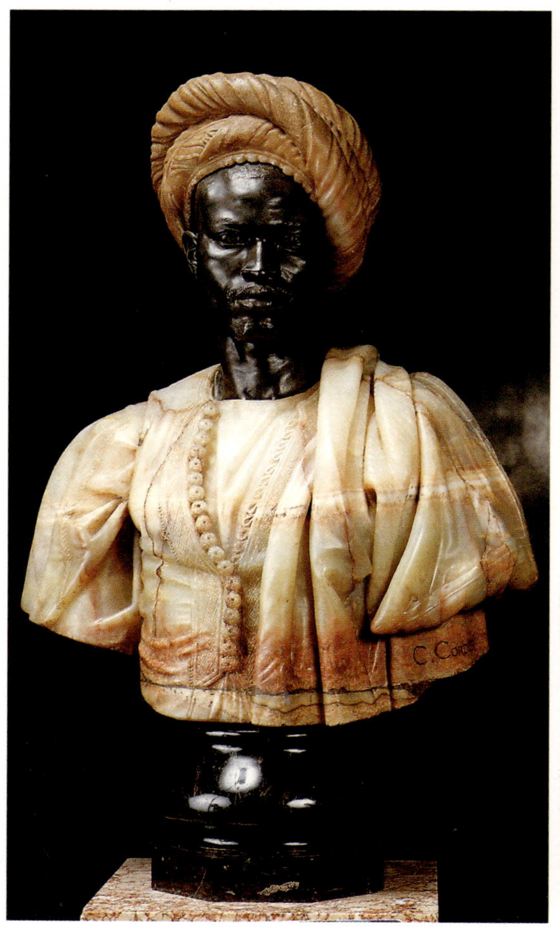

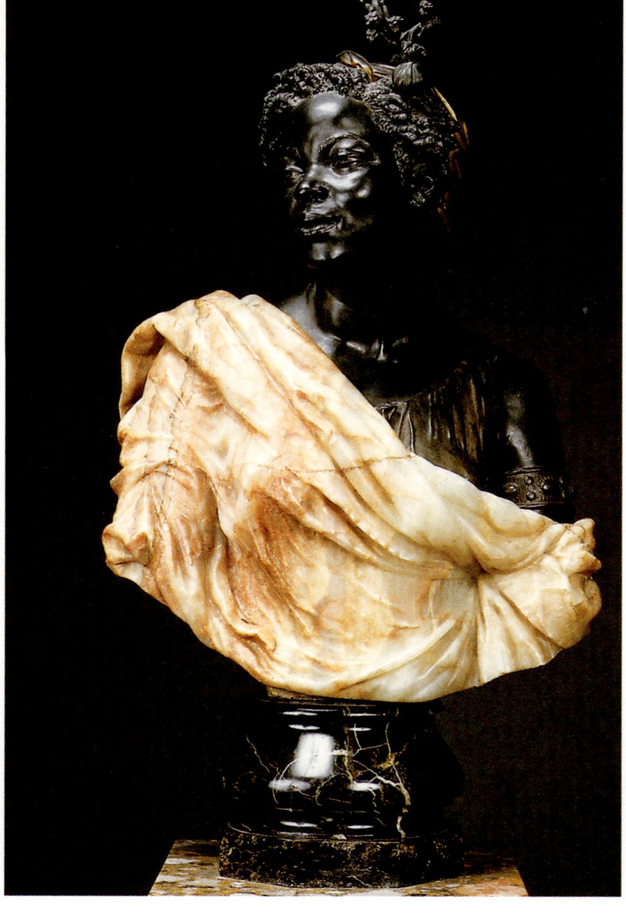

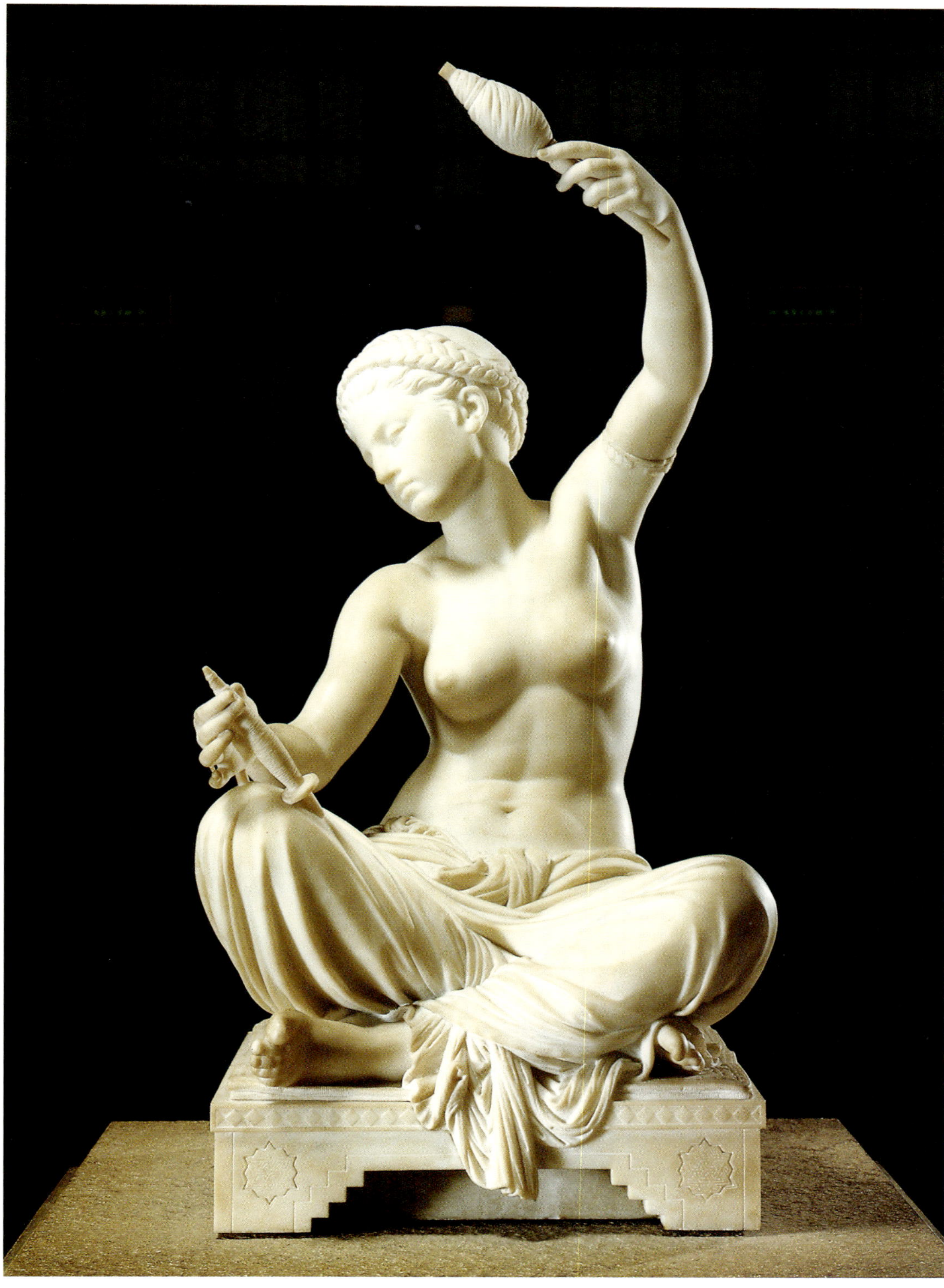

Louis-Ernest Barrias
Paris 1841 – Paris 1905
Young Girl of Megara, 1870
Marble statue. 1.26 x 0.63 x 0.66 m
Plaster executed in Rome, 1867;
Acquired from the 1870 Salon;
Luxembourg Museum, 1872; Louvre, 1923;
Orsay, 1986.
RF 159

Cordier wanted to 'widen the circle of beauty ... by initiating the study of different races'. His bust of *Saïd Abdalah of the Kingdom of Darfour* exhibited at the Salon of 1848 was his first 'ethnographic' study. It owed nothing to science and everything to the sensibility of an artist who set about exploiting the vivid colours of exotic materials that appealed both to Queen Victoria and to Napoleon III. The *Young Girl of Megara* by Barrias is more orientalist in the version of 1890, which he made to mark the grave of the painter Guillaumet in the Montmartre Cemetery.

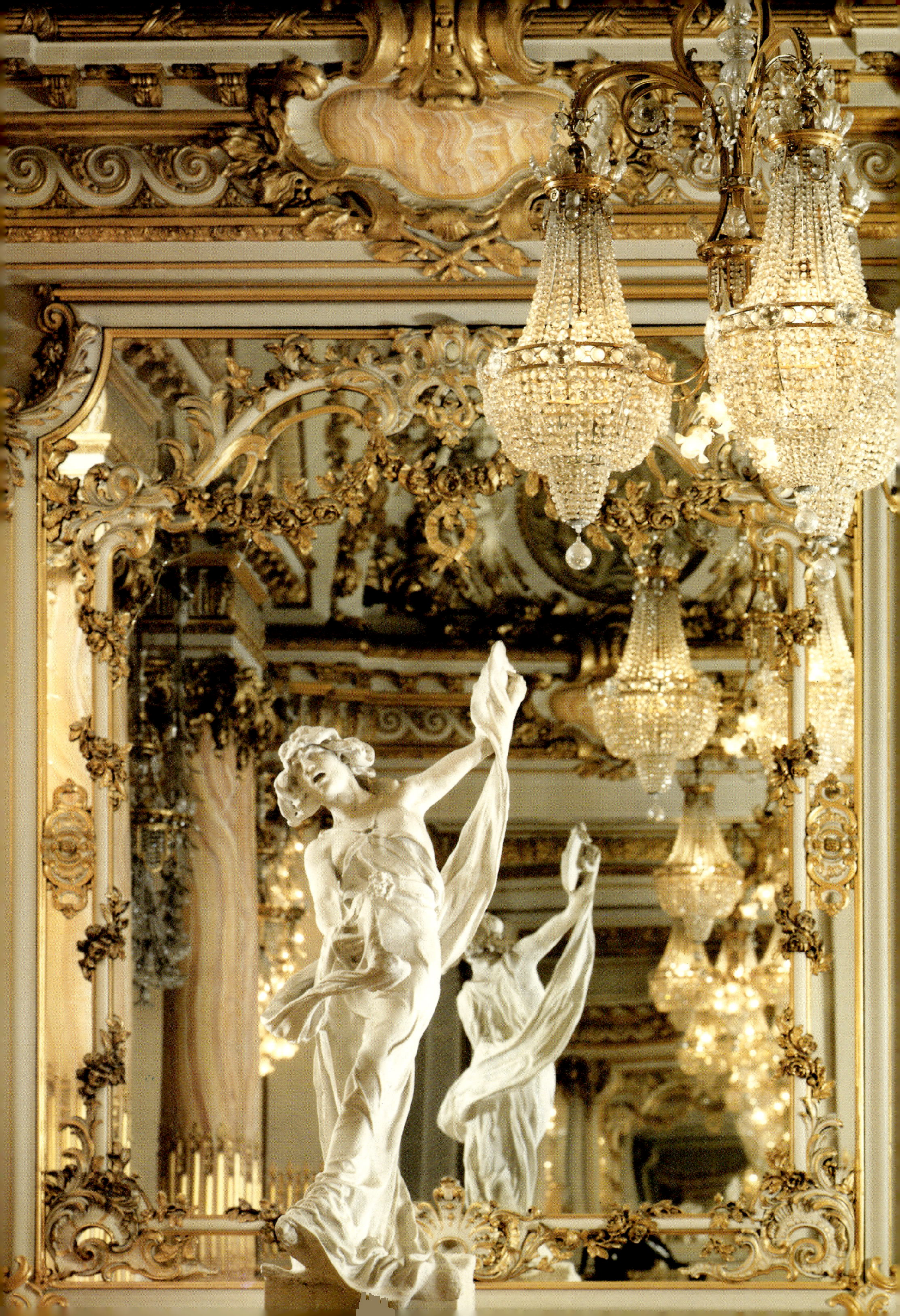

Electicism and the Third Republic

The ballroom (1900) of the hotel built into the Gare d'Orsay railway station was modelled on the Hall of Mirrors at Versailles – gilding, plaster mouldings, allegorical paintings, mirrors reflecting to infinity the crystal chandeliers and garlands that conceal – a novelty – electric-light fixtures. It seemed no more than fitting to use this room for displaying the Salon prize-winners saved from cellars and attics where they languished for 50 years under layers of dust.

The Florentine style popular during the Second Empire was followed by Neo-Baroque. This sea change washed over the republic and culminated in the World's Fair of 1900, for which the broad avenue that runs from Louis XIV's Les Invalides, across the Alexander III bridge and between the Petit Palais and the Grand Palais was built. The republicans wanted to outdo the monarchs who had designed Paris. They appreciated the triumphal style, but could not forget that their own lives had been marked by France's defeat in the Franco-Prussian War of 1870, and patriotic statuary thus began a reign prolonged by the two wars yet to come. Following the triumph of the true republicans in 1879, numerous sculpture competitions were launched for pieces to commemorate the new regime. Previously erected monuments did not survive the test of time. The Arc de Triomphe at the Etoile lost Fremiet's quadrigae *The Triumph of the Revolution*, which in plaster survives only in photographs of Victor Hugo's funeral, and in wax at the Musée d'Orsay (study from the Général de Beylie collection, Grenoble Museum Depository). The Louvre's Cour Napoléon lost the *Monument to Gambetta* erected by international public subscription (1884–8), one 'detail' of which, discovered after having been hidden away for 38 years, was placed behind the Town Hall of Paris's 20th *arrondissement* in 1982 to celebrate the centenary of the populist leader's death. The Pantheon lost Falguière's colossal plaster statue, *The Triumph of the Republic*, from its choir (studies on display at the Musée d'Orsay). On the other hand, historical sites that had never been commemorated received monuments still standing today – by the Morice brothers in the Place de la République; and by Dalou in the Place de la Nation. The latter is the largest bronze monument in Paris except for the columns in the Place Vendôme and at the Bastille.

Eclecticism dominated a bourgeoisie entranced with Henri II dining-rooms, Louis XV living-rooms and Louis XVI bedrooms. This public wanted versatile sculpture that would fit into their interior decoration schemes. Miniaturization, sand-casting and auction catalogues all fostered the proliferation of statuettes. Some of these miniatures were originals designed for sale (by Moreau, Picault, etc.). Others were reduced-size replicas of museum pieces, such as the small bronzes based on *the Sacred Dance* by Prix de Rome laureate Ségoffin, the sinuous lines of its cymbal-player heralding the transition from Neo-Baroque to Art Nouveau.

Victor Ségoffin
Toulouse 1867 – Paris 1925
War Dance or *Sacred Dance*, 1905
Marble statue.
2.50 x 1.40 x 0.80 m
Commissioned in 1904 for the gardens of the Elysée Palace (broken arm); National Depository; transferred to Orsay and restored, 1984.
RF 3686

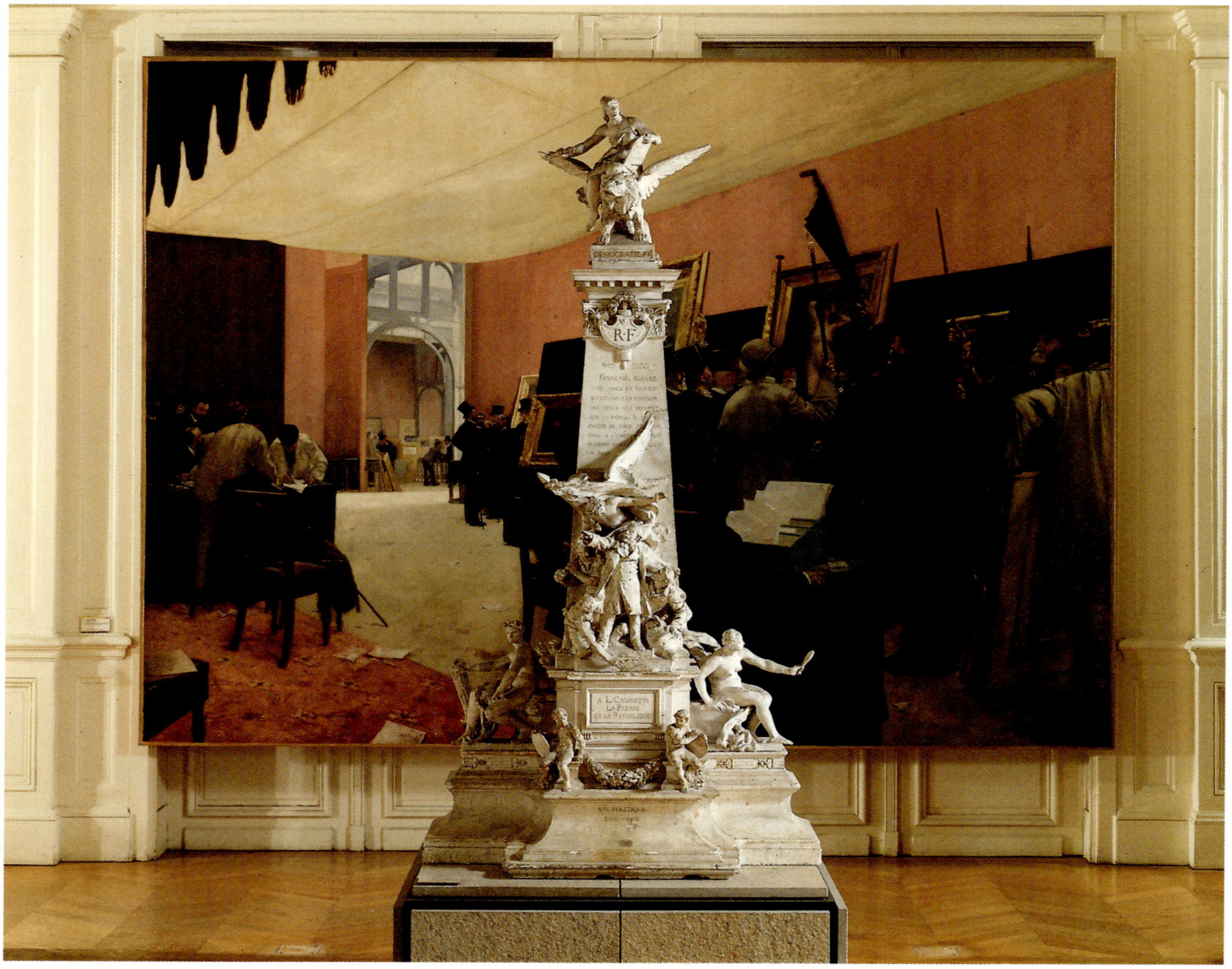

Jean-Paul Aubé
Longwy 1837 – Capbreton 1916
Monument to Léon Gambetta (1838–1882), 1884
Plaster model to 1/90 scale. 2.40 x 1.22 x 0.98 m
The 1884 competition winner. The monument was inaugurated in the Cour Napoléon of the Louvre on 14 July 1888, stripped of its bronzes during the occupation, and removed in 1954.
Museum of Decorative Arts Depository; Orsay, 1980.
DO 1980–13

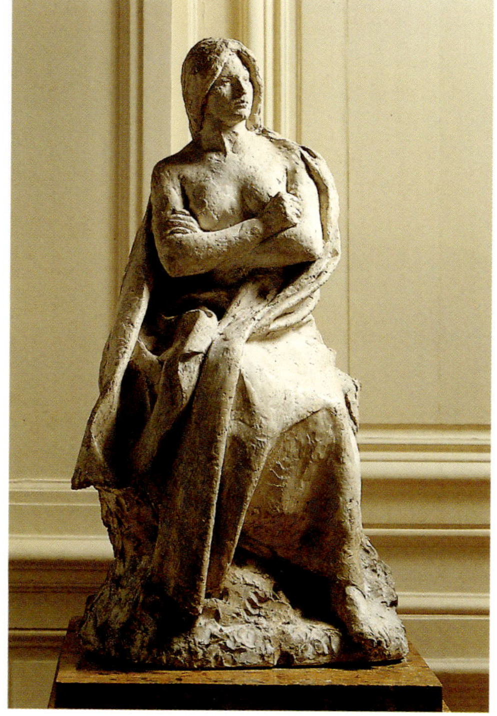

Alexandre Falguière
Toulouse 1831 – Paris 1900
Resistance, 1870
Plaster model. 1.10 x 0.63 x 0.55 m
Commemoration of the snow statue built on the ramparts of Paris during the siege of 1870, described by Théophile Gautier and Théodore de Banville. Gift of Gustave Sins 1950; Louvre, 1950; Orsay, 1986.
RF 2672

1871: Rude's son-in-law Cabet sculpts a *Nation in Mourning*, Falguière models a *Resistance* in snow on the ramparts of besieged Paris, Aubé depicts Gambetta's call to arms from the centre of a group similar to the one on the Arc de Triomphe, and Mercié executes his *Gloria Victis*.

Paul Cabet
Nuits-Saint-Georges 1815 – Paris 1876
Eighteen Hundred and Seventy-One, 1877
Marble statue. 1.25 x 0.66 x 1.01 m
Plaster, 1872 Salon; commissioned by the Nation, 1873;
Realized by Daumas after Cabet's death; 1877 Salon;
Luxembourg Museum, 1877; Douai Museum, 1886;
Dijon Museum, 1890; Nuits-Saint-Georges Town Hall, 1970;
Orsay, 1986.
RF 747

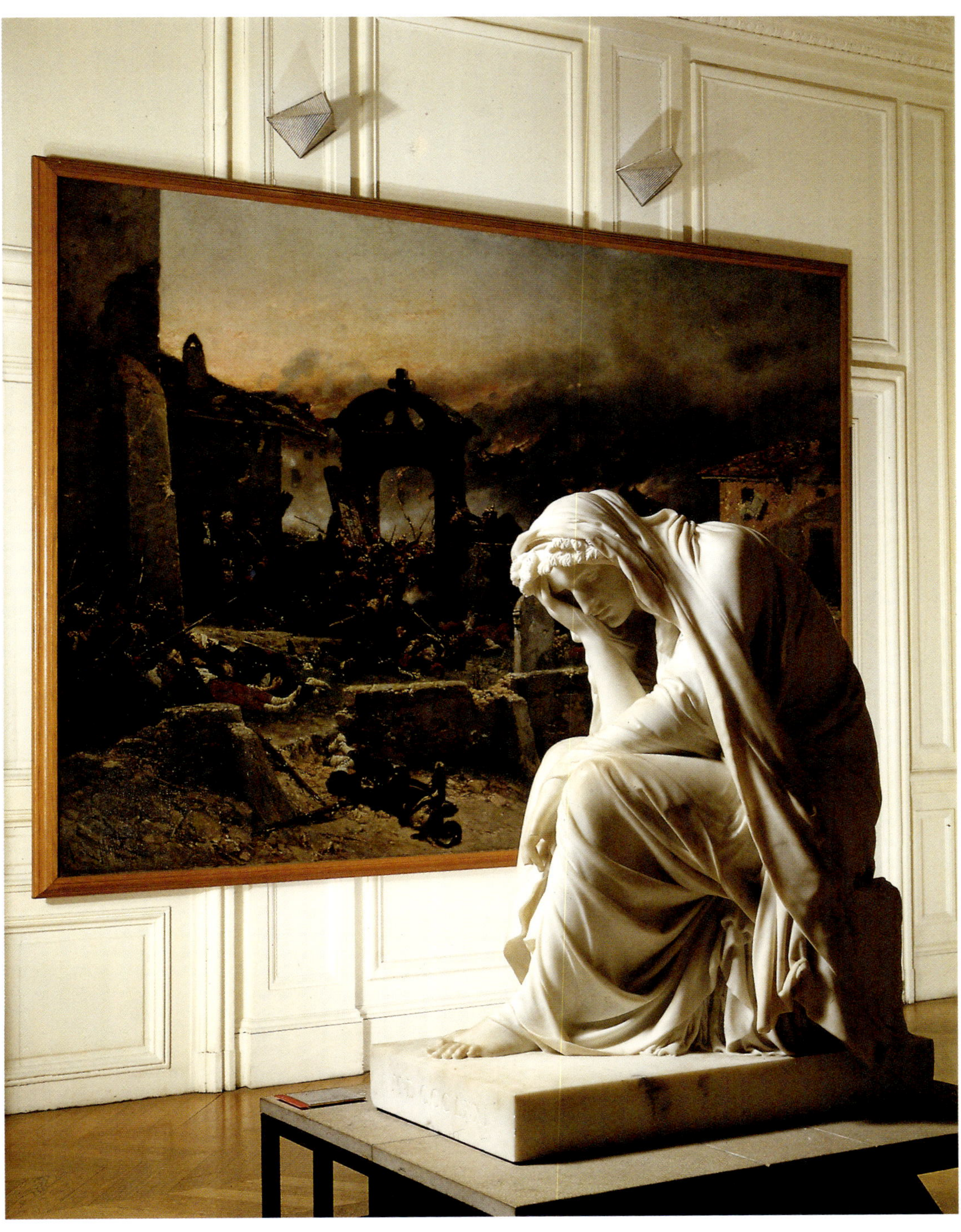

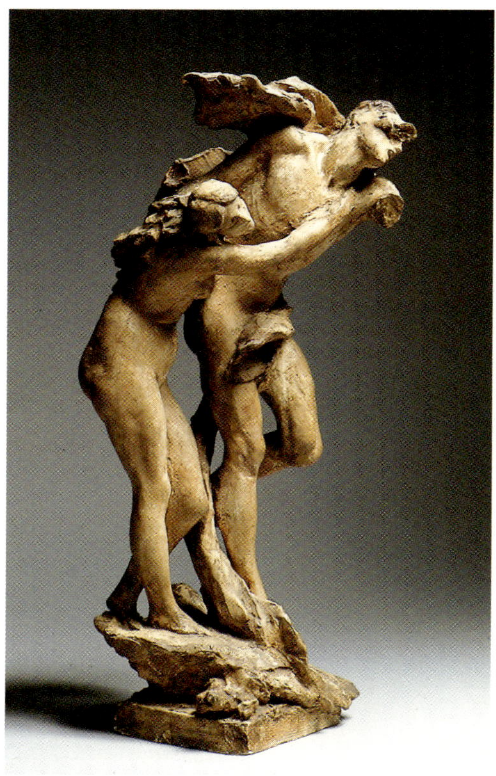

The common feature uniting these sculptures is the posture and drapery: on the left: Michelangelo's influence destroys classic balance of literary and allegorical nudity. On the right: Fremiet's historical realism underpins the stasis of an unequal combat with its centred windmill silhouette. In each case, floating drapery restores the balance.

Emmanuel Fremiet ▷
Paris 1824 – Paris 1910
Saint Michael and the Dragon, 1897
Beaten copper enlargement. 6.17 x 2.60 x 1.20 m
Based on a gilded bronze statue shown at the 1879 Salon; commissioned in 1897 by the Nation from Monduit to serve as a weathervane on the steeple of Mont Saint-Michel; replica donated by Mme G. Pasquier to the French Department of Historical Monuments; Orsay Depository, 1983.
DO 1983-80

Joan of Arc on Horseback
Plaster miniature of the original monument in the Place des Pyramides, Paris.
0.75 x 0.46 x 0.22 m
Gift of Blanche Fauré-Fremiet, 1979.
RF 3437

Wandering Knight
Plaster study for the large 1878 Salon plaster model based on Victor Hugo's *La Légende des siècles* held by the Lille Musée des Beaux-Arts. 0.42 x 0.355 x 0.155 m
Gift of Blanche Fauré-Fremiet, 1979.
RF 3431

Jean Hugues
Marseilles 1849 – Paris 1930
Shades of Paolo and Francesca da Rimini, 1877
Plaster. 0.53 x 0.21 x 0.23 m
Sketch for the second submission from Rome; 1879 Salon (unplaced);
Gift of Messrs Hugues, grandsons of the sculptor, 1979.
RF 3445

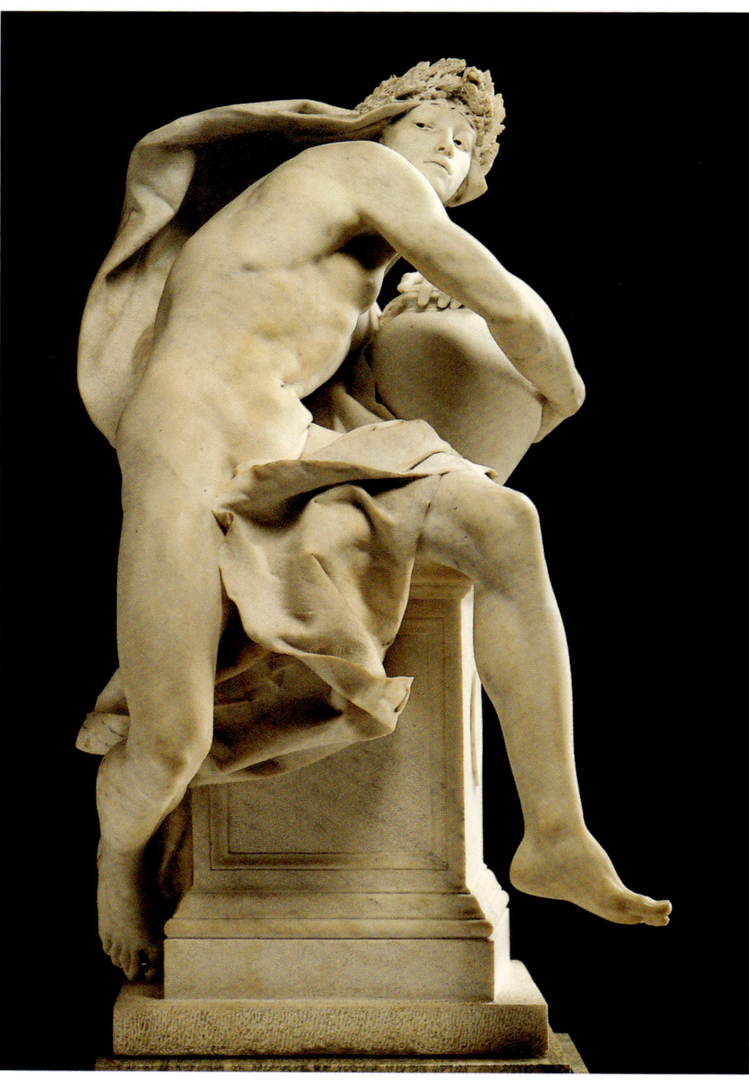

Charles René de Paul de Saint-Marceaux
Rheims 1845 – Paris 1915
Spirit Guarding the Secret of the Tomb, 1879
Marble group. 1.68 x 0.95 x 1.19 m
Acquired by the Nation from the 1879 Salon (1st-place medal and Medal of Honour); Luxembourg Museum, 1879;
Louvre, 1933; Orsay, 1986.
RF 300

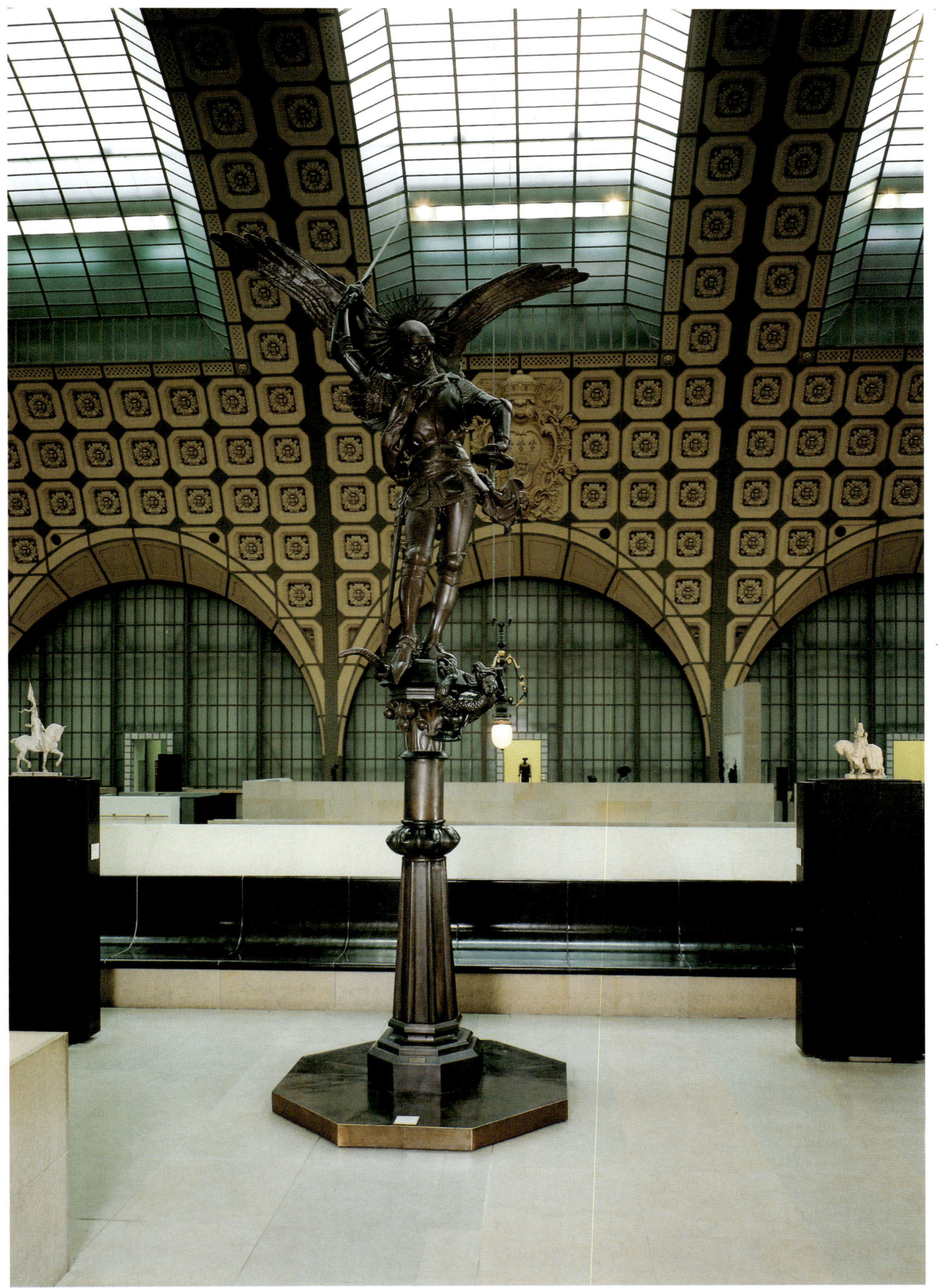

Antonin (Jean Antoine) Injalbert
Béziers 1845 – Paris 1933
Vase with Mascarons, Nymphs and Satyrs, 1905
Marble. 1.04 x 1.40 x 1.10 m
SNBA Salon, 1905; acquired by the Nation, 1906; Luxembourg Museum, 1907; Senate, 1917; Orsay, 1984.
RF 1402

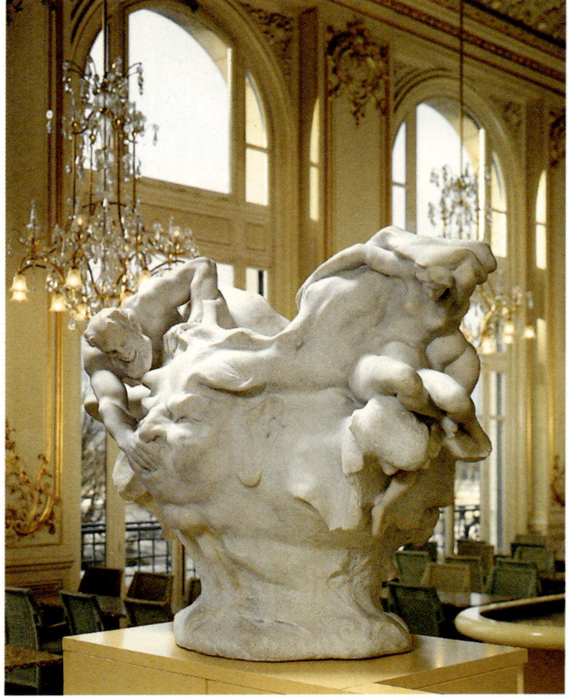

Théophile Barrau
Carcassone 1848 – Paris 1913
Suzanne, 1895
Marble statue. 2.13 x 0.59 x 0.658 m
Acquired by the Nation from the 1895 SAF Salon; Chamber of Deputies, 1901; damaged 1908; Louvre, 1935; restored, 1961; Orsay, 1986.
RF 2441

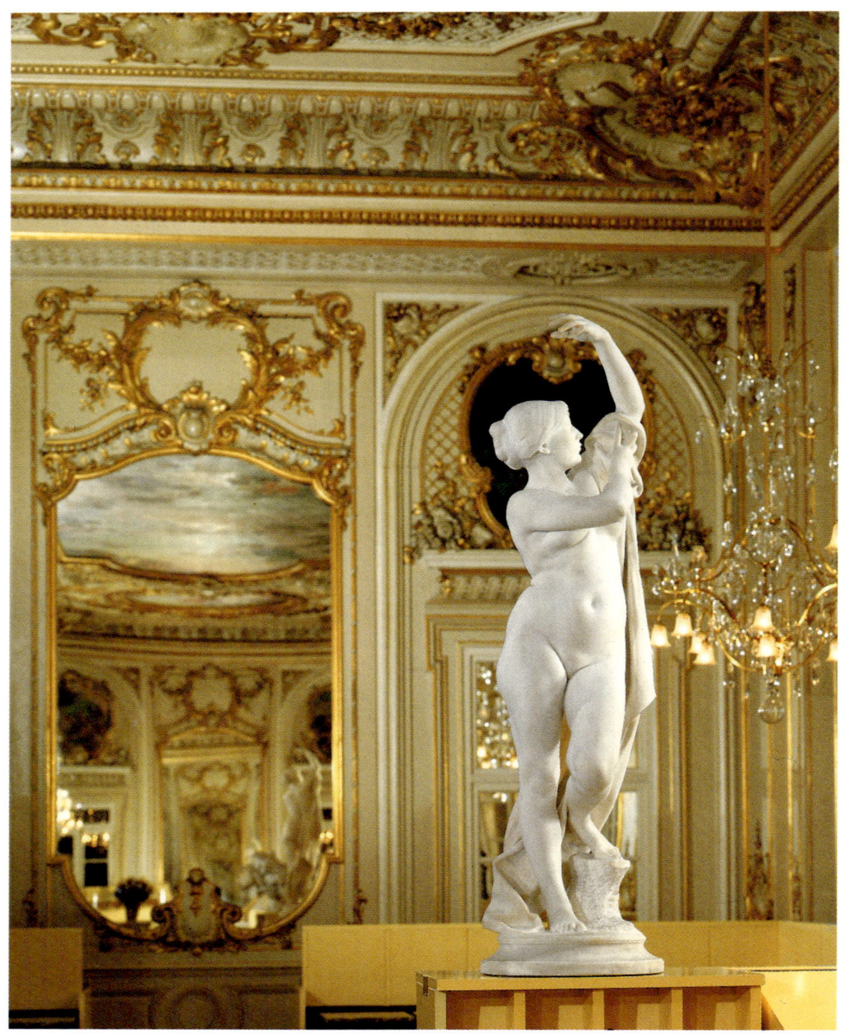

Denys Puech ▷
Gavernac 1854 – Rodez 1942
Aurora, 1900
White and pink marble. 1.16 x 0.80 x 0.59 m
SAF Salon, 1901; Chauchard bequest, 1909; National Trust, 1961; Palais de Tokyo, 1981; Orsay, 1986.
Ch M 138

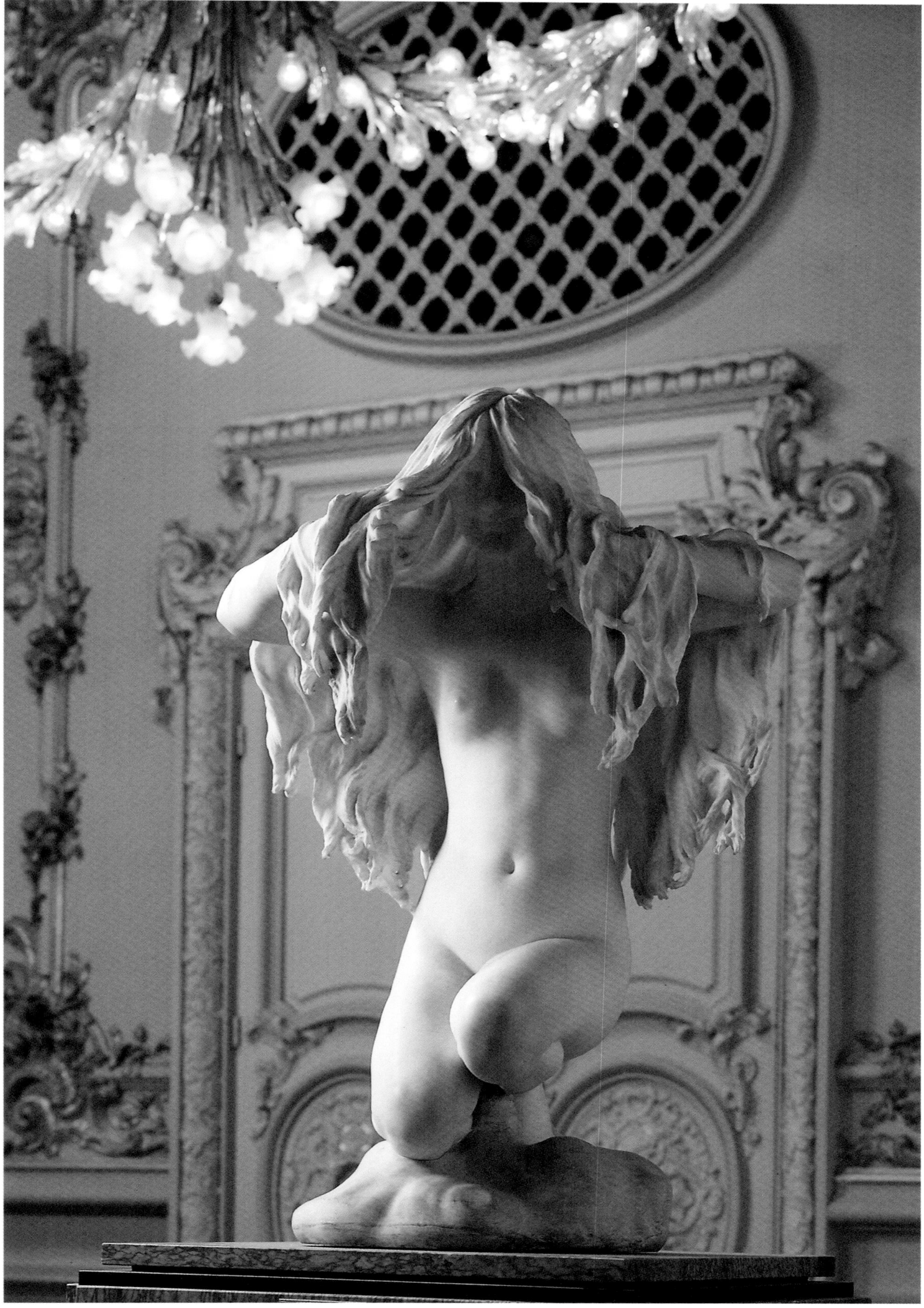

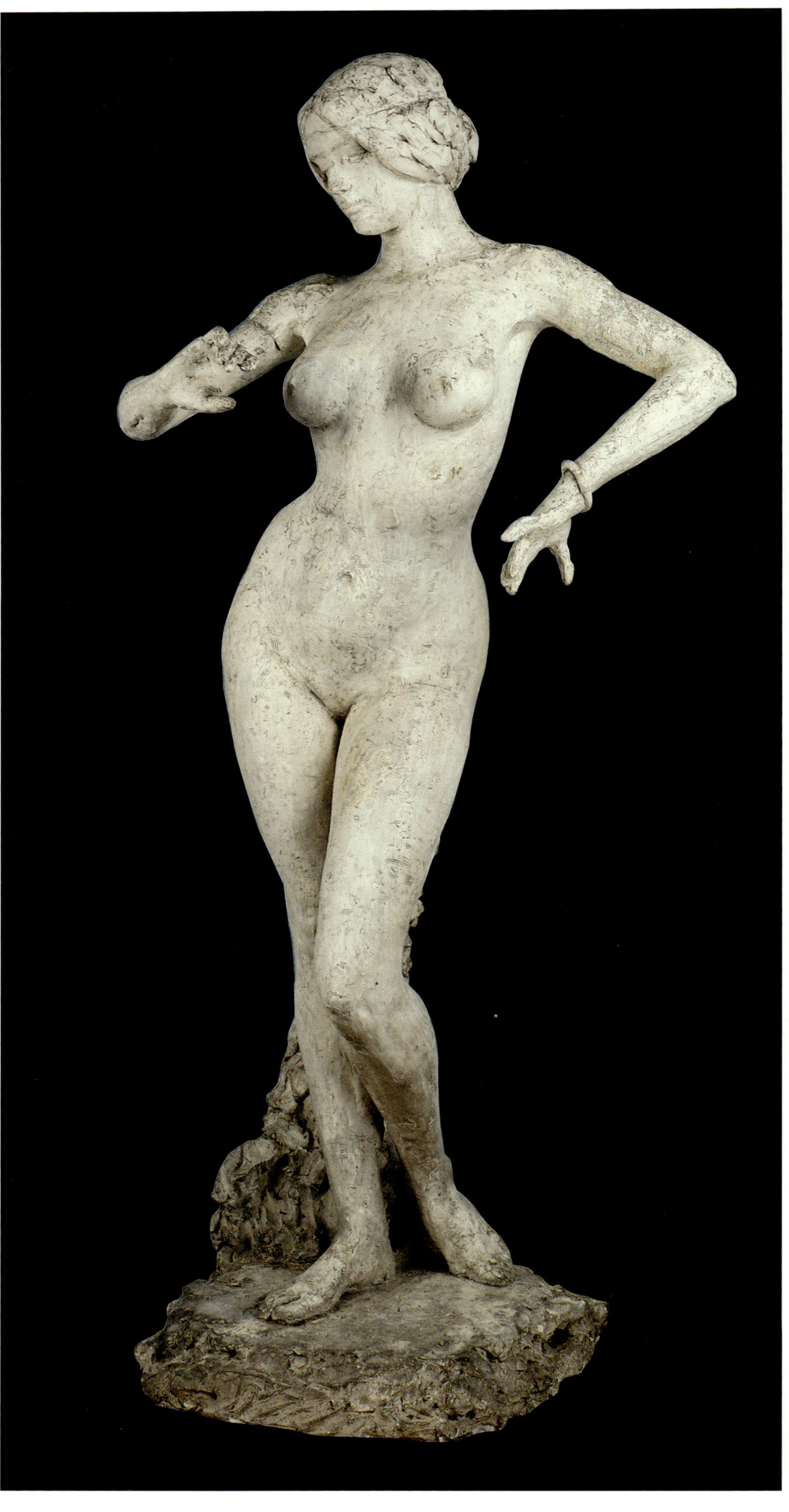

Cléo de Mérode, who posed for Degas and Forain, was the most photographed woman of her time. Elected Queen of Beauty over 131 other celebrities by the readers of *L'Illustration* (1896), she fell victim to the scandal surrounding the Salon of 1896 which displayed the marble (location unknown) based on the model that was moulded live. The famed bandeau coiffure betrayed the identity of the 'Dancer'.
In March 1895 Gauguin stated to *Echo de Paris*: 'Perfect mouldings can be taken from life; a skilled moulder can make a Falguière statue for you any time you like!'

Alexandre Falguière
Toulouse 1831 – Paris 1900
Dancer (Cléo de Mérode, 1881–1966), c.1896
Plaster. 1.65 x 0.77 x 0.57 m
Moulded live to serve as the model for the marble exhibited at the 1896 Salon under the title *Danseuse* (unplaced). Gift of Gustave Sins, husband of Falguière's natural daughter, 1950; Orsay, 1986.
RF 2674

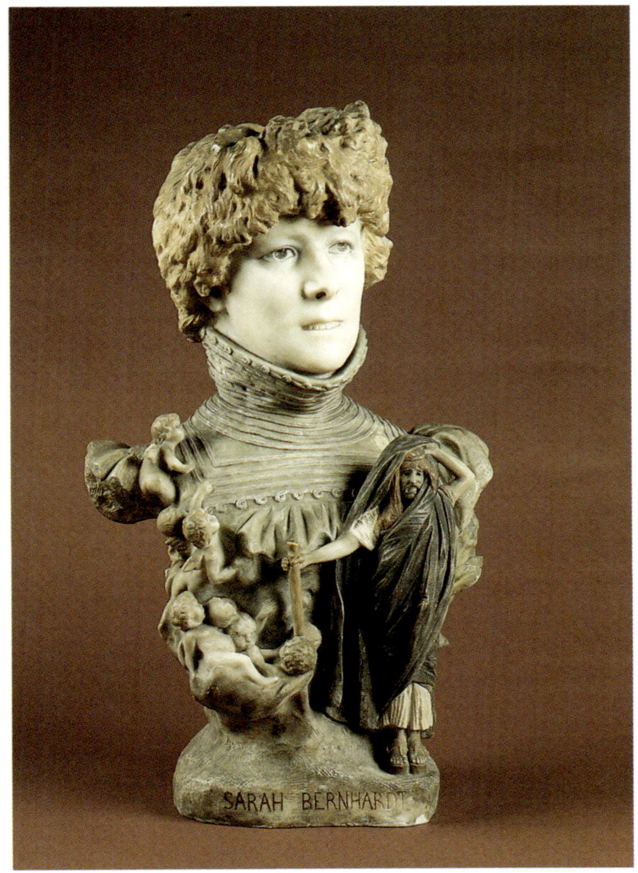

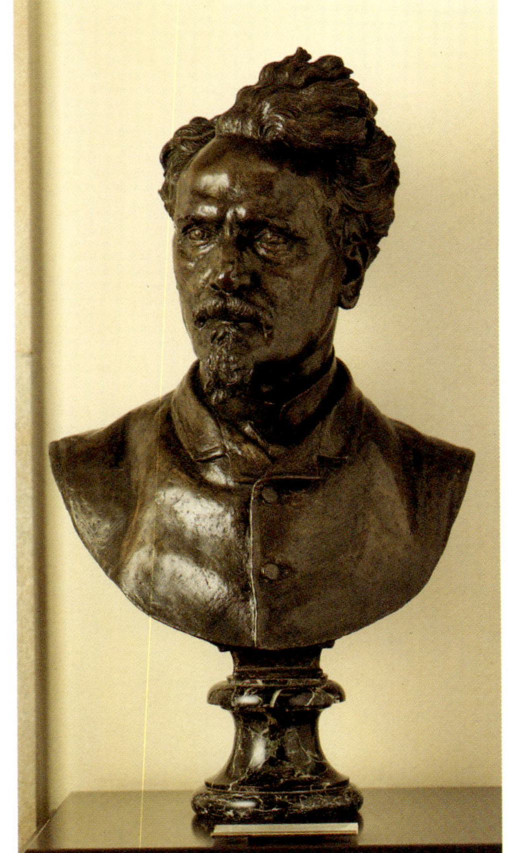

Aimé-Jules Dalou
Paris 1838 – Paris 1902
Henri Rochefort (1831–1913), journalist and politician, 1888
Bronze bust cast by Bingen. 0.715 x 0.41 x 0.26 m
1888 Salon; acquired from Mme Segard, Rochefort's first wife; Louvre, 1946; Orsay, 1986.
RF 2577

Jean-Léon Gérôme
Vesoul 1824 – Paris 1904
Sarah Bernhardt (1844–1925), actress, c.1895
Tinted marble bust. 0.69 x 0.42 x 0.29 m
Gérôme bequest (1896 will); Luxembourg Museum, 1904; Château de Lunéville Museum, 1924; Orsay, 1981.
RF 1393

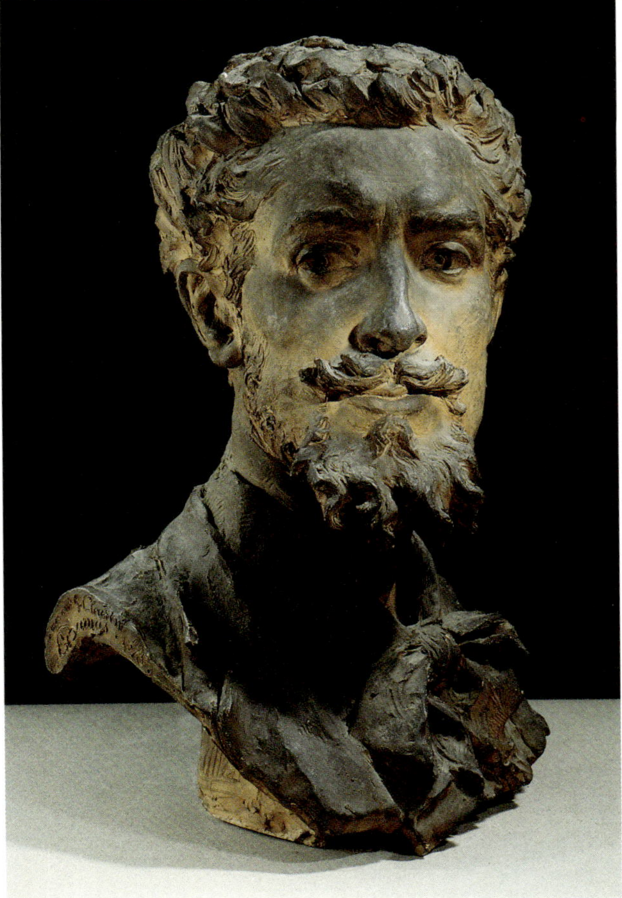

Louis-Ernest Barrias
Paris 1841 – 1905
Georges Clairin (1843–1919), painter, 1875
Terra-cotta bust. 0.429 x 0.28 x 0.27
Gift of M. Petit de Villeneuve at the request of his mother, Clairin's sister, 1931; Louvre, 1931; Orsay, 1986.
RF 2138

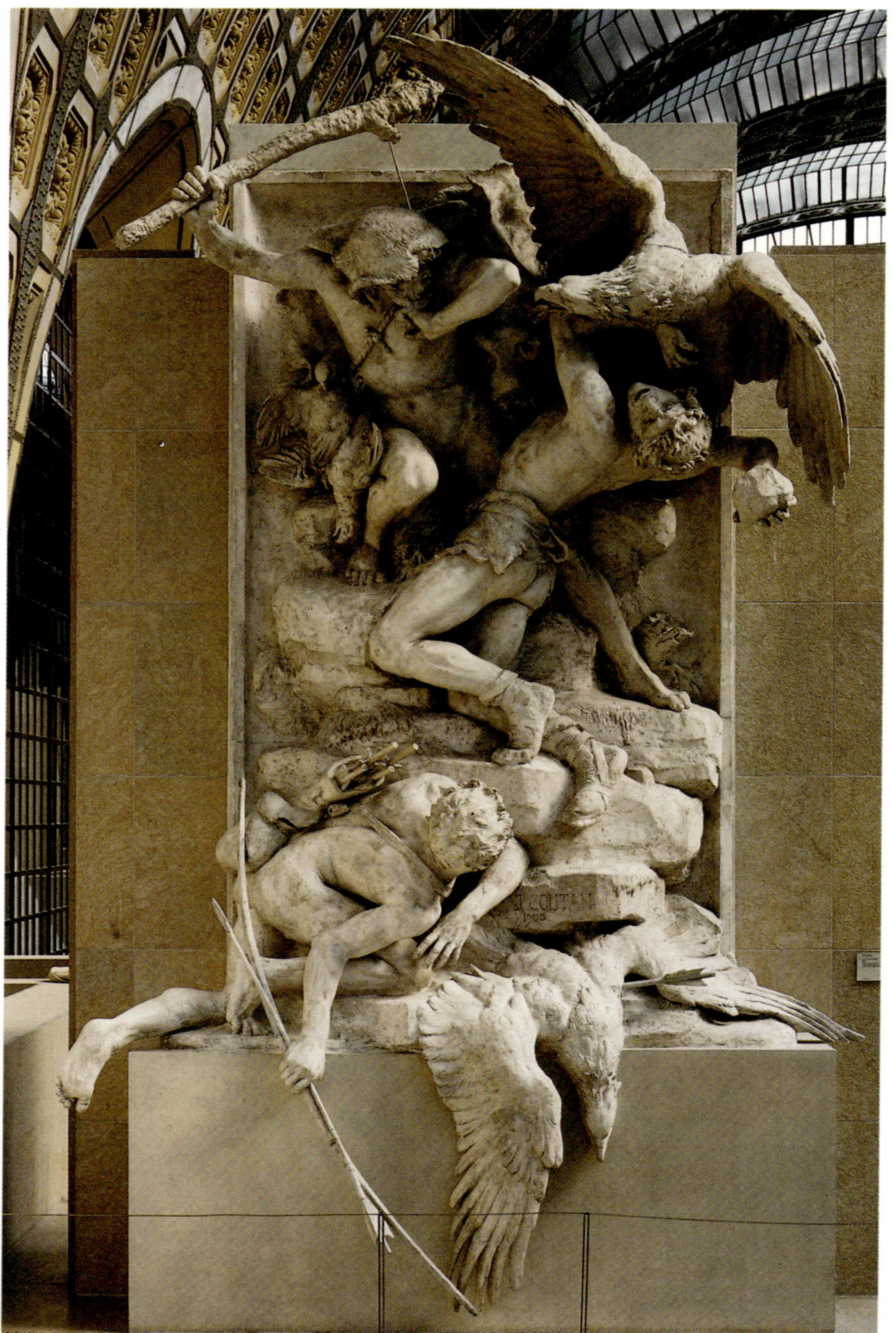

Jules Coutan
Paris 1848 – 1939
The Eagle Hunters, 1900
Plaster. 5.35 x 3.05 x 1.20 m
Commissioned in 1893 for the Museum's anthropology gallery (Ferdinand Dutert, architect); Roubaix Depository; Ecole Nationale Supérieure des Arts et Industries Textiles (Dutert, architect), 1903; transferred to Orsay, 1986.
REF 3741

Louis-Ernest Barrias ▷
Paris 1841 – Paris 1905
Nature Revealed to Science, 1899
Statue in marble, onyx, granite, malachite and lapis-lazuli.
2 x 0.85 x 0.55 m
Commissioned for the Conservatoire des Arts et Métiers in 1895; SAF Salon, 1899; Luxembourg Museum, 1903; Conservatoire des Arts et Métiers, 1931; Orsay, 1986.
RF 1409

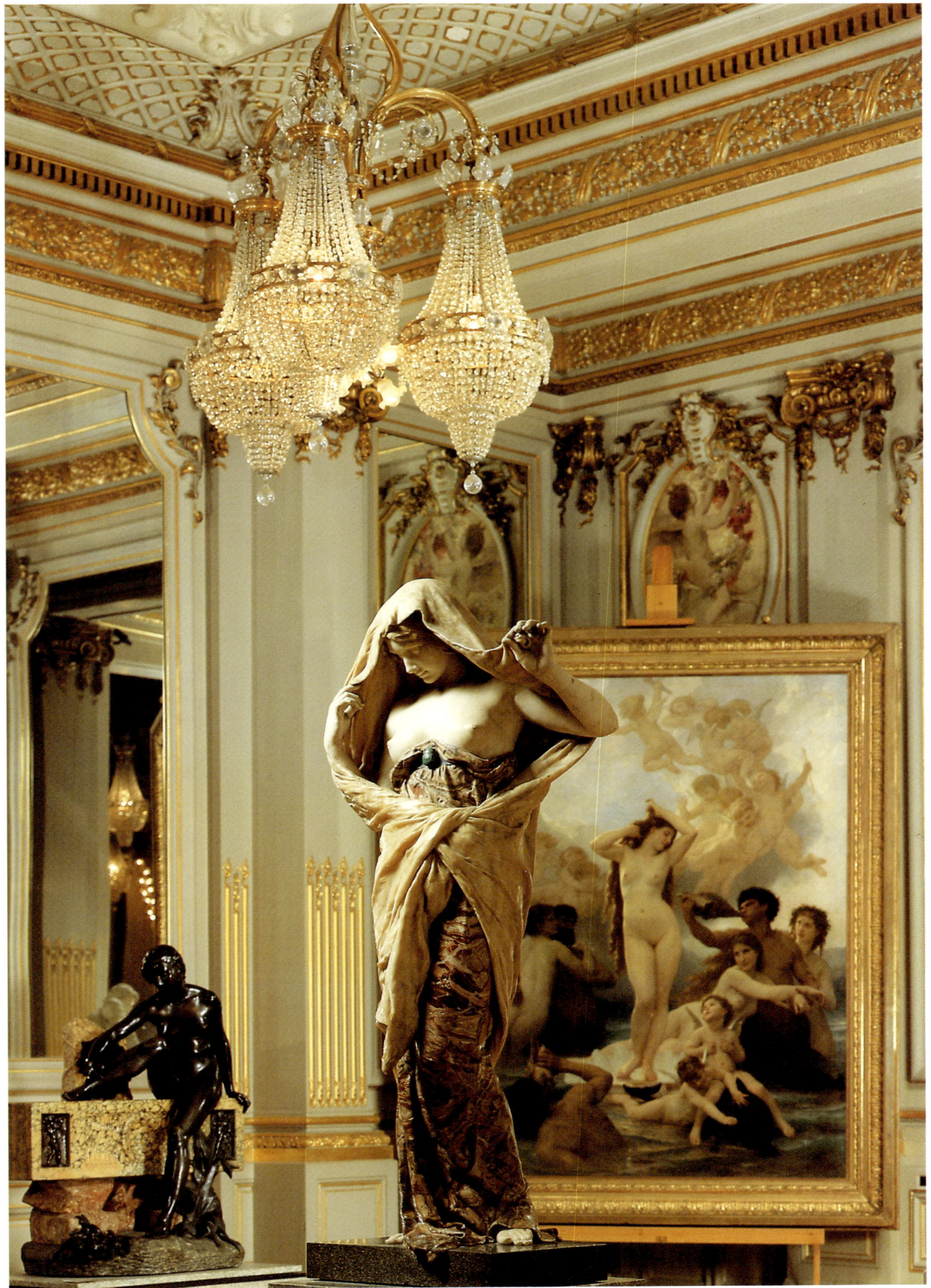

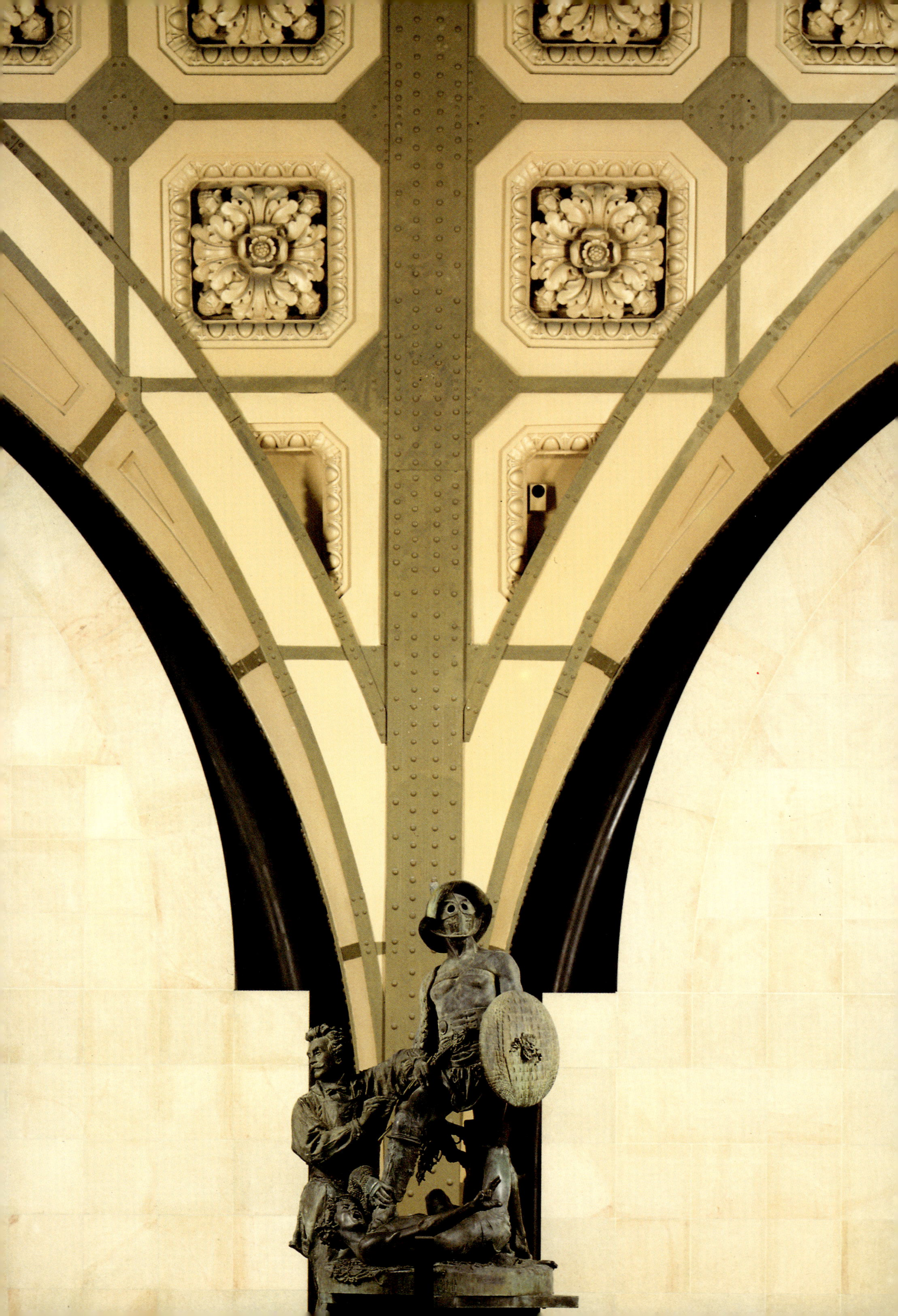

Realism

Realism – photographic, historical, caricatural and social – may take many forms in reflecting sculpture's capacity to mimic life all too closely. From the creation of Adam out of a lump of clay, to the myth of Pygmalion breathing life into *Galatea*, the transformation of inert matter into vibrant life has haunted mankind. So has its opposite; one has only to think of all the humans turned to pillars of salt or stone in the Bible, myth, legend and fiction. Formal congruity suggests the possibility of moving from one world to the other and back again. The invention of photography provided a further incentive to exploit this back-and-forth movement, which is why we have included Gérôme's *The Gladiators* here. Gérôme, a fierce adversary of the Impressionists, sent away to Naples for replicas of antique armour for his models to wear. His son-in-law then used the work as the basis for his *Monument to Gérôme*. Here, Gérôme's effigy is shown sitting near a real stool, half-turned as if to observe his costumed models more minutely. The second part of the monument, done from a photograph, is as much a *tableau vivant* as the first.

This is the kind of historical realism film-makers were later to strive for; their forerunners in attempting to re-create exact replicas of the past were Fremiet and Bartholdi.

Caricature draws on reality, exaggerating details in order to reveal character. Daumier, with his biting wit, was one of the first 19th-century artists to revolutionize sculpture by using realism to pierce his models' façades and reveal their underlying character.

Depicting the world of manual labour would seem perforce to require a 'realistic' approach. Although the first life-sized labourer in 19th-century French sculpture was the child in clogs standing at the foot of Chapu's monument to *Eugène Schneider* and symbolizing 'gratitude' (1878, Le Creusot), the first adult worker to play a heroic role was Dalou's *The Blacksmith*. Dalou had fled to London to escape the death sentence pronounced in absentia and condemning him for his participation in the Paris Commune. With the amnesty of 1879, he submitted the study for the *Triumph of the Republic* (Paris, Petit Palais) to the Salon. Dalou's labourer with cart, the first glorification of manual labour and the worker under the new regime, did not have the heroic mien of a Vulcan. This was because, despite his powerful muscles, the face is lined and the back bent.

By contrast, the Belgian Constantin Meunier, who became famous in 1886 in Paris when his life-size plaster *Hammersmith* shown at the Salon was praised by Octave Mirbeau in *La France* and Gustave Geffroy in *La Justice*, often did tend to model his figures on Vulcan. His workers were athletes only minimally marked by fatigue, which enhanced the impact of exceptions such as his relief *The Clod of Earth*, acquired in 1892 by the Luxembourg Museum. Alexandre Charpentier mined the realistic vein gloriously inaugurated by Zola's novel *Germinal* (1885) and collaborated with Constantin Meunier on the Zola monument in Paris (since destroyed). The German Hoetger went through several artistic phases, but his Paris period sensitized him to proletarian expressionism.

Jean-Léon Gérôme
Vesoul 1824 – Paris 1904
Aimé Morot
Nancy 1850 – Dinard 1913
Monument to Gérôme. Gérôme Sculpting the Gladiators, 1878 and 1909
Monument to Gérôme, wax-cast bronze group by A.A. Hébrard in 1909, incorporating *The Gladiators*, wax-cast bronze group by E. Gonon in 1878. Total: 3.60 x 1.82 x 1.70 m
Commissioned by the Nation, 1905; inaugurated in garden of the Louvre Oratory, 1909; removed in 1967 for foundation work on the colonnade; Fort du Mont Valérien, 1971; Orsay, 1980.
RF 3517

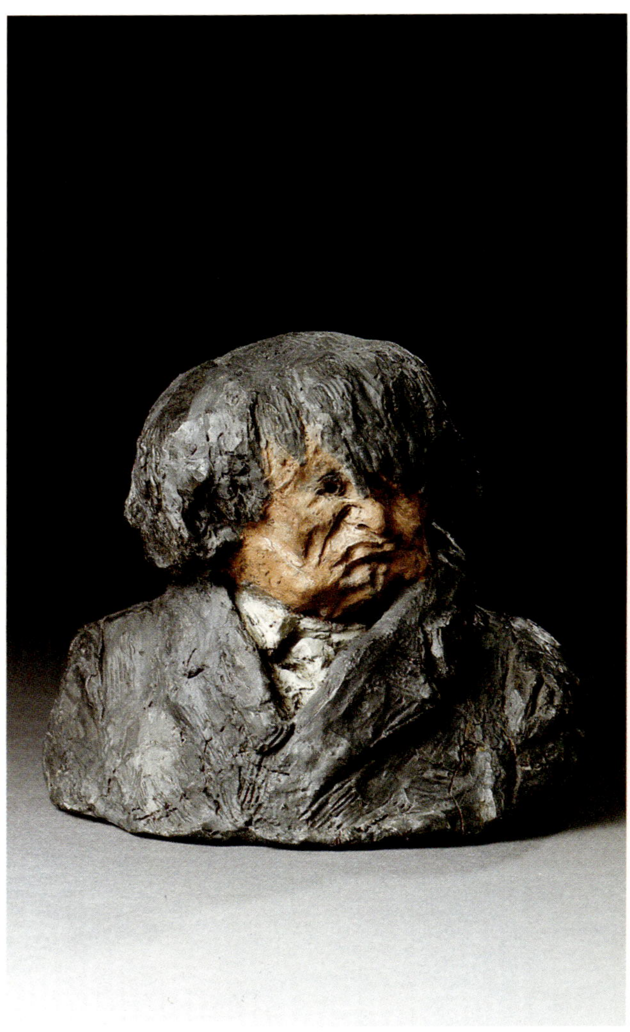

Honoré Daumier
Marseilles 1808 – Valmondois 1879
Doctor Clément François Victor Gabriel Prunelle (1774–1853), deputy
Small tinted unbaked clay head. 0.134 x 0.152 x 0.159 m
Group acquired for the Musée d'Orsay from the Le Garrec heirs with assistance from Michel David-Weill of the Lutèce Foundation, 1980.
RF 3506

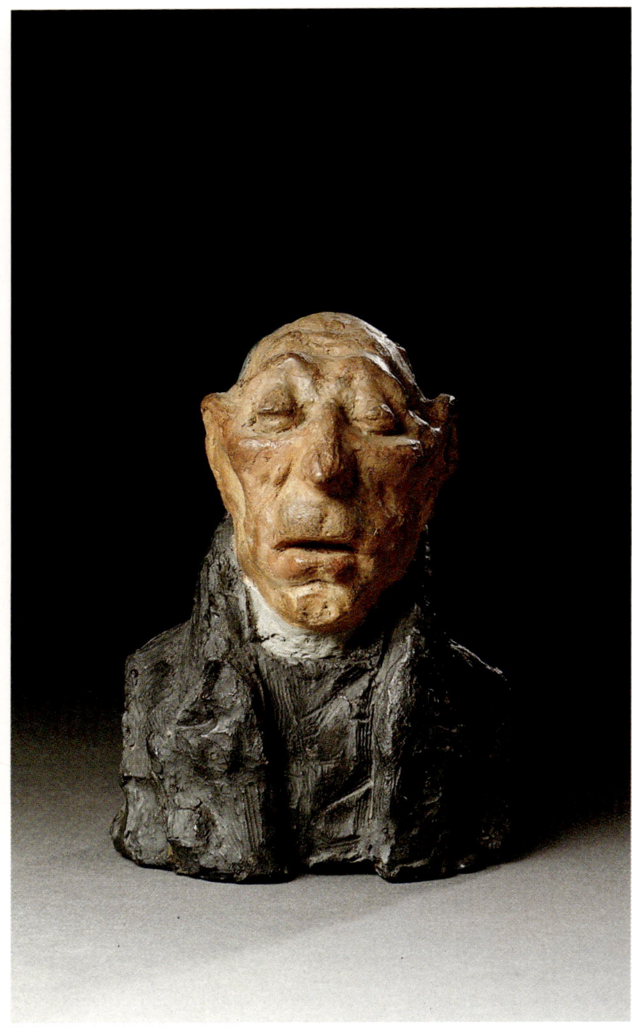

Honoré Daumier
Marseilles 1808 – Valmondois 1879
Jean-Claude Fulchiron (1774–1859), poet and deputy
Small tinted unbaked clay head. 0.173 x 0.129 x 0.118 m
Provenance as before.
RF 3489

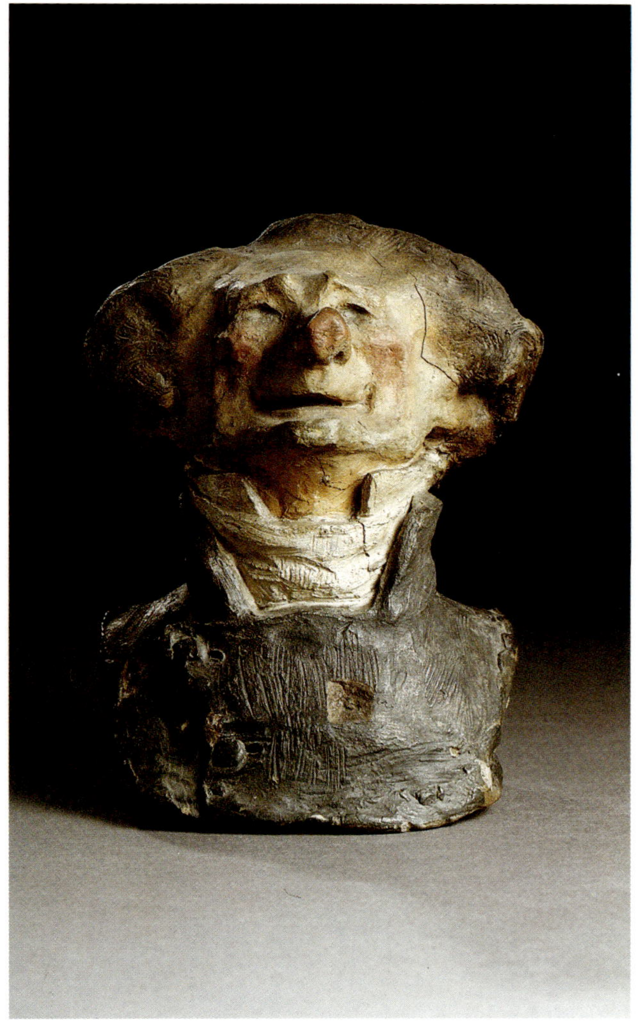

Honoré Daumier
Marseilles 1808 – Valmondois 1879
Charles Philipon (1800–1862), journalist, newspaper owner and editor
Small tinted unbaked clay head. 0.164 x 0.130 x 0.106 m
Provenance as before.
RF 3504

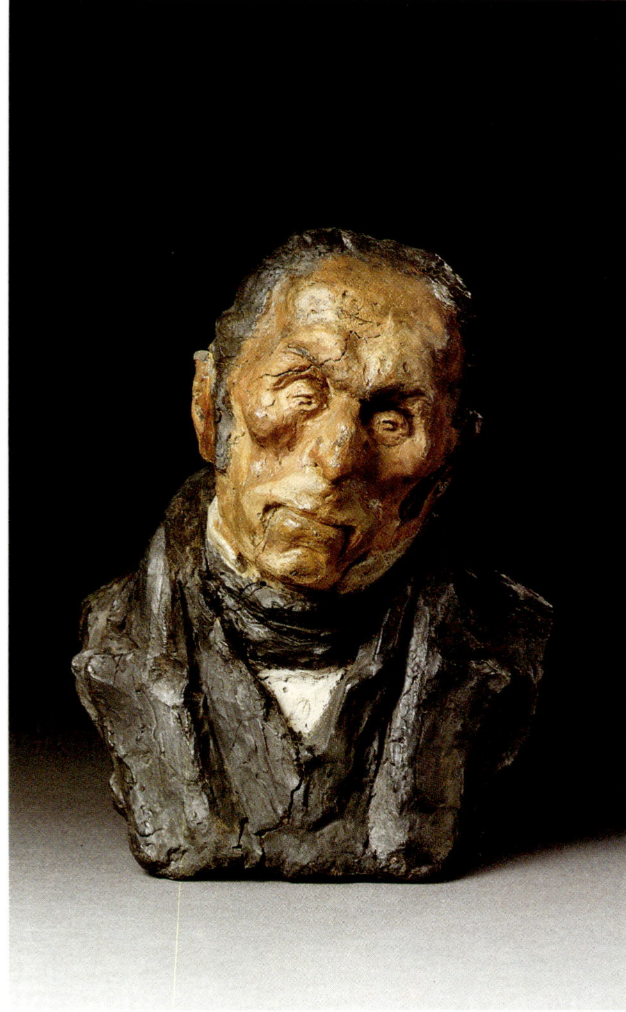

Honoré Daumier
Marseilles 1808 – Valmondois 1879
François Guizot (1787–1874), deputy, minister, president of the Conseil, historian
Small tinted unbaked clay head. 0.225 x 0.175 x 0.154 m
Provenance as before.
RF 3493

The 1830 Revolution that put Louis-Philippe on the throne also provided a degree of freedom to the press, but Fieschi's attempt on the king's life in 1835 restored censorship for drawing and engravings. Between those two dates, however, although frequently seized or fined, newspapers flourished. Outstanding among them were *La Caricature*, founded in 1831, and *Le Charivari*, in 1832. Their director, Charles Philipon – the 'Juvenal of caricature' and inventor of Louis-Philippe-the-pear – spent many months in prison along with one of his best cartoonists, Daumier. Reports to the contrary notwithstanding, Daumier probably did not work from life inside the Chamber itself, 'his marvellous, almost divine memory recalling his models for him'. During 1831, when Dantan the younger exhibited his true-to-life portraits, the Phrenology Society of Paris was created popularizing Gall's theory that 'the inner man can be divined from the outer form, the moral man from the physical'. Baudelaire celebrated Daumier thus: 'The energy with which/He paints Evil and its works/Proves the beauty of his heart'.

Although chronologically Daumier belongs in the Louvre, he has been given a place in the first gallery at the Musée d'Orsay so that this prodigious draughtsman, painter and sculptor will be recognized as the forerunner he was. Maurice Gobin's captions (1952) add nothing to the impact of the portraits themselves ('The Snob', 'The Hypocrite', 'The Toothless Smile' and 'The Bore').

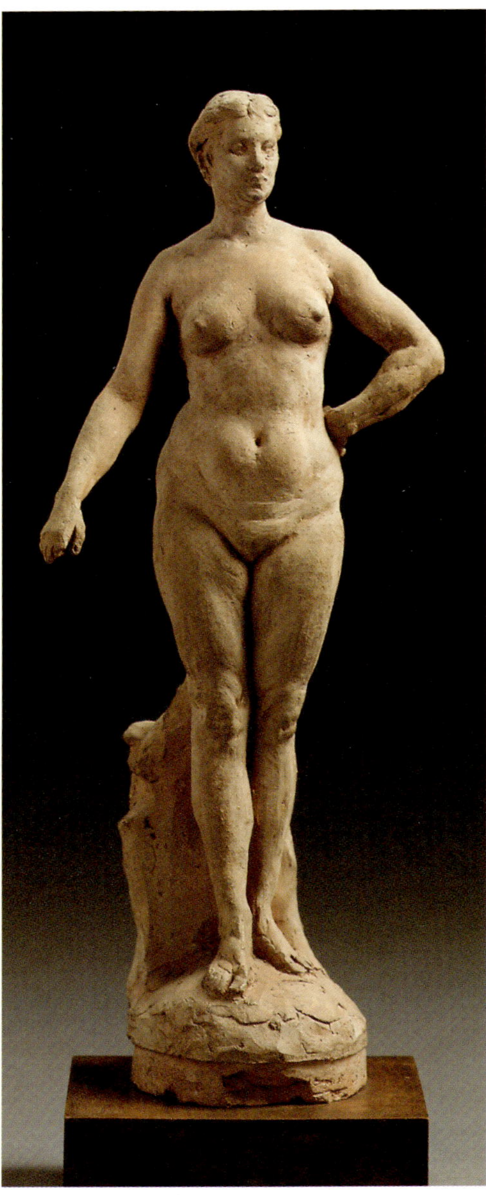

In April 1897 Dalou wrote, 'I resolve to undertake without delay the monument to the glory of the workers I have been dreaming of since 1889. This subject is in the air; it is timely and will be done by someone else if I do not act today. The future has arrived; this is the cult that will replace the mythologies of the past.' However, Constantin Meunier had in 1895 already exhibited *The Glorification of Labour* at the Salon de la Libre Esthétique in Brussels. Neither Meunier, Dalou, Rodin, Van der Stappen nor Henri Bouchard ever executed the *Monument to Labour* of which they all dreamed.

Aimé-Jules Dalou ▷
Paris 1838 – Paris 1902
The Peasant, 1897–1902
Bronze statue cast by Susse Frères.
1.97 x 0.70 x 0.68 m
Plaster model for projected *Monument to the Workers*, 1902 SNBA Salon; bronze acquired in 1905; Luxembourg Museum, 1905; Louvre, 1920; Orsay, 1986.
RF 2999

Aimé-Jules Dalou
Paris 1838 – Paris 1902
The Republic, 1879
Terra-cotta study. 0.338 x 0.141 x 0.09 m
Nude study of clothed allegory for *Monument to the Republic*, 1879–89. Gift of Mmes Brodin et de Massary (daughters of Etienne Moreau-Nélaton), 1927; Louvre, 1927; Orsay, 1986.
RF 1911

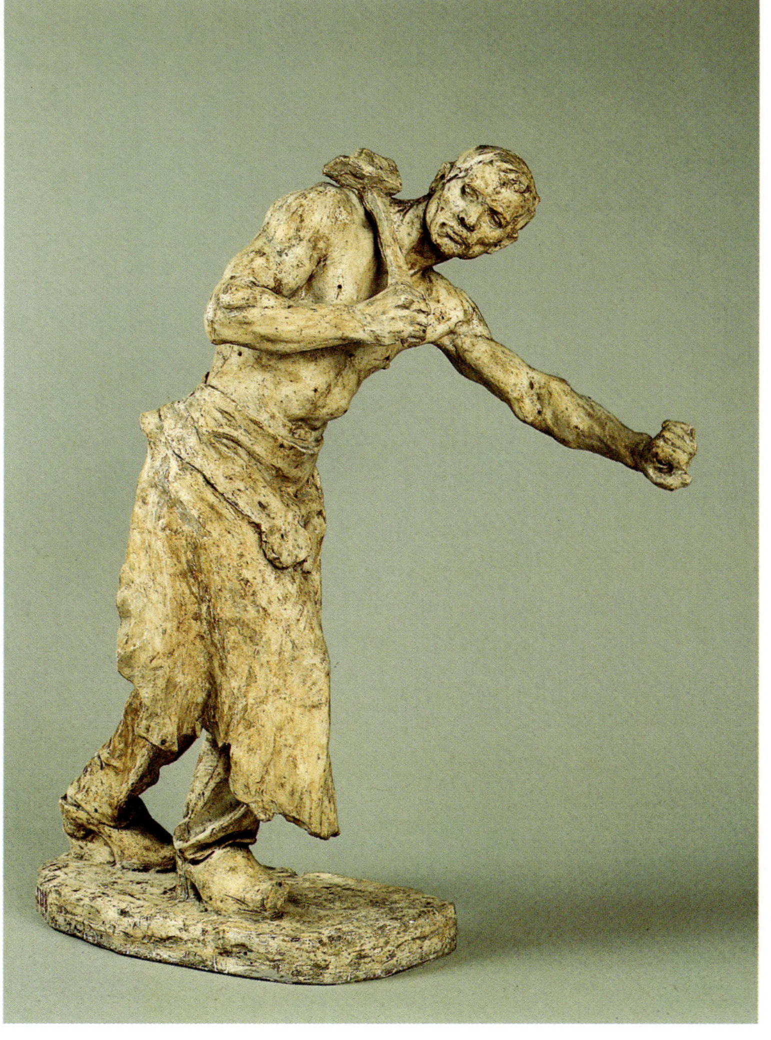

Aimé-Jules Dalou
Paris 1838 – Paris 1902
The Blacksmith, 1886
Model to 1/6 scale, patinated plaster with gradations.
0.678 x 0.37 x 0.62 m
Study for the same monument; gift from August Biaggi (Dalou's pupil), 1952; Louvre, 1952; Orsay, 1986.
RF 2738

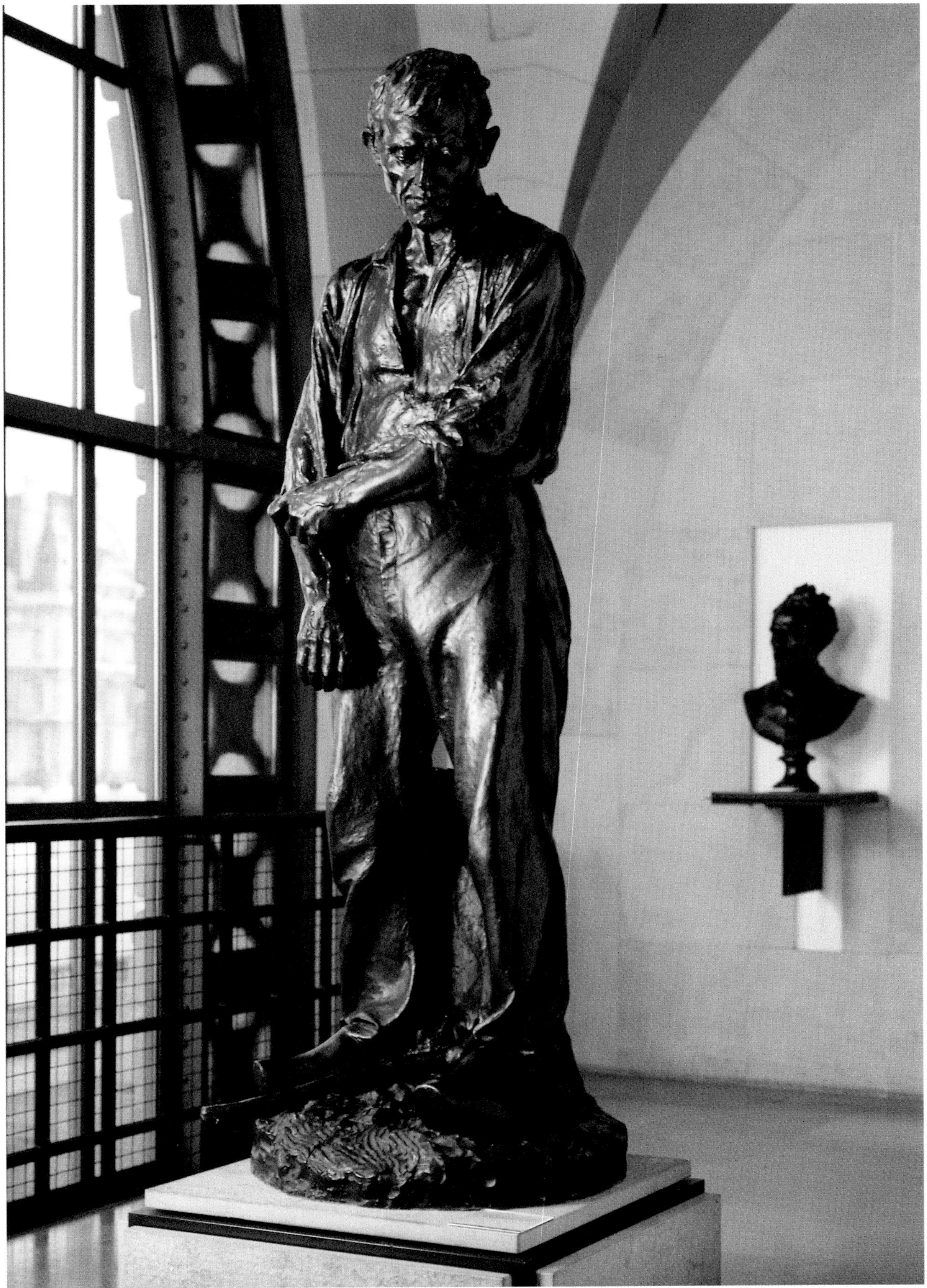

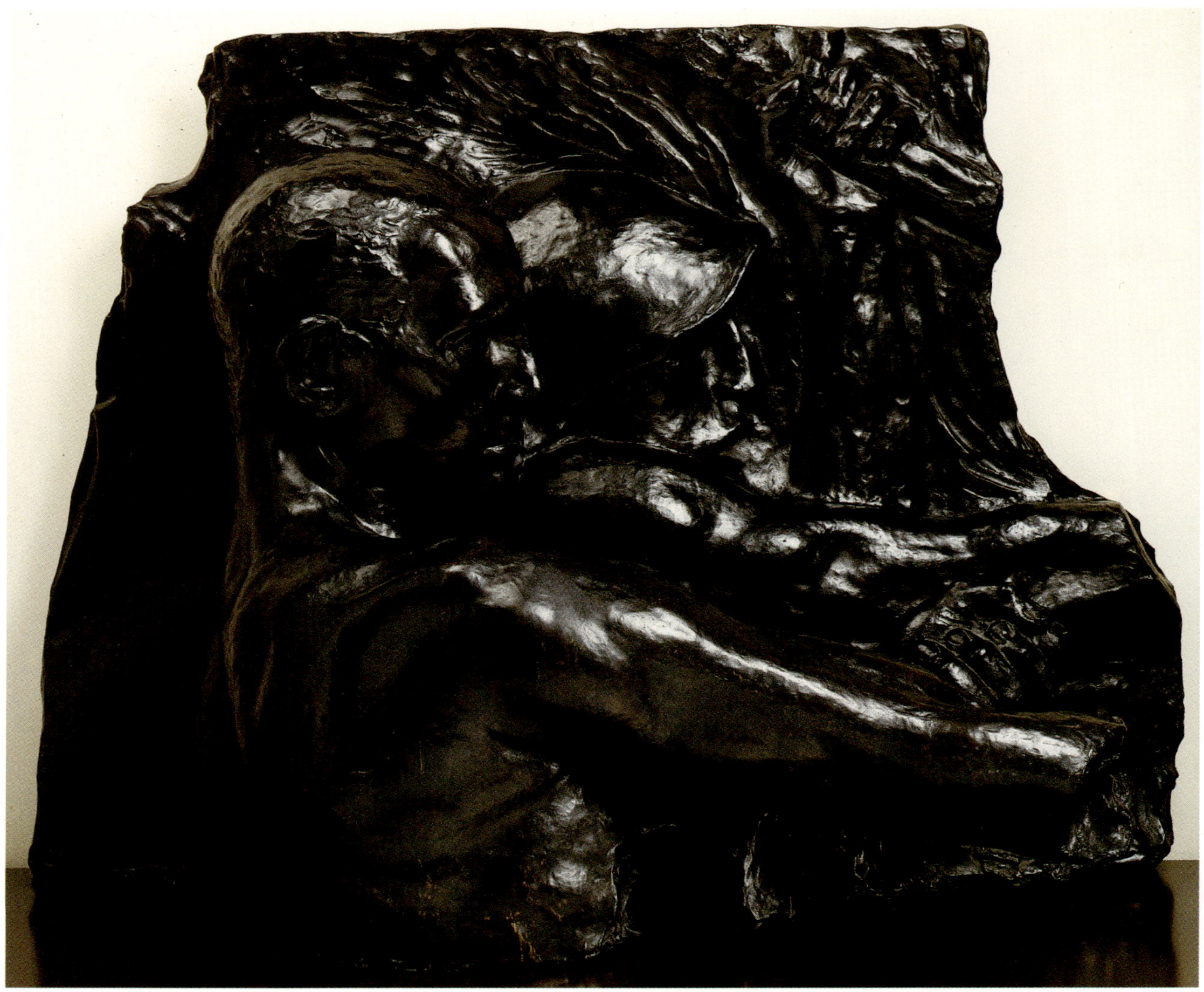

Constantin Meunier
Etterbeck 1831 – Ixelles (Belgium) 1905
Industry, 1892–6
Bronze bas-relief cast by J. Petermann, Brussels.
0.68 x 0.91 x 0.36 m
Commissioned for the Luxembourg Museum; acquired in 1897;
Musée des Ecoles Etrangères, 1923; National Museum of Modern Art, 1940;
Louvre, 1977; Orsay, 1986.
RF 3254

Georges Clemenceau declared that Constantin Meunier, when he exhibited at Siegfried Bing's Art Nouveau gallery in Paris in 1896, had perfectly rendered the 'epic of labour'. Bas-reliefs for the projected monument in honor of this novel virtue retained links with the four elements: *Industry* or *Fire*, *The Harvest* or *Air*, *The Port* or *Water*, *The Mine* or *Earth*. The fragment shown above, drawn from the larger work, was an exception in the oeuvre of Meunier, who otherwise produced finished pieces. Meunier shows all the excess of a Zola in this *harvest* scene, in which barefoot peasants move through looming wheat fields in search of a stray cow. The monument was installed temporarily in 1909 following Meunier's death, and then permanently, at Laeken, in 1930.
Roty's allegory, also barefoot, has had the great good fortune – even though she's sowing against the wind – to find a home in every coin purse and pocket in France.

Oscar Roty
Paris 1846 – Paris 1911
The Sower, 1887–96
Wax on slate. 0.50 x 0.50 x 0.26 m
Study for Ministry of Agriculture monument (unrealized), 1887; engraved on 50-centime coin, 1897;
used again for postage stamps, 1903–40;
and again for the 'heavy' franc, 1959; acquired in 1991.
RF 4374

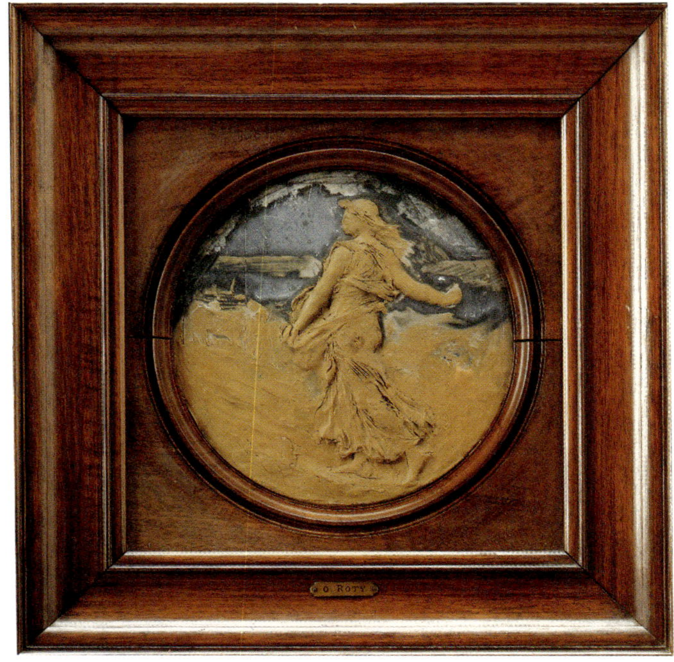

Constantin Meunier
Etterbeck 1831 – Ixelles (Belgium) 1905
The Harvest or *Earth*, 1895
Bronze relief cast by J. Petermann, Brussels.
0.635 x 0.83 x 0.17 m
Plaster, 1895 SNBA Salon; acquired in 1986.
RF 4102

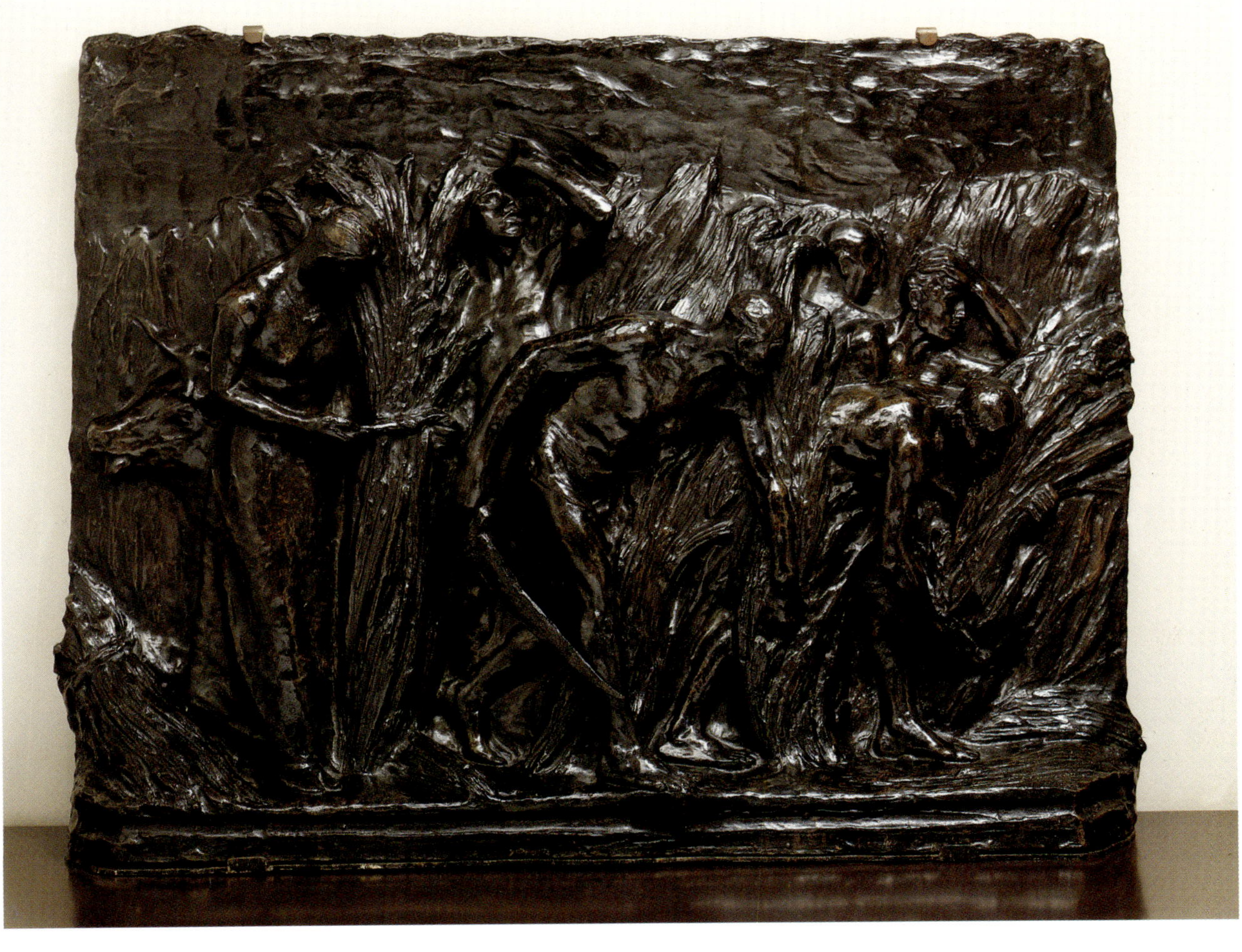

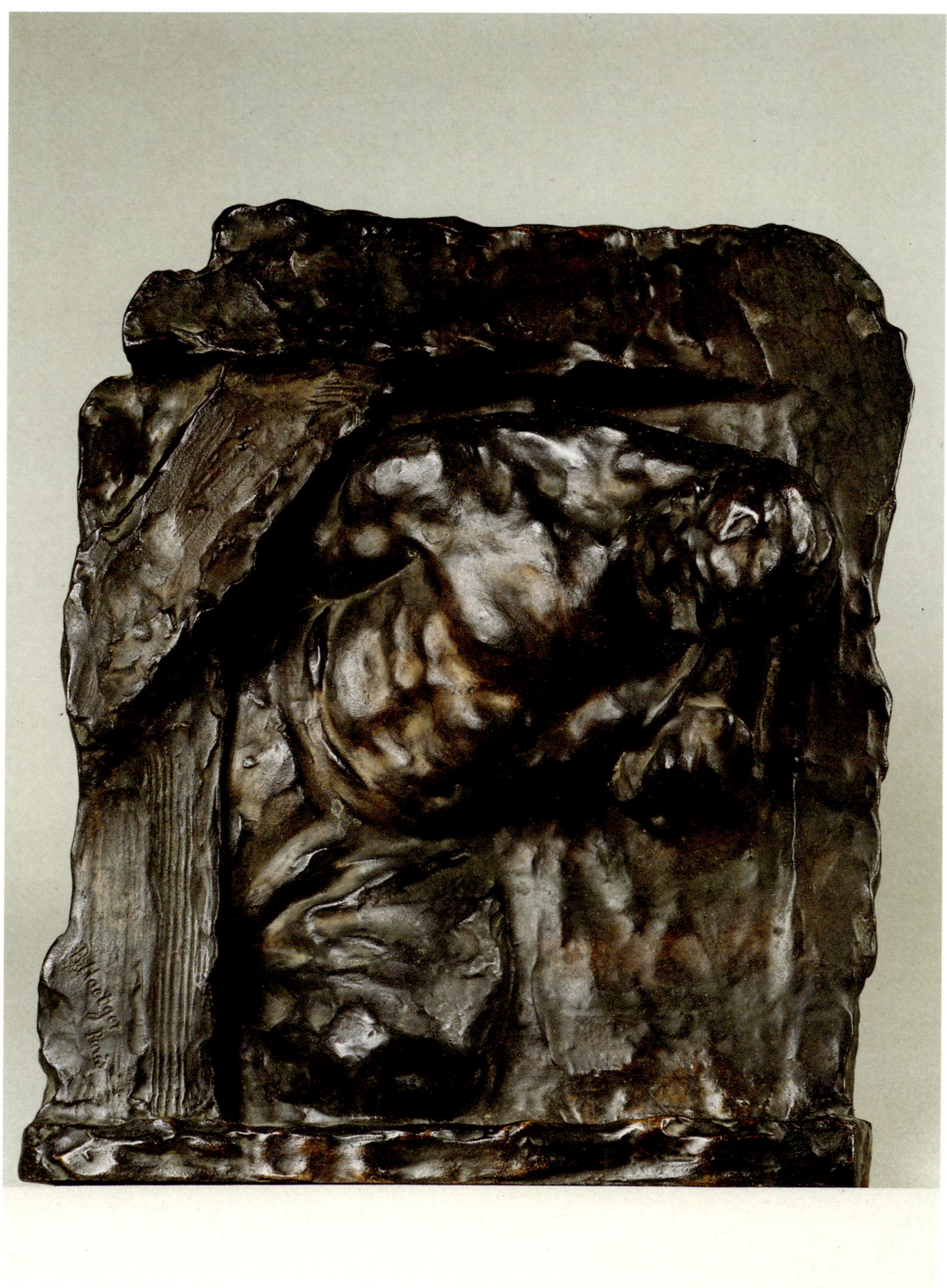

Bernhardt Hoetger
Hörde 1874 – Beatenburg (Germany) 1949
The Human Machine, 1902
Bronze relief cast by Eugène Blot. 0.44 x 0.37 x 0.18 m
Gift from Mme Marcel Duchamp to the National Museum of Modern Art, 1977;
Orsay Depository, 1983.
DO 1983 –75

Henri Bouchard ▷
Dijon 1875 – Paris 1960
Stevedore, 1905
Bronze statuette cast by Bisceglia Frères, Paris.
0.71 x 0.28 x 0.39 m
Acquired in 1907 by the Nation from *Les Onze*,
Galerie des Artistes Modernes; Luxembourg Museum, 1909;
National Museum of Modern Art, 1940; Orsay
Depository, 1983.
DO 1983–73

Note here that a subtle allusion can be more telling than exact representation. The details of Bouchard's *Stevedore* tell us less about social reality than Hoetger's straining muscles, the image reproduced as a drawing on the cover of *L'Assiette au beurre* for 10 December 1903.

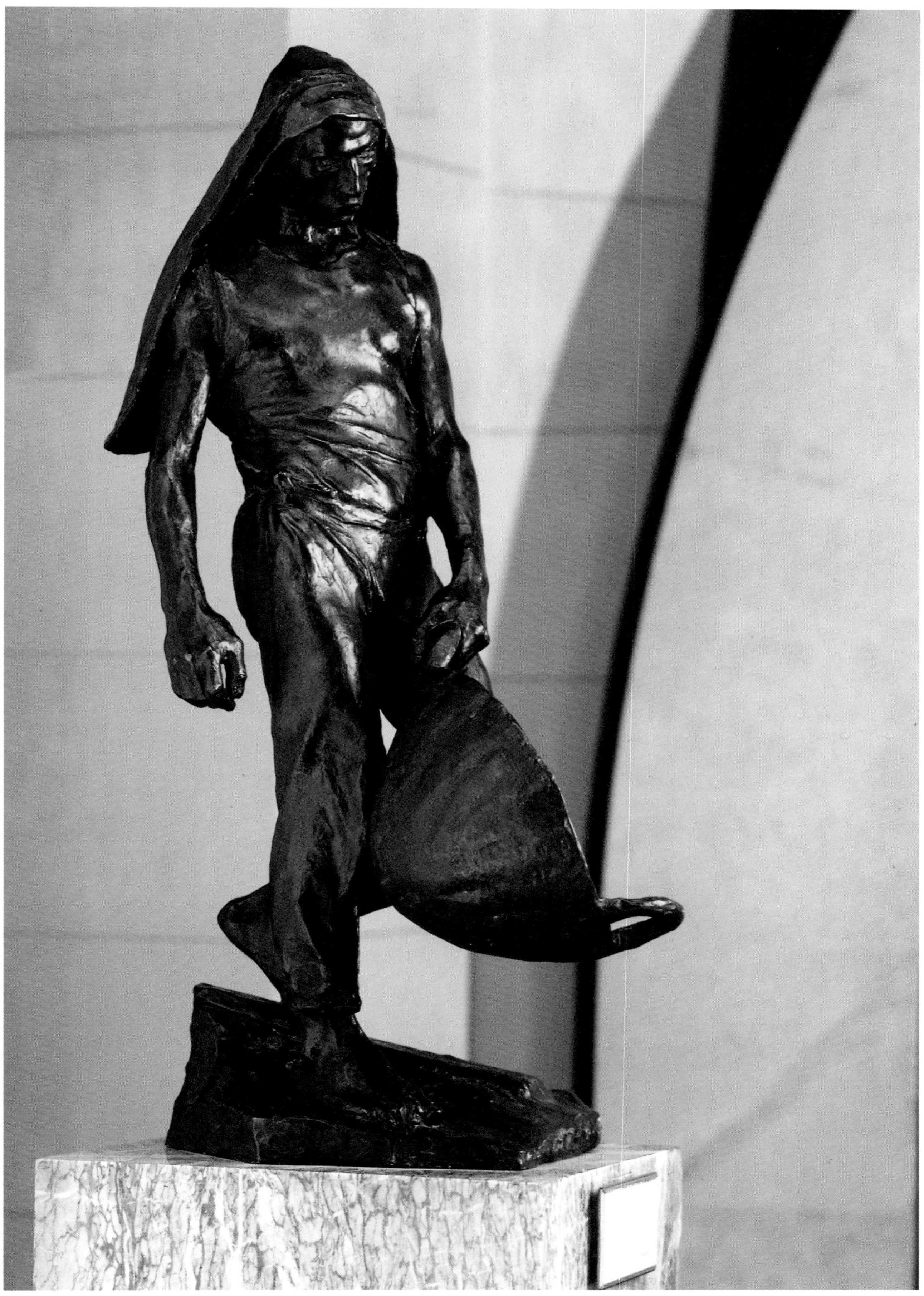

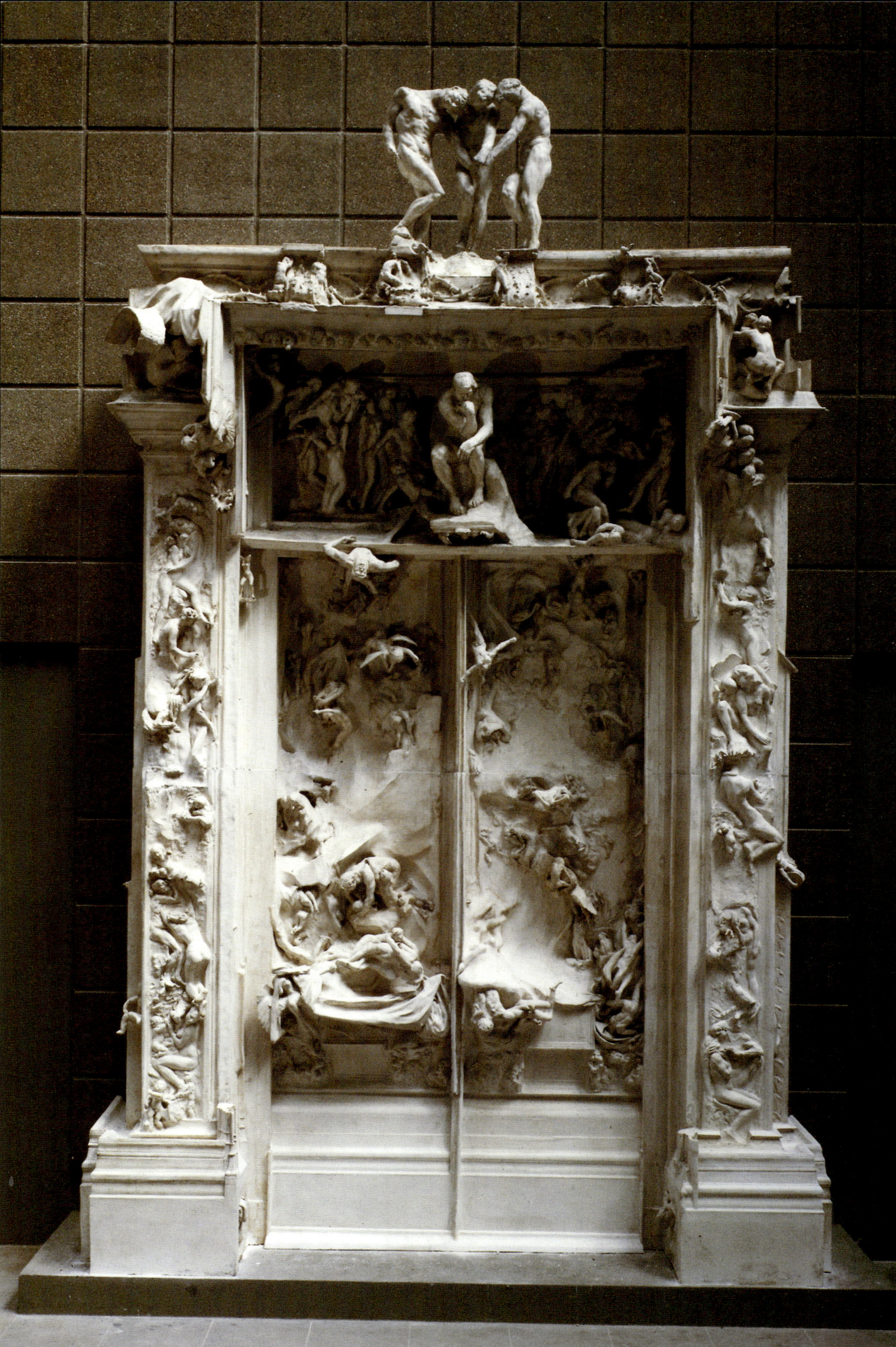

Auguste Rodin

The Musée d'Orsay has been compared to a church, with forecourt, narthex, transept and choir. Perhaps this is because the former station points eastwards, now that it is no longer entered from the side. Visitors approaching from beneath the canopy will see opposite them a sort of white flame, Rodin's *Balzac*; and, next to Gae Aulenti's left-hand tower, his *Gate to the Inferno* or *Gate of Hell*. Rodin thus occupies the museum's 'choir'. These two plaster casts, which Rodin never saw in bronze, were installed in the Pavillon de l'Alma where Rodin exhibited his work at the World's Fair of 1900: *Balzac* in the centre, and *Gate to the Inferno* to the left, on the supporting slab. In fact the outline of the gate is less important than the inferno it encloses, which should be viewed from close up. Rodin learned to draw from memory when he was a pupil at the Petite Ecole between the ages of fourteen and seventeen, but was otherwise self-taught. He thrice failed the entrance competition for the Ecole des Beaux-Arts, served a novitiate at a monastery (1862–3) following the death of his sister Maria, and then, returning to the secular world, followed his patron Carrier-Belleuse to Brussels. After a seven-year stay in Belgium, where he was joined by his companion Rose Beuret, and his Michelangelo pilgrimage in Italy, he exhibited the plaster *Vanquished* first in Brussels, and then in Paris under the new title *Bronze Age* in 1877. Rodin was accused of modelling this figure live, which could have destroyed his reputation. To put an end to the rumours, the Under Secretary of State for Fine Arts Edmond Turquet not only purchased the bronze in 1880, but the same year also commissioned a gate for the Museum of Decorative Arts. The original plan in 1882 was to build a new museum on the ruins of the old Cour des Comptes, the very site later to be occupied by the Gare d'Orsay. It took 104 years for this sculpture to be installed on this site – not in the originally planned Museum of Decorative Arts (which was inaugurated in 1905 in the Pavillon de Marsan of the Louvre), but in the Musée d'Orsay. This commission won Rodin a state-subsidized studio at the Marble Depository on 182 rue de l'Université. He stopped working for Carrier-Belleuse at the Sèvres porcelain works, met Camille Claudel in 1883, and with her experienced the creative passions whose torments are depicted in the *Gate to the Inferno*. A number of successful commissions, such as the *Monument to the Burghers of Calais* (1884–95), were counterbalanced by the refusal of others, such as *Victor Hugo* for the Pantheon (1889; refused in 1890) and *Balzac* (1891; refused in 1898). Rodin was ahead of his time. He moved away from single-figure works when he replicated *Adam* for the *Three Shades* placed above the *Gate to the Inferno*; and from completed works, as indicated by his titles (Georges Petit's catalogue of 1889, 'No.6, *Two old women*. One needs work.'); and also from works in their entirety (ibid., 'No.27, *The Thinker*; *the Poet. Fragment of Gate*.'). His *Man Walking* rightly belongs to the 20th century, as do his torsos. Rodin eliminated details to gain expressiveness – which he had already begun doing when he removed the lance from his *Bronze Age* in 1877. Raymond Duchamp-Villon said, 'Compressing an idea increases its power', and Rodin made significant progress towards this goal, while also exploring other libertarian avenues with his drawings.

Auguste Rodin
Paris 1840 – Meudon 1917
Gate to the Inferno
(or *Gate of Hell*), 1880–1917
Plaster haut-relief. 6.25 x 4 x 0.94 m
Commissioned by the Nation for a projected Museum of Decorative Arts, 1880; Rodin Donation, 1916; Rodin Museum, 1919; Orsay Depository, 1986.
DO 1986–4

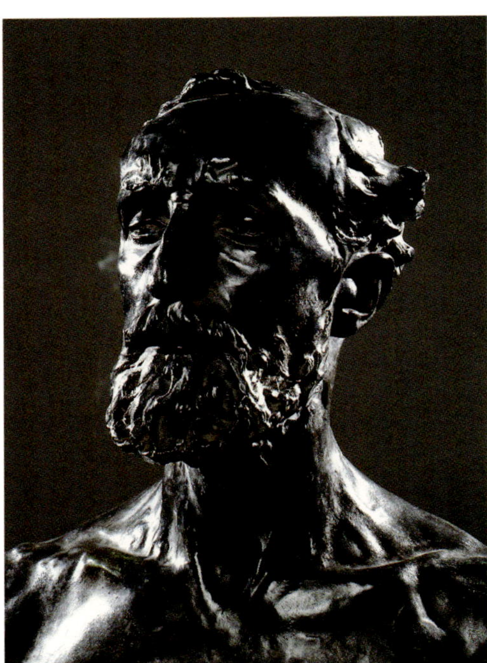

Auguste Rodin
Paris 1840 – Meudon 1917
Aimé-Jules Dalou (1838–1902), 1884
Bronze bust cast by Alexis Rudier. 0.545 x 0.455 x 0.234 m
Acquired by the Nation, 1906; Luxembourg Museum, 1908; Louvre, 1933; Orsay, 1986.
RF 2244

Auguste Rodin
Paris 1840 – Meudon 1917
The Bronze Age, 1877
Bronze statue cast by Thiébaut Frères. 1.78 x 0.59 x 0.651 m
Acquired from the 1880 Salon (3rd-place medal); Luxembourg Gardens, 1884; Luxembourg Museum, 1901; Louvre, 1933; Orsay, 1986.
RF 676

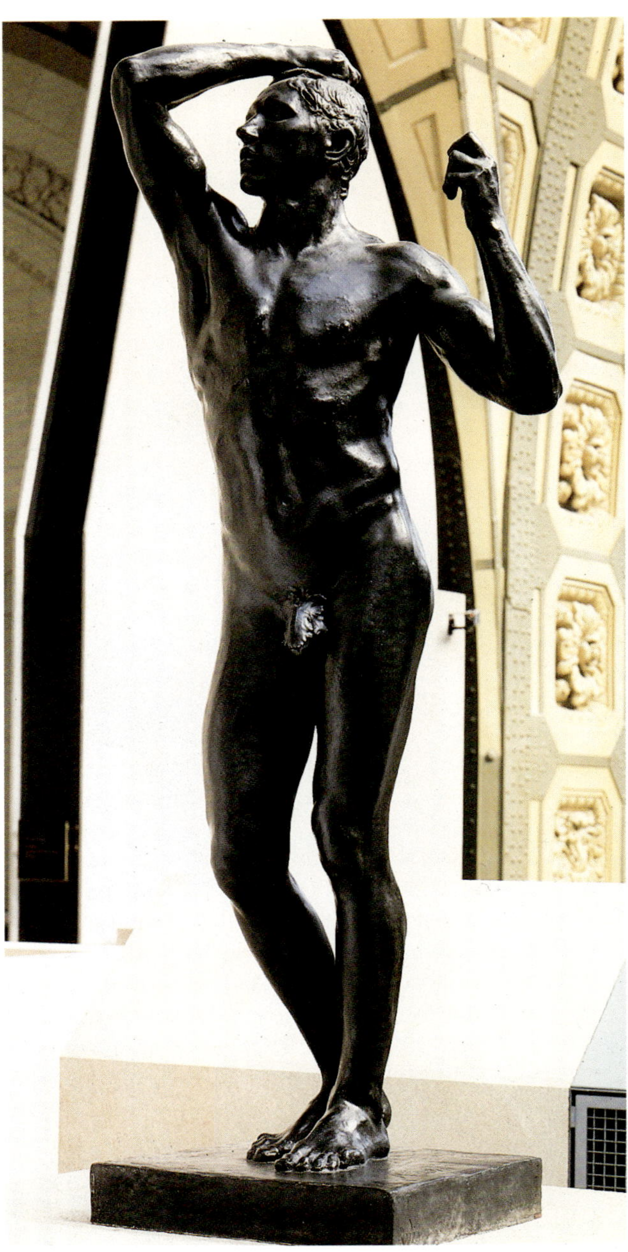

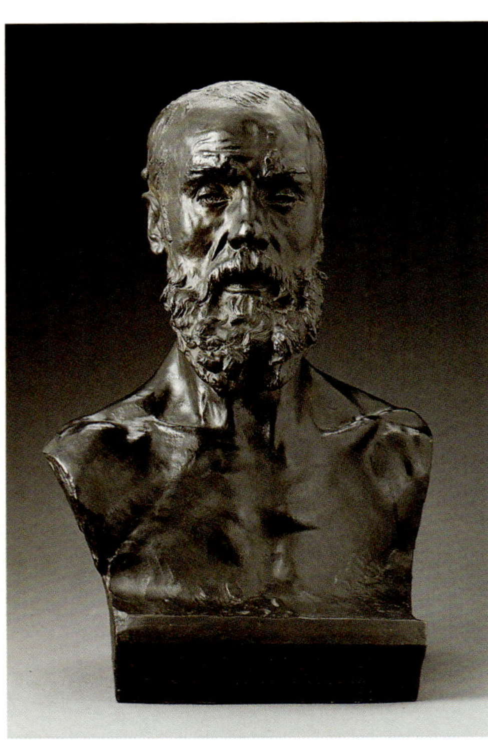

Auguste Rodin
Paris 1840 – Meudon 1917
Jean-Paul Laurens (1838–1921), 1882
Bronze bust cast by F. Rudier, Griffoul & Cie.
0.582 x 0.385 x 0.325 m
Gift from pupils in the J.P. Laurens Studio, 1892; Luxembourg Museum, 1895; Louvre, 1929; Orsay, 1986.
RF 1049

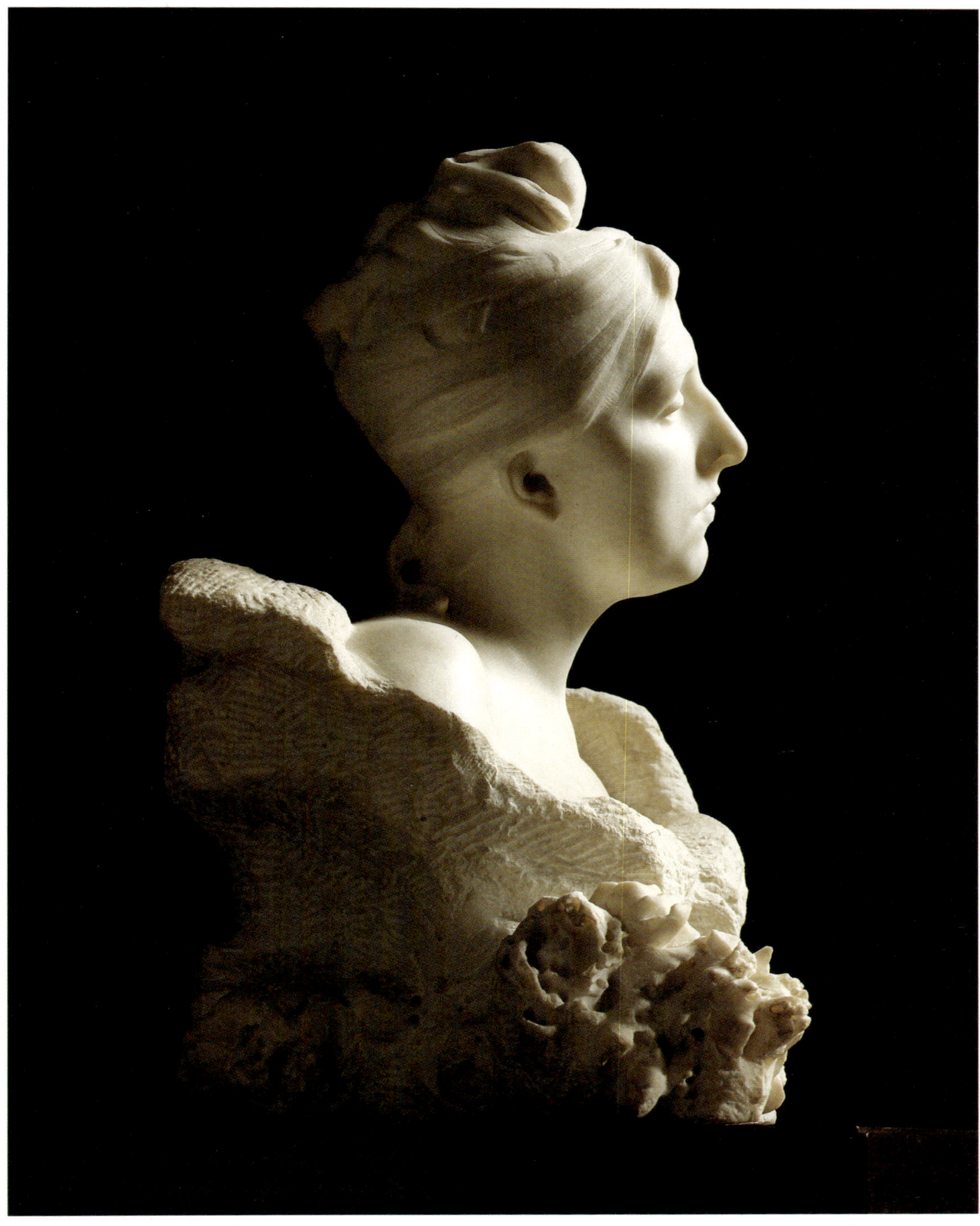

Auguste Rodin
Paris 1840 – Meudon 1917
Madame Vicuña, 1888
Marble bust chiselled by Escoula. 0.569 x 0.499 x 0.37 m
Acquired by the Nation from the 1888 Salon;
Luxembourg Museum, 1888; Rodin Museum, 1919;
Orsay, 1986.
RF 793

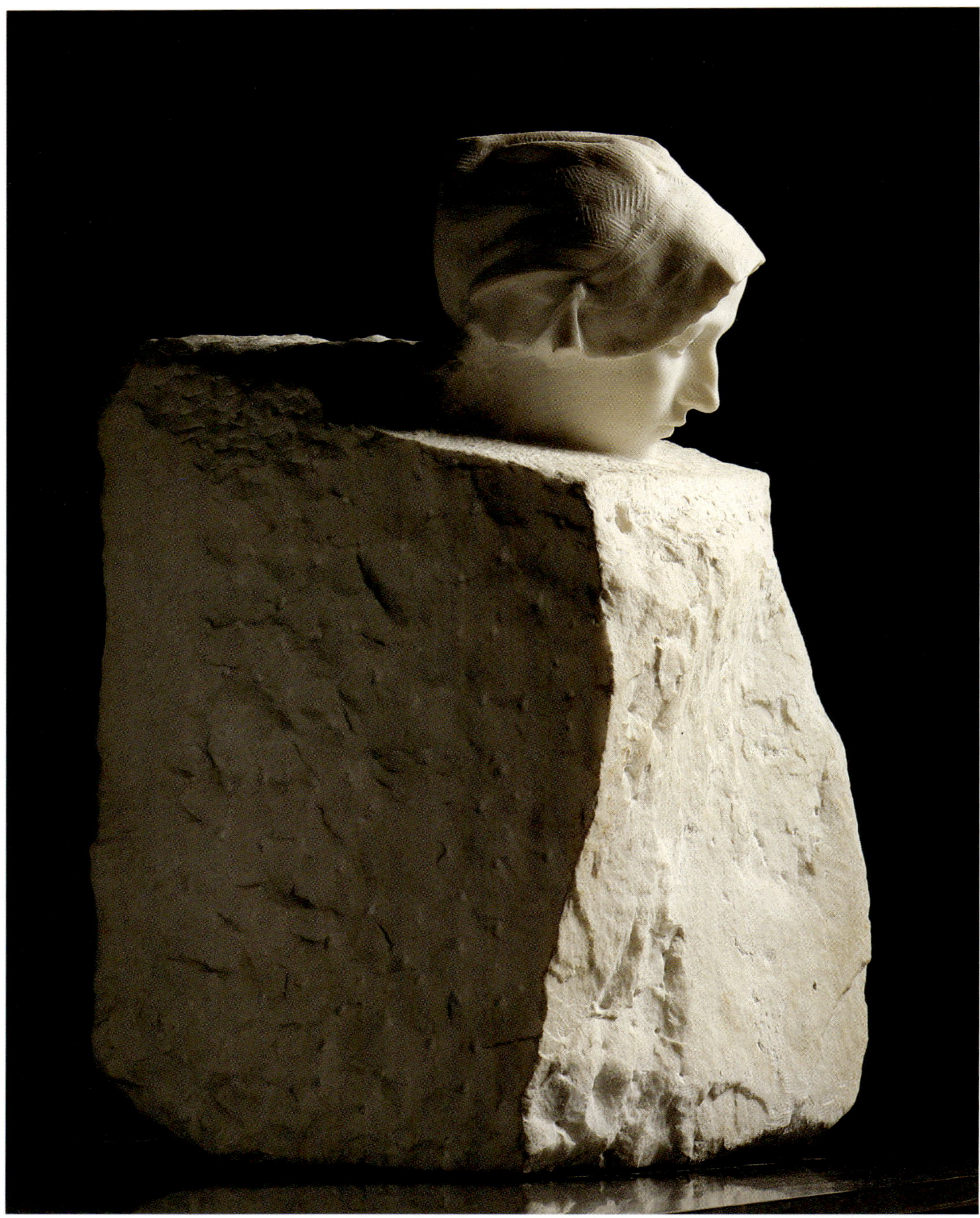

Auguste Rodin
Paris 1840 – Meudon 1917
Thought, 1886–9 (portrait of Camille Claudel, 1864–1943)
Marble chiselled by Victor Peter. 0.742 x 0.435 x 0.461 m
Acquired by Mme Durand for the Luxembourg Museum, 1902; Rodin Museum, 1919; Orsay, 1986.
RF 4065

Taken from the *Gate to the Inferno*, where it appears twice, Rodin's *Fugit Amor* is a reply to Camille Claudel's *Maturity*, described thus by her brother Paul: 'this composition, whose unity springs from a rupture ... this naked young woman, is my sister! My sister Camille. Imploring, humiliated, on her knees, this superb, proud woman ... and do you know what is being torn from her, at that very moment, before your very eyes – her soul!'

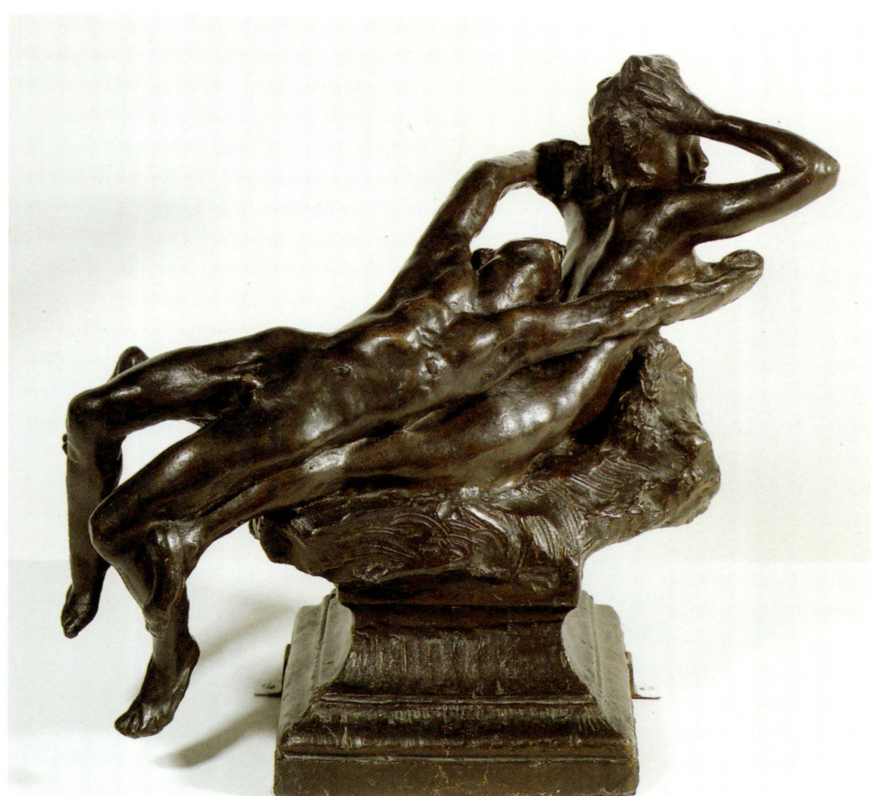

Auguste Rodin
Paris 1840 – Meudon 1917
Fugit Amor, c.1881
Small bronze group. 0.388 x 0.46 x 0.335 m
Dedicated to 'his dear friend and pupil G. Natorp'.
Part of the See collection until 1913; Cosson collection; Cosson bequest, 1926; Luxembourg Museum, 1926; Louvre, 1929; Orsay, 1986.
RF 2241

Camille Claudel
Fère-en-Tardenois 1864 – Montfavet 1943
Maturity, 1893–1903
Bronze group cast by Thièbaut Frères, Fumière & Gavignot. 1.14 x 1.63 x 0.72 m
First casting. Commissioned by Captain Tissier; 1903 SAF Salon; acquired in 1982 from Tissier's son who donated to the Musée d'Orsay eight letters from Camille Claudel to his father.
RF 3606

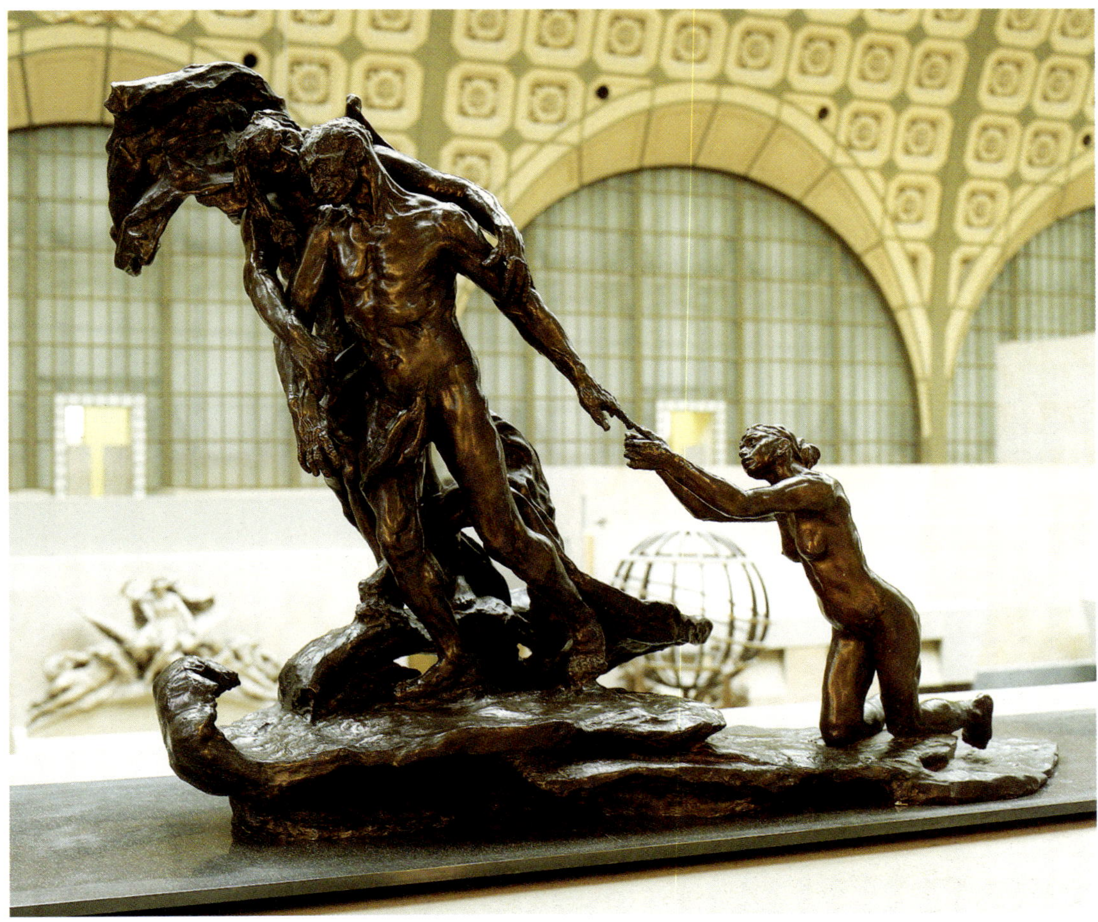

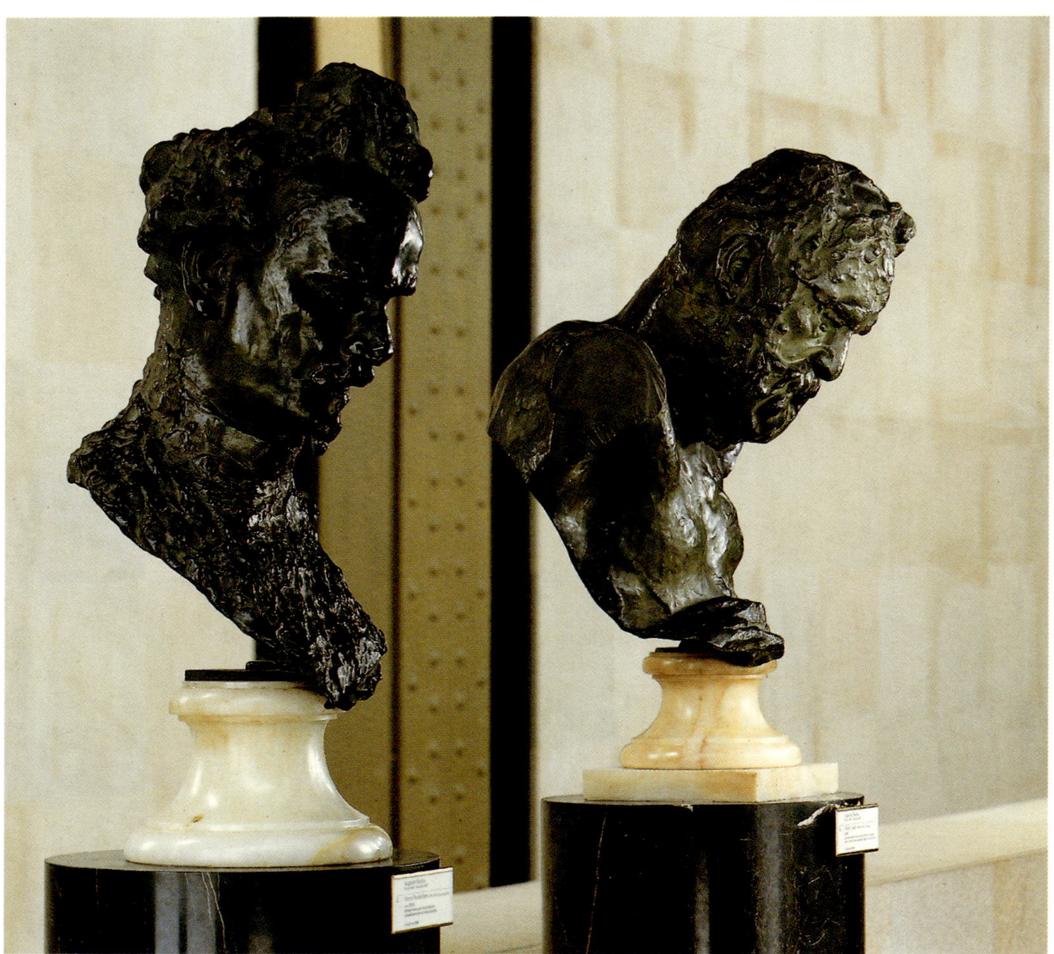

Auguste Rodin
Paris 1840 –
Meudon 1917
Henri Rochefort
(1831–1913), 1884–90
Bronze bust cast
by Alexis Rudier.
0.715 x 0.414 x 0.38 m
Acquired by the Nation, 1906;
Luxembourg Museum, 1908;
Rodin Museum, 1919;
Orsay, 1986.
RF 4067

Victor Hugo
(1802–1885), 1897
Bronze bust.
0.706 x 0.615 x 0.568 m
Fragment of the *Monument*
commissioned by the
Pantheon, rejected in 1890,
erected in the Palais Royal
gardens in 1909; acquired by
the Nation, 1906;
Luxembourg Museum, 1908;
Rodin Museum, 1919;
Orsay, 1986.
RF 4066

Auguste Rodin ▷▷
Paris 1840 – Meudon 1917
Monument to Balzac (1799–1850), 1897
Plaster model. 2.75 x 1.21 x 1.32 m
When Chapu died in 1891, Emile Zola, the new president of the Société des Gens de Lettres, had the commission transferred to Rodin. Endless studies from the nude, plus the influence of Medardo Rosso, resulted in this symbol of shining intellect rejected by the Société des Gens de Lettres when it was shown at the 1898 SNBA Salon. Rodin Donation, 1916; Orsay Depository, 1986.
DO 1986–2

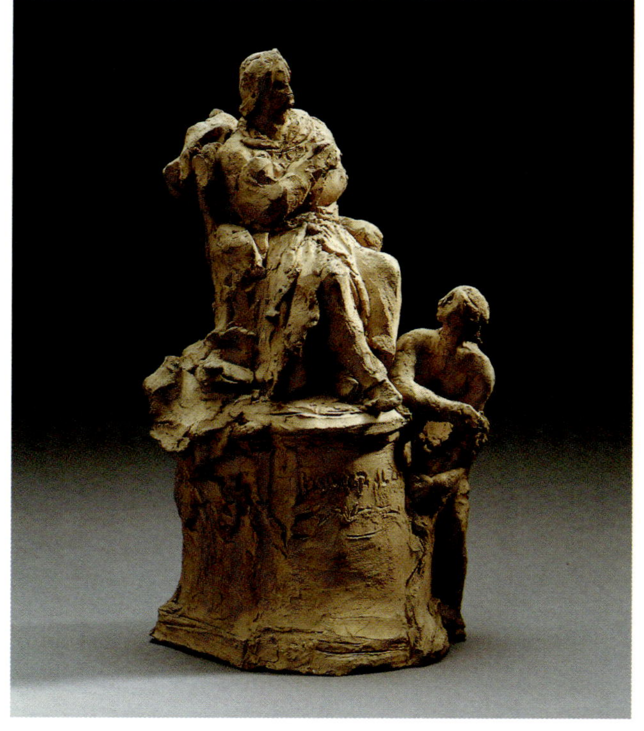

Henri Chapu
Le Mée 1833 – Paris 1891
Monument to Balzac (1799–1850),
between 1888 and 1891
Terra-cotta study. 0.24 x 0.126 x 0.128 m
Commissioned by the Société des Gens de Lettres in 1888 for the Galerie d'Orléans of the Palais Royal; acquired from Mme L.S. Berryer, 1922; Louvre, 1922; Orsay, 1986.
RF 1764

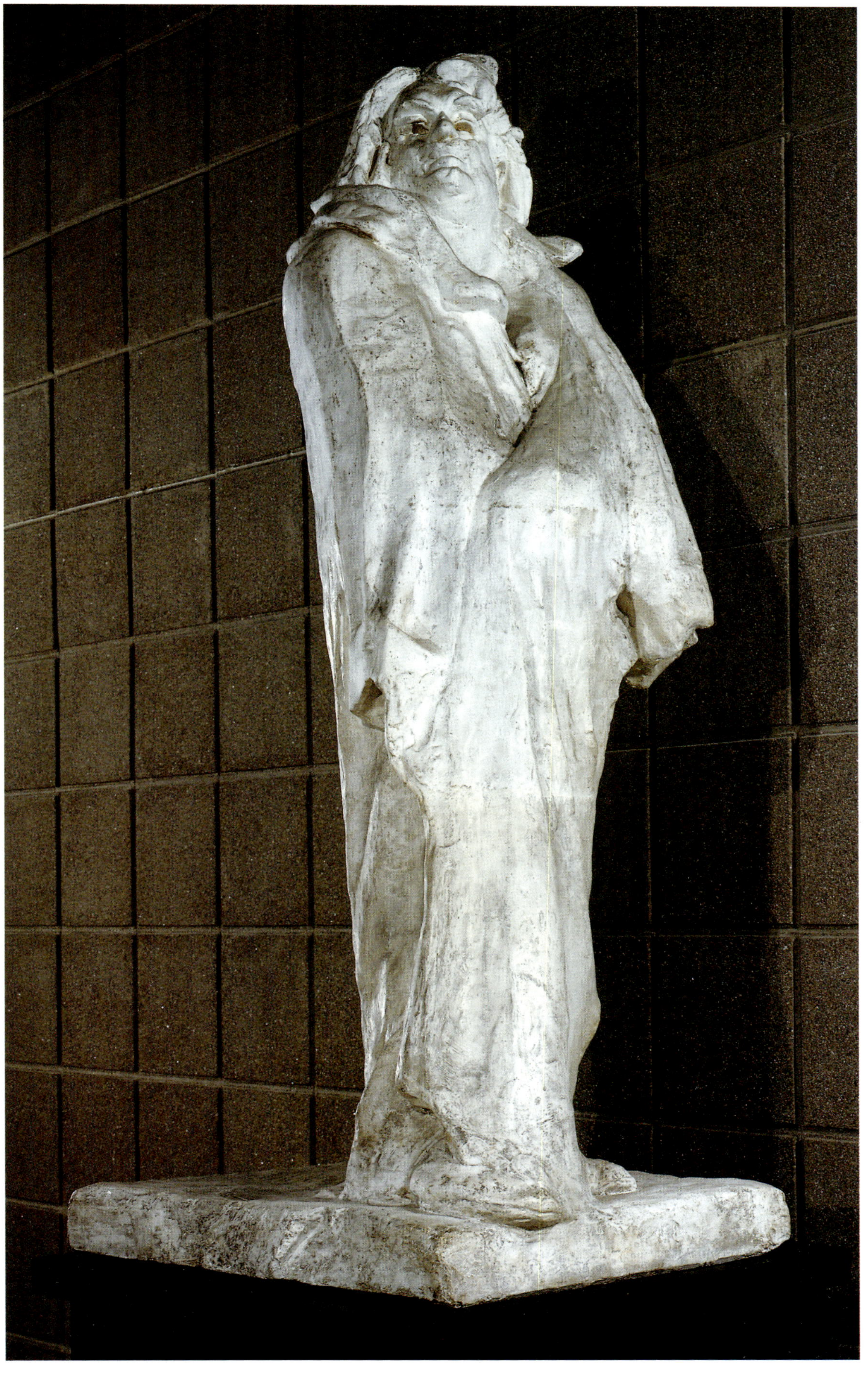

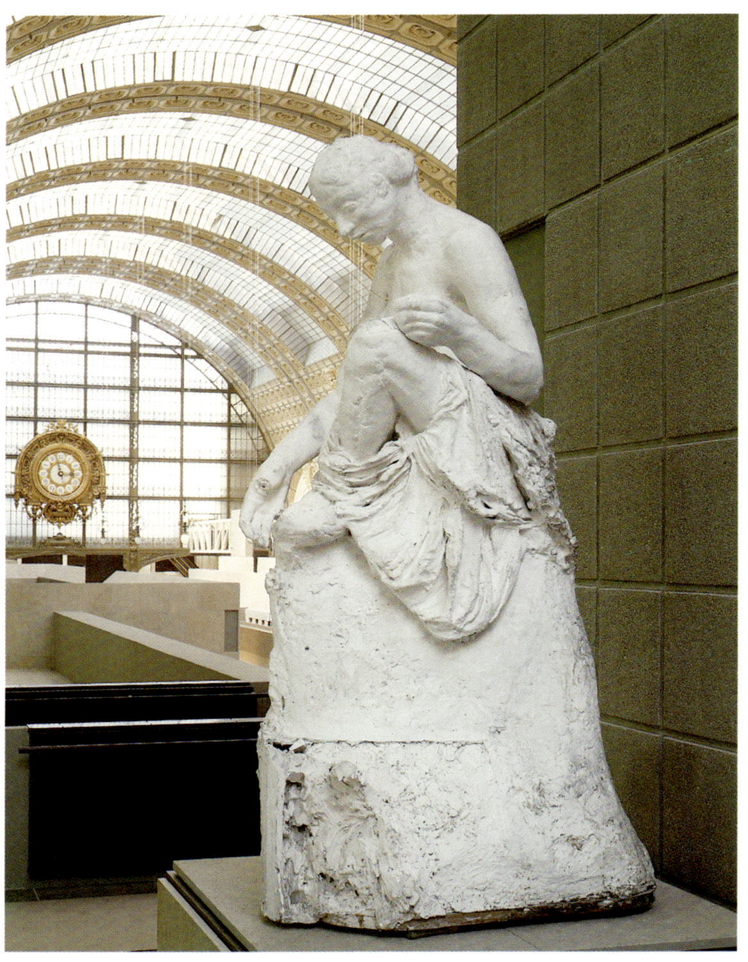

Auguste Rodin ▷
Paris 1840 – Meudon 1917
Man Walking, 1905
Bronze statue cast by Alexis Rudier. 2.13 x 1.61 x 0.72 m
Enlargement of the 1900 plaster made in 1905
by Henri Lebossé with a study for *Saint John the Baptist*
(c.1877–8) and the *Male Bust* (1877). Gift of Messrs.
Fenaille, Goloubeff, Joanny, Peytel and Léon Grunbaum
to the French Nation, 1911; Rome, Palazzo Farnese, 1911;
Lyon, Musée des Beaux-Arts, 1923; Orsay, 1986.
RF 4094

Auguste Rodin
Paris 1840 – Meudon 1917
Apotheosis of the Muse
from the *Whistler Monument*, 1908
Plaster model. 2.40 x 1.30 x 1.50 m
1908 SNBA Salon (arm missing; portrait of Whistler missing).
Unfinished monument.
Rodin Donation, 1916; Orsay Depository, 1986.
DO 1986–3

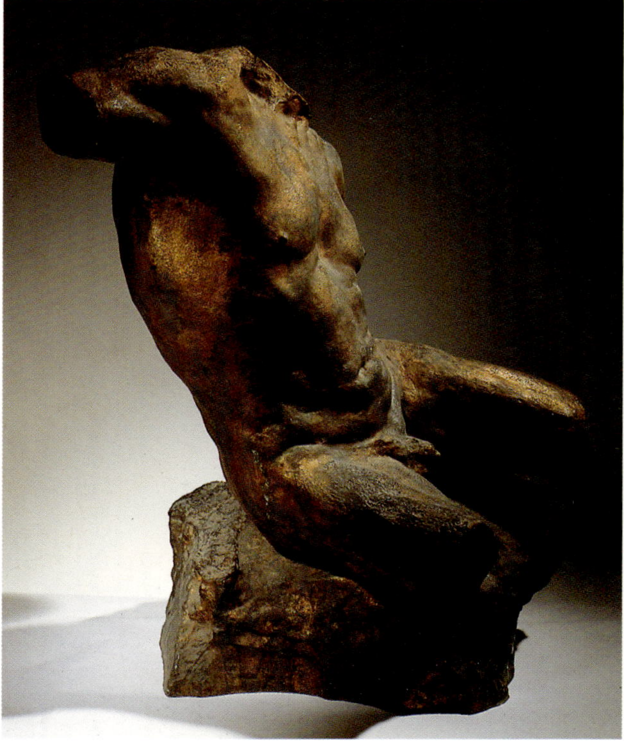

Jules Desbois
Parçay-les-Pins 1851 – Paris 1935
Male Bust, 1910–34
Gilded bronze statue cast by Alexis Rudier.
1.28 x 1.05 x 0.90 m
Fragment of the *Rock of Sisyphus*, 1910 SNBA Salon;
commissioned by the Nation, 1934;
Luxembourg Museum, 1935; National Museum of Modern Art, 1940;
Louvre, 1977; Orsay, 1986.
RF 3204

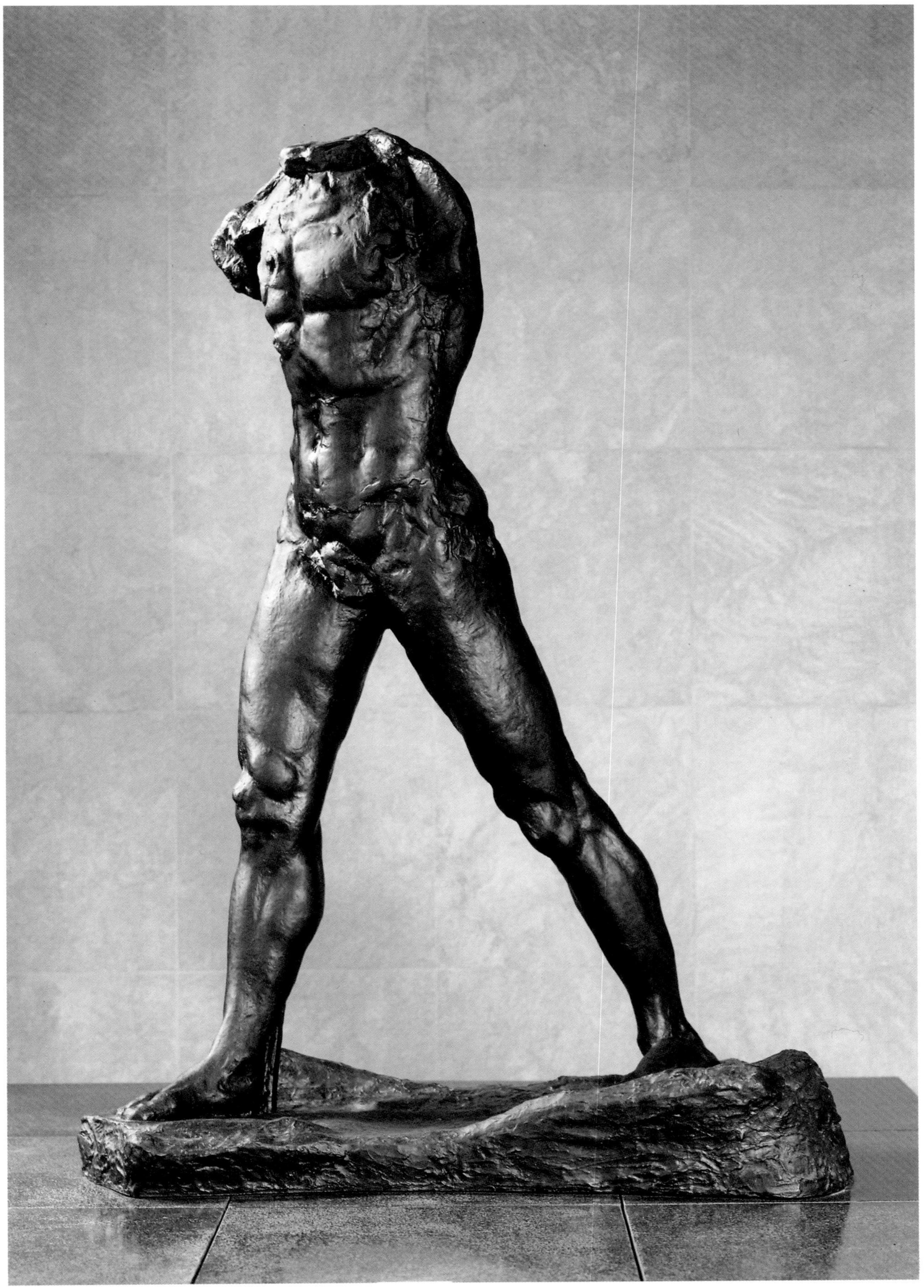

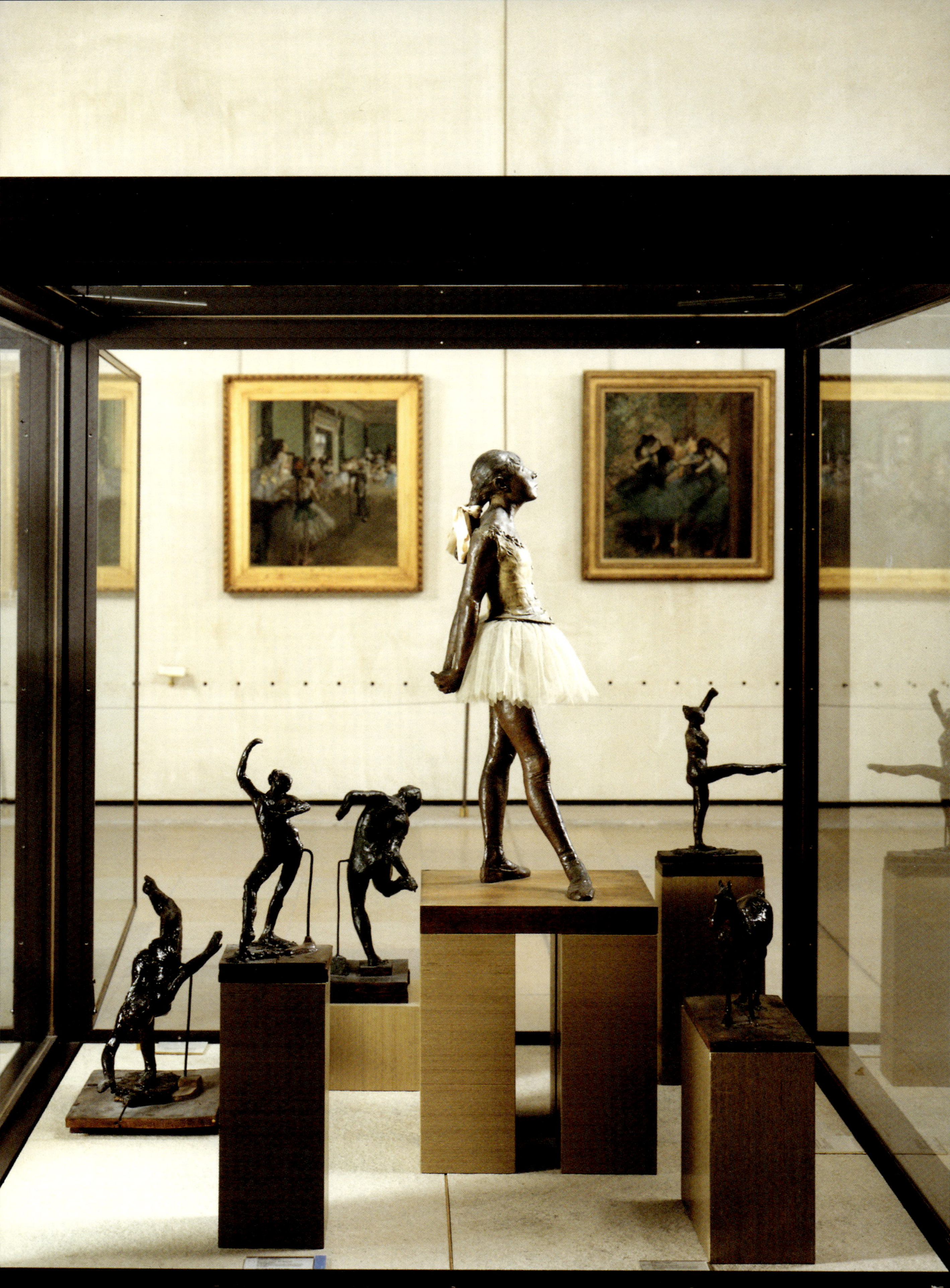

Is There Such a Thing as Impressionist Sculpture?

Sculpture, the enduring art, would seem antithetical by nature to feeling; and also, because of its immobility, to modern life. But this is to forget that the play of light over sculpted surfaces, and the relationship between shadow and volume are essential aspects of this medium. The play of light had lent expression to sculpted studies on which the imprint of the fingers is still visible since the 18th century. Some 19th-century sculptors left a visible trace of the creative process in the finished work.

Daumier, a genius of both line and surface and always ahead of his time, had explored the impression made by a passing crowd emerging from a frieze he called the *Emigrants.* At a time when Impressionist painters were separating their brushstrokes, Carpeaux captured light by fragmenting the surfaces touched by it. A lover of the 18th century and of movement, he retained the dash of the preliminary study in the definitive work – or at least until the plaster model stage, since the transition to marble chilled a vitality that is nevertheless still perceptible in the stone of *The Dance.*

Rodin, despite his patterns of curve and hollow, adopted a less spontaneous approach. Symbolism and expressionism dominated his work. His *Balzac* might be said to reflect both approaches, had it not been adduced by so many as a prime example of Impressionist sculpture. Could this be attributed to Rodin's meeting with Medardo Rosso, from the Milan *scapigliatura*? The 'secret of the atmospheric ambience, the throb of life' was announced by Rosso in his titles: *Impression from an Omnibus* (1885), *Impression of Woman with Umbrella* (1894), *Impression of Boulevard by Night* (1895). The breath of fresh air Rosso brought with him – long after the First Impressionist Exhibition in 1874 – the dissolution of volume in light, the choice of a single viewpoint, gained from Rodin the declaration that 'I was struck with wild admiration.' Rodin's goal, however, was to subsume form to an idea, rather than to dissolve it in light.

Degas, in his sculpture, was no more concerned with literature than with psychology. For him, sculpture was an exercise, a means to create better paintings. 'To achieve the kind of precision that gives a sense of life', he declared to Thiebault-Sisson, 'you must work in three dimensions ... because [in sculpture] approximations will not do'. The only one of his sculptures he exhibited was the *Young Dancer of Fourteen,* which he had promised for the Fifth Impressionist Exhibition but did not show until the sixth in 1881. He refused Vollard's suggestion that he cast his studies in bronze, 'that material made for eternity' which precludes 'the pleasure of starting over again'. After his death, his heirs asked the sculptor A. Bartholomé and bronze caster A.A. Hébrard to create a posthumous series. At the Musée d'Orsay, these 'P' series bronzes can be compared to the five wax originals donated by the great American collector Paul Mellon.

Edgar Degas
Paris 1834 – Paris 1917
Young Dancer of Fourteen,
1881
Bronze statuette cast by A.A. Hébrard (P), polychromatic patinas, tulle, satin.
1.038 x 0.488 x 0.50 m
Acquired with assistance from the heirs of Degas and the caster, 1930; Jeu de Paume, 1973; Orsay, 1986.
RF 2137
Shown with four *Dancers* and one *Horse,* wax models donated by Paul Mellon, 1956 and 1992.

Vollard succeeded with Renoir where he had failed with Degas. This explains why under the painter's supervision the young Guino created works closer to classical immobility than to Impressionism.

'Society' sculpture often has an Impressionist feel because the swift movements of the artist's hand remain imprinted on the material, as in the portraits by the international artist Troubetzkoy.

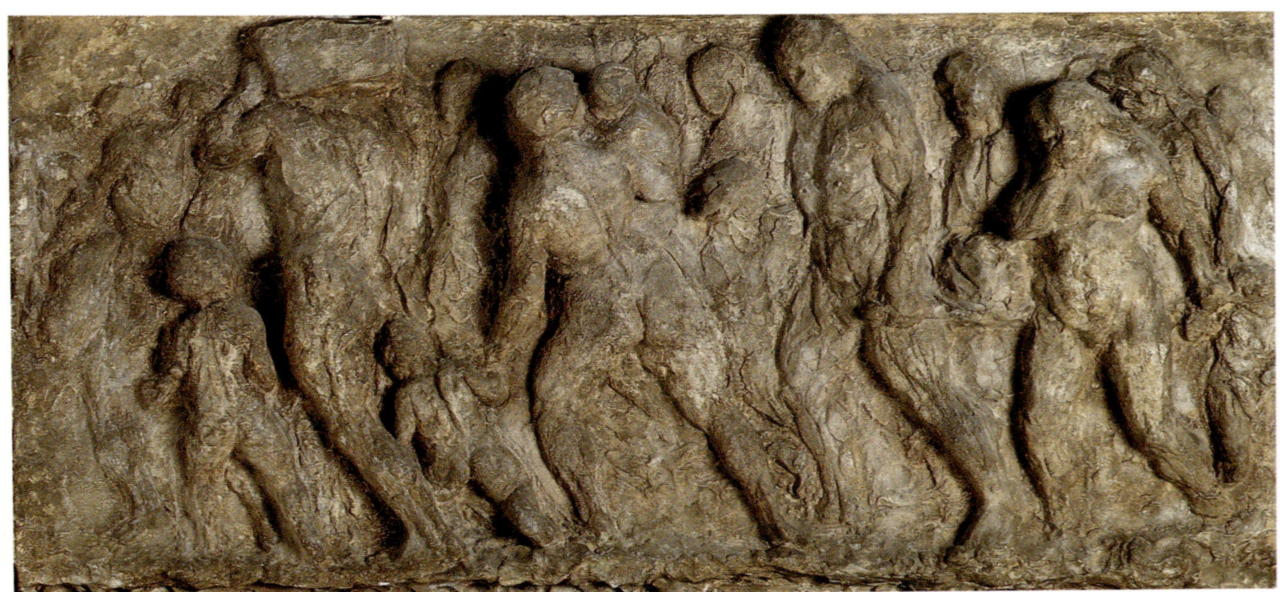

Honoré Daumier
Marseilles 1808 – Valmondois 1879
The Emigrants, c.1848
Plaster relief. 0.28 x 0.66 x 0.08 m
Executed by the sculptor Victor Geoffroy-Dechaume from a clay mould destroyed in the process.
Acquired 1960; Louvre, 1960; Orsay, 1986.
RF 2830

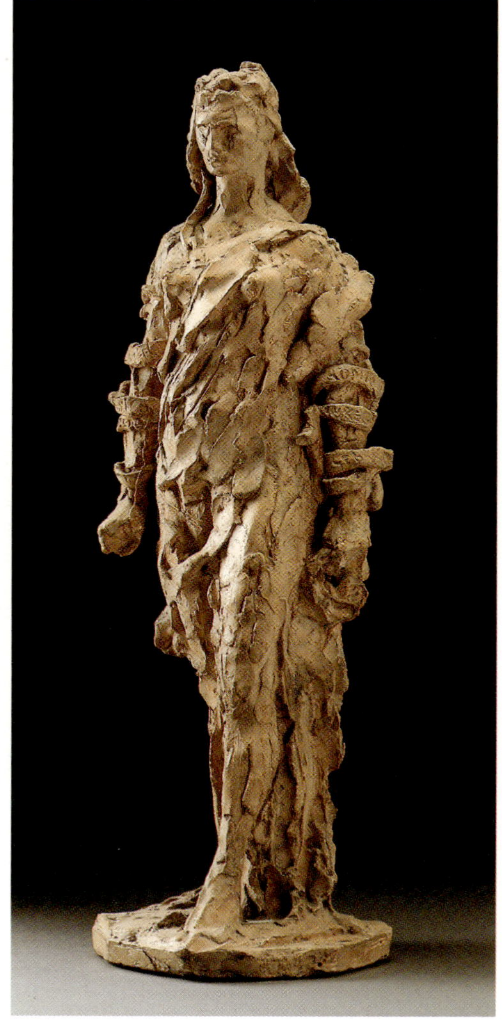

Jean-Baptiste Carpeaux
Valenciennes 1827 – Courbevoie 1875
The Motherland, c.1870
Patinated terra-cotta plaster study.
0.659 x 0.215 x 0.23 m
Acquired from Louis Holfeld (heir of Louise Clément-Carpeaux, the sculptor's daughter), 1962; Louvre, 1962; Orsay, 1986.
RF 2844

Medardo Rosso
Turin (Italy) 1858 – Milan (Italy) 1928
(Naturalized French, 1902)
Ecce Puer, 1906

Portrait executed in London, in December 1905, of Alfred William Mond, aged eight, hiding behind a curtain in his father Emile Mond's house on Hyde Park Square.
Bronze head. 0.44 x 0.37 x 0.27 m
Gift of Francesco Rosso (the sculptor's son), 1928, in exchange for a plaster acquired in 1907 by Clemenceau; Musée des Ecoles Etrangères, 1922; National Museum of Modern Art, 1940; Louvre, 1977; Orsay, 1986.
RF 4231

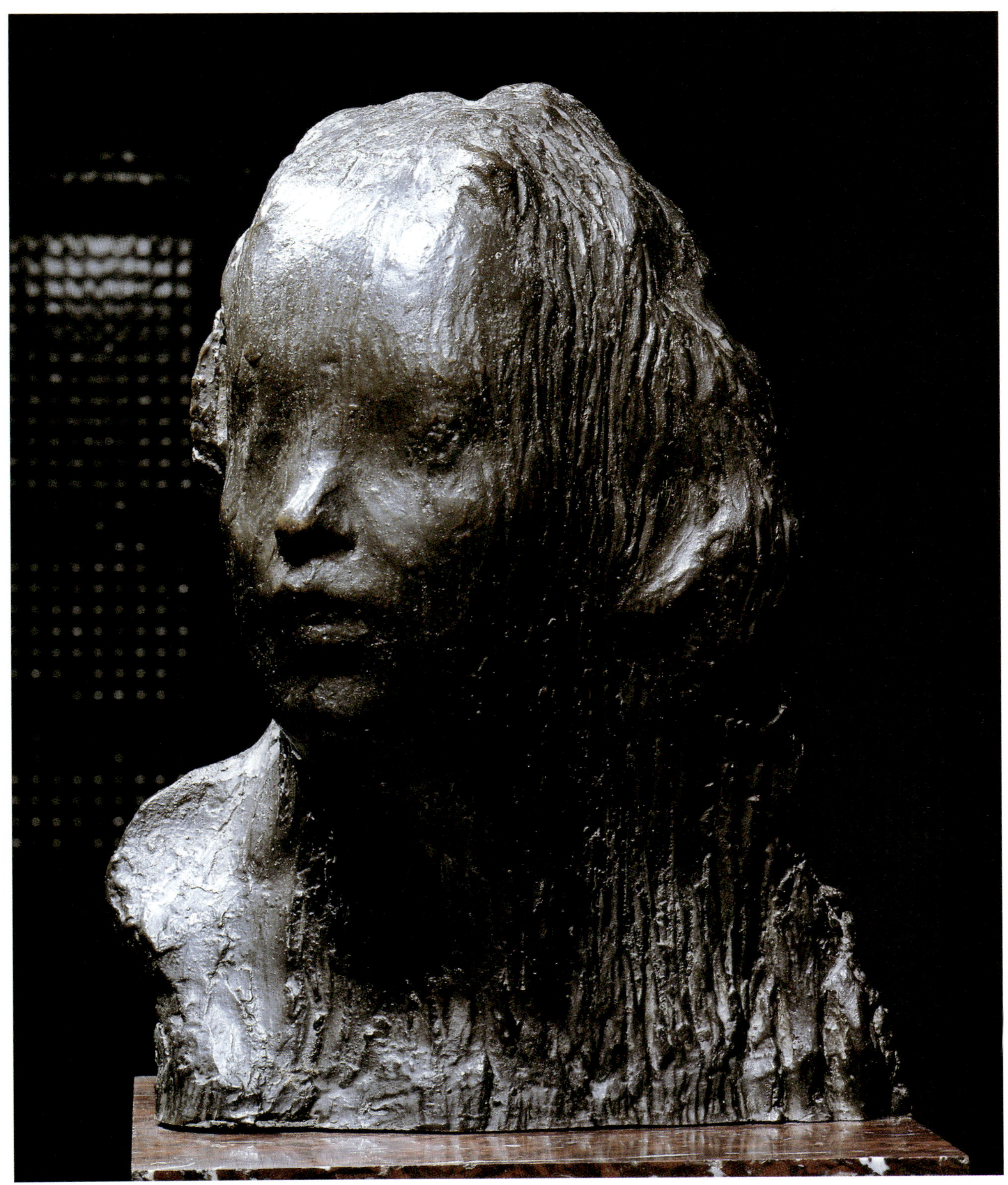

Vollard's archives, donated to the Musée d'Orsay in 1988, contained 72 photographs of 53 Degas wax models. When we discovered that these photographs had been taken by Gauthier after Degas's death, between 29 December 1917 and 28 March 1918 (on behalf of the dealers responsible for making an inventory of his last studio, 6 boulevard de Clichy), we realized that we at last had evidence of the state in which Degas left his sculptures. By comparing these photographs with the waxes and bronzes, we are now in a position to evaluate the fidelity of the reproductions.

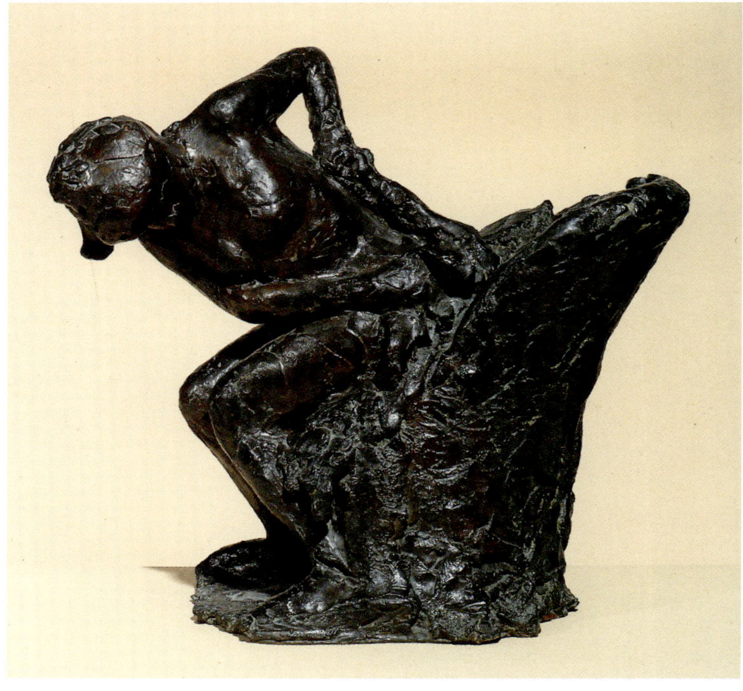

Edgar Degas
Paris 1834 – Paris 1917
Seated Woman Drying her Left Side, 1896–1911
Bronze statuette cast by A.A. Hébrard (54/P). 0.455 x 0.305 x 0.304 m
Acquired with assistance from the heirs of Degas and the caster, 1930; Louvre, 1930; Orsay, 1986.
RF 2131

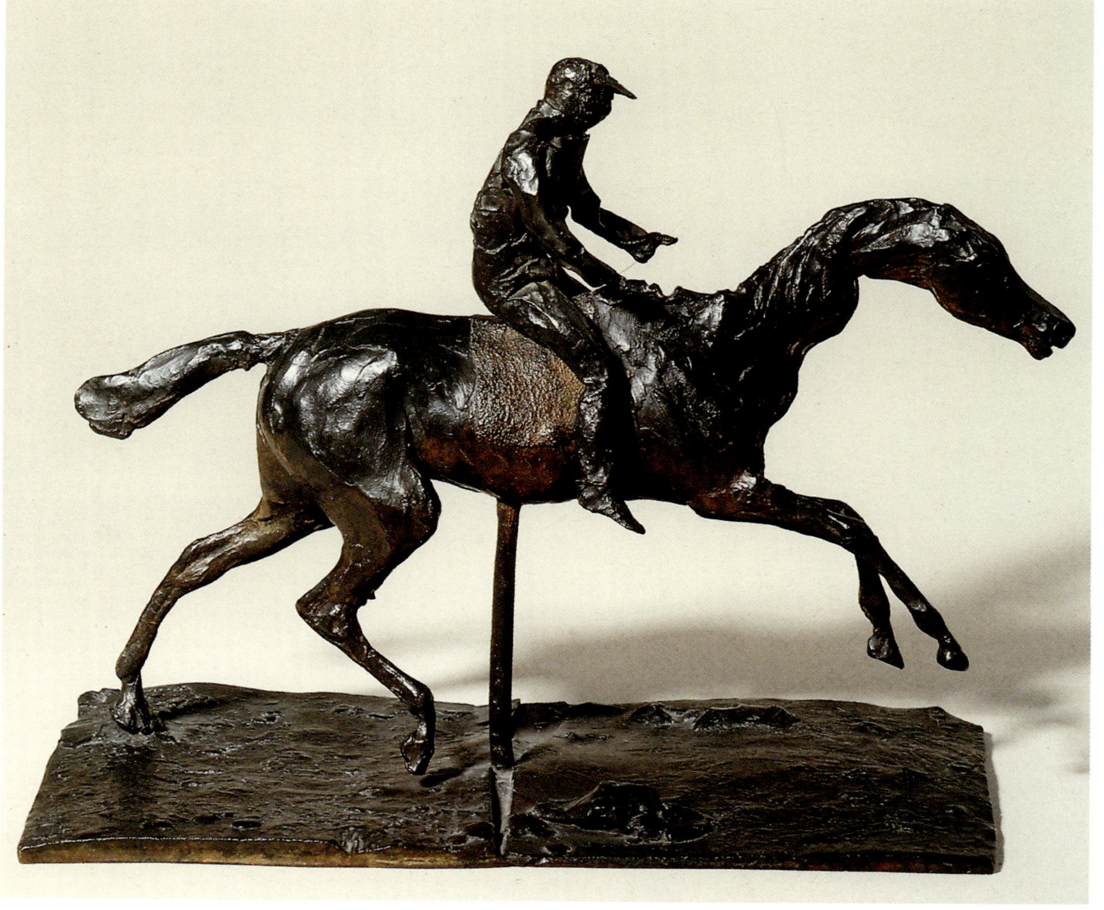

Edgar Degas
Paris 1834 – Paris 1917
Jockey on Cantering Horse, Right Legs Forward, 1865–90
Bronze statuette cast by A.A. Hébrard (25/P and 35/P). 0.20 x 0.182 x 0.335 m
Acquired with assistance from the heirs of Degas and the caster, 1930; Louvre, 1930; Jeu de Paume, 1974 ; Orsay, 1986.
RF 2113–2114

Edgar Degas
Paris 1834 – Paris 1917
Study for Spanish Dance, 1896–1911
Original wax.
0.452 x 0.21 x 0.195 m
Donated by Paul Mellon through the Foundation for French Museums, on the Musée d'Orsay's fifth anniversary, in memory of his friend Ambassador Emmanuel de Margerie, 1992.
RF 4396

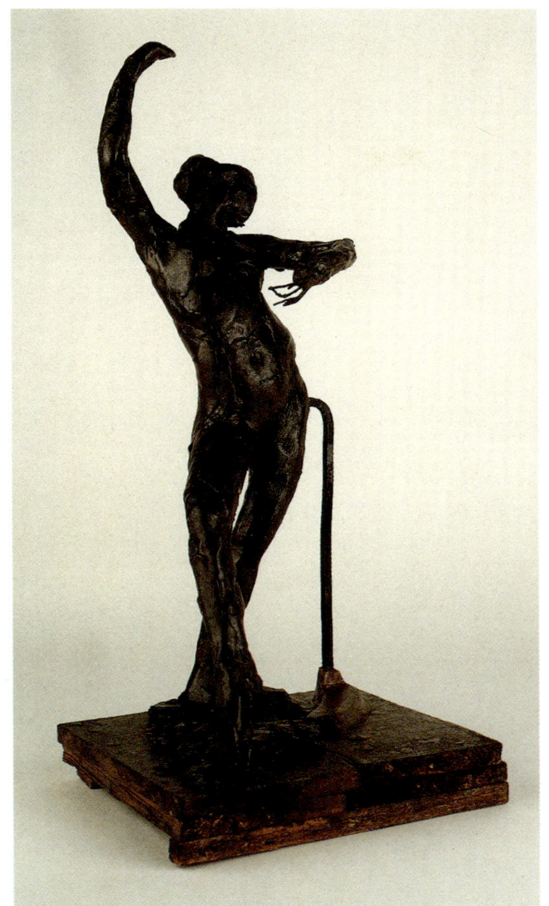

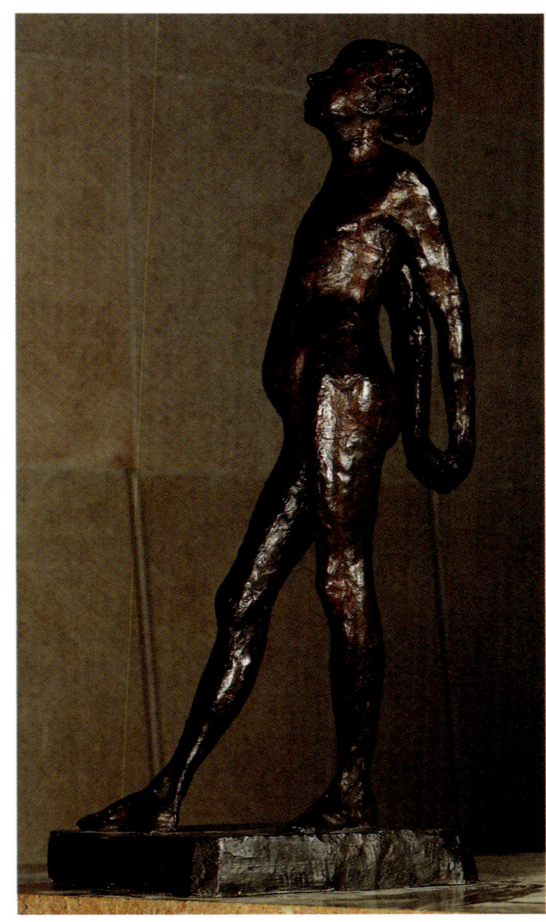

Edgar Degas
Paris 1834 – Paris 1917
Nude Study for Clothed Dancer, 1878–80
Bronze statuette cast by A.A. Hébrard (56/P).
0.735 x 0.349 x 0.31 m
Acquired with assistance from the heirs of Degas and the caster, 1930; Louvre, 1930; Orsay, 1986.
RF 2101

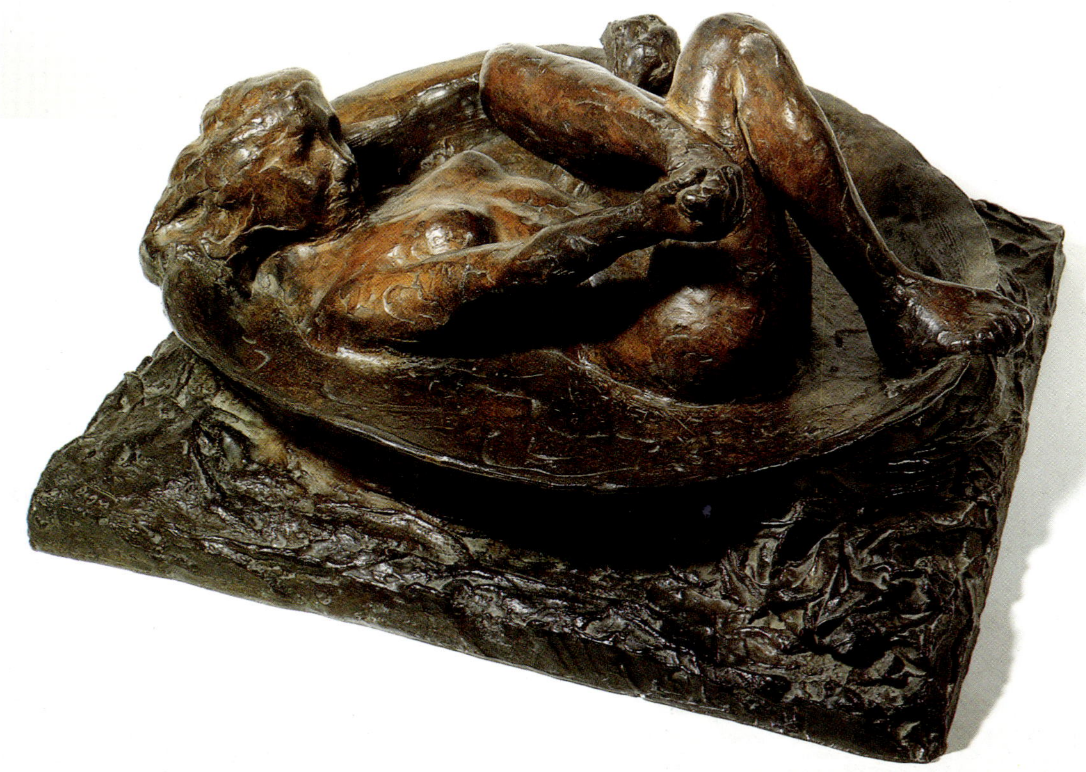

Edgar Degas
Paris 1834 – Paris 1917
The Tub, 1888–9
Bronze statuette cast by A.A. Hébrard (26/P).
0.225 x 0.438 x 0.458 m
Acquired with assistance from the heirs of Degas and the caster, 1930; Louvre, 1930; Orsay, 1986.
RF 2120

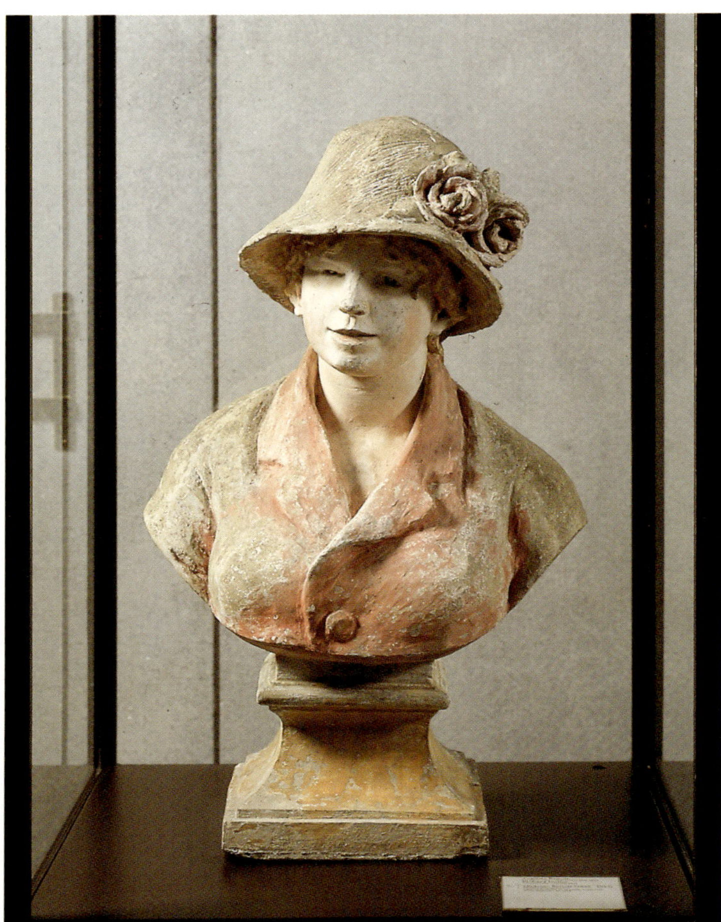

Pierre-Auguste Renoir
Limoges 1841 – Cagnes-sur-Mer 1919
Richard Guino
Gerone, Catalonia (Spain) 1890 –
Antony (Spain) 1973
(Naturalized French, 1925)
Mme Renoir, née Aline Charigot
(1859–1915), 1916
Polychromatic mortuary bust. 0.824 x 0.53 x 0.345 m
Enlargement by Guino, for Mme Renoir's grave at Essoyes, of the upper part of *Mother and Child*, a small group based on the portrait executed by Renoir in 1885 (Philadelphia Museum of Art). Acquired 1955; Louvre, 1955; Orsay, 1986.
RF 2764

Pierre-Auguste Renoir
Limoges 1841 – Cagnes-sur-Mer 1919
Richard Guino
Gerone, Catalonia (Spain) 1890 –
Antony (Spain) 1973
(Naturalized French, 1925)
Judgment of Paris, 1914
Plaster relief. 0.762 x 0.945 x 0.10 m
Acquired at public auction, 1954;
Jeu de Paume, 1954; Orsay, 1986.
RF 2745

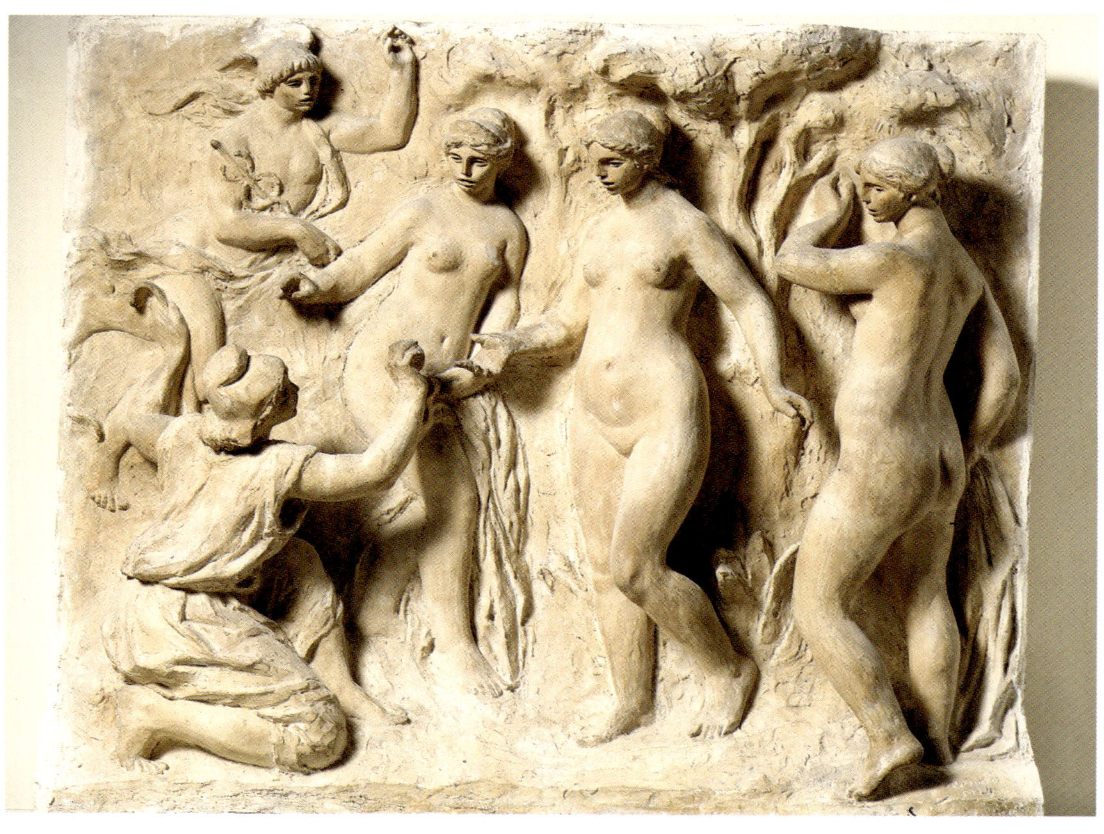

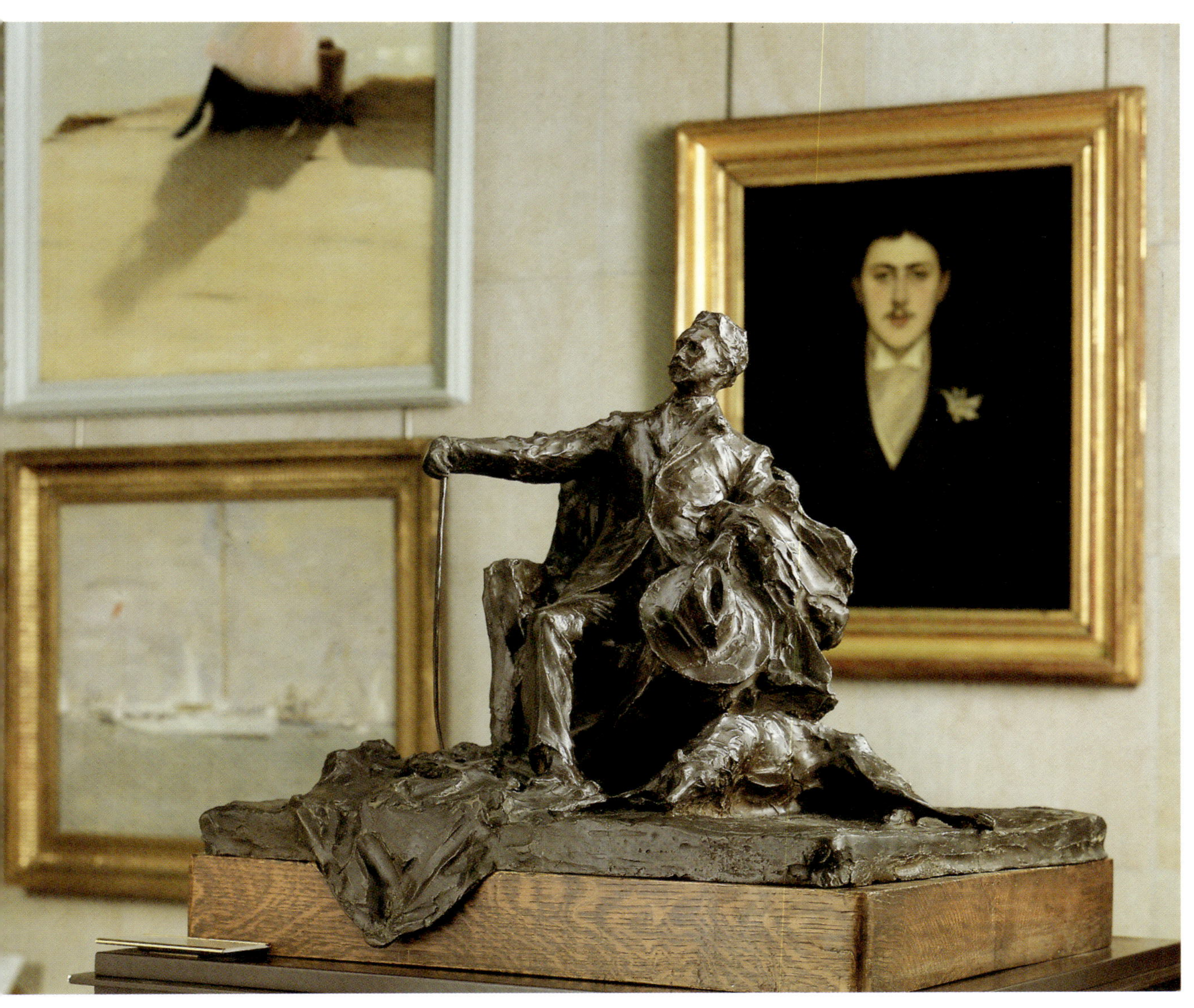

Paul Troubetzkoy
Intra (Italy) 1866 – Suna (Italy) 1938
Comte Robert de Montesquiou (1855–1921), 1907
Small bronze group cast by C. Valsuani. 0.56 x 0.62 x 0.565 m
Acquired at public auction in Enghien, 1980.
RF 3476
In the background is the portrait of *Marcel Proust* by Jacques-Emile Blanche.
Baron de Charlus, in Proust's *A la recherche du temps perdu* (1913–28),
is partly based on Robert de Montesquiou.

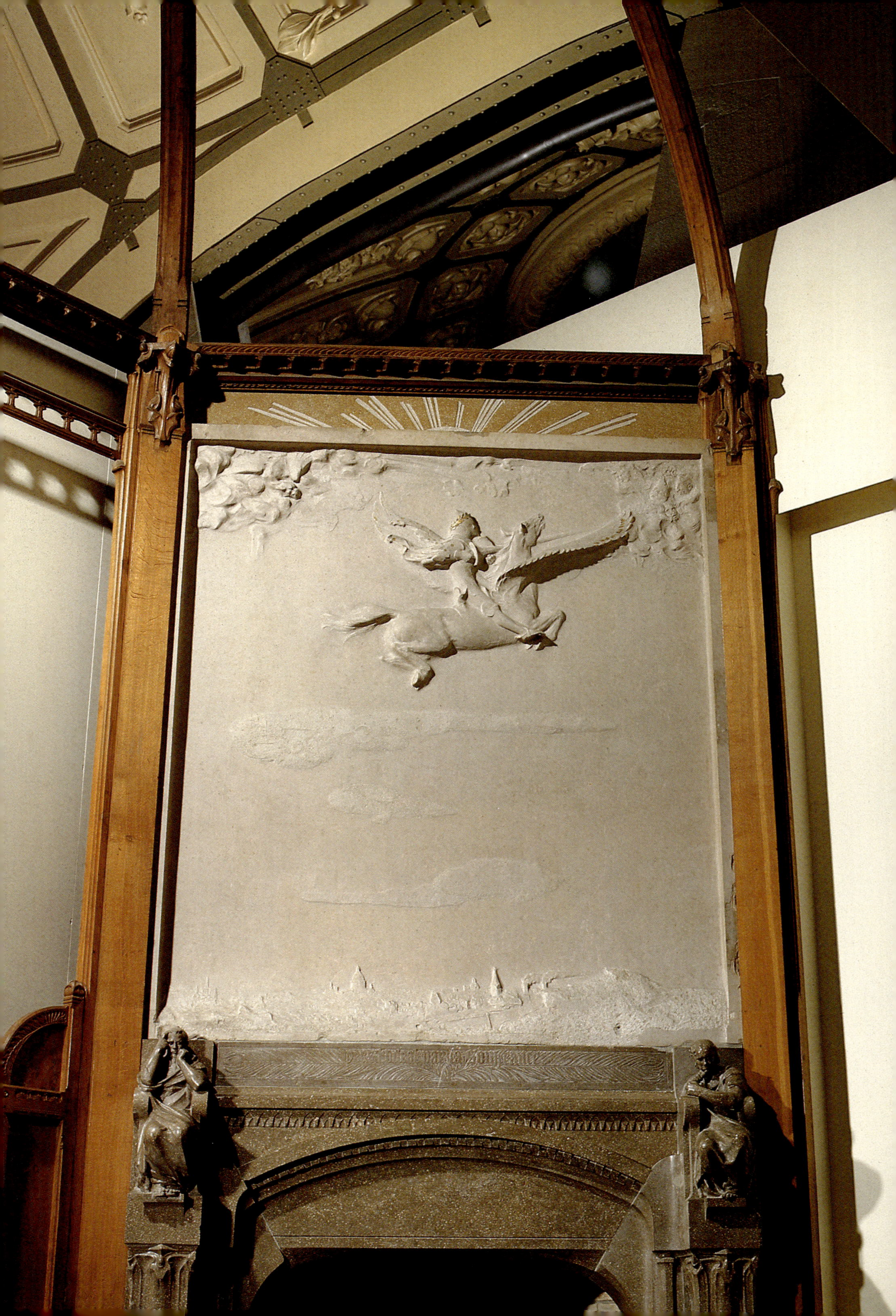

Symbolism

Nature is a temple whose living colonnades
Breathe forth a mystic speech in fitful sighs;
Man wanders among symbols in those glades
Where all things watch him with familiar eyes.

Like dwindling echoes gathered far away
Into a deep and thronging unison
Huge as the night or as the light of day,
All scents and sounds and colors meet as one.

Perfumes there are as sweet as the oboe's sound,
Green as the prairies, fresh as a child's caresss,
- And there are others, rich, corrupt, profound

And of an infinite pervasiveness,
Like myrrh, or musk, or amber, that excite
The ecstasies of sense, the soul's delight.

('Correspondences', tr. by Richard Wilbur, NY, New Directions, 1989)

This fourth poem in 'Spleen et idéal' from Baudelaire's *Fleurs du mal* (1857) expresses the very essence of symbolism. Long before Baudelaire, however, sculpture had already been using symbolism since the dawn of time. Before the prodigious miracle of classical Greek sculpture, correspondences were more natural to this medium than imitation. Representation vanquished the symbol only when, before the dawn of our own era, the Athenians achieved their perfection in portraying the figure. This hierarchy was confirmed by the Renaissance and not contested until the end of the 19th century. It was then that a few artists sated with sculptural mimesis decided to go beyond the purely visual. Literature and music were to provide powerful assistance in this response to the call of the undefinable. Symbolism in sculpture – like romanticism – sought the freedom of textured reliefs for expression. Curiously, these reliefs were also gates – allusions to the myth of passage, perhaps? Among them are Rodin's *Gate to the Inferno*, a landmark of symbolism; Carriès's *Parsifal Manuscript*, left unfinished; and even Bartholomé's *Monument to the Dead* in the Père Lachaise Cemetery, which is not a gate, properly speaking, but a gaping hole ready to swallow all who come near it.
The Middle Ages also contributed illuminated dreams and echoes from a period when symbolism held sway. Martine de Béhague, Comtesse de Béarn, who was a patron of Henri de Régnier and Paul Valéry, had in her town house on rue Saint Dominique a copy of the Queen's staircase at Versailles, a Neo-Byzantine music room and a special room reserved for artistic conversation. The latter was commissioned from the sculptor Jean Dampt, 'inspiration, supervisor, worker', and formed a single work of art, from the walls (oak, ash and elm featuring an interplay of knots and grains), to the furniture, curtains and fire tongs. Two pensive philosophers are carved into the red Jura granite chimneypiece. Between them, inscribed on palm fronds (symbolizing martyrdom?) is the motto '*Vers l'idéal par la souffrance*'. Above the huge, slightly protuberant sculpted Comblanchien marble slab lies a void which separates a laurel-wreathed knight mounted on a steed with gold-tipped wings from the city roofs far below him.

Jean Dampt
Venarey 1853 –
Venarey 1946
'Vers l'idéal par la souffrance' chimneypiece in the Parfit Gentle Knight's Room,
1900–06
Bas-relief in gilded pink Comblanchien marble.
1.965 x 2.24 x 0.14 m
Museum of Decorative Arts Depository to Orsay, 1980.
DO 1980–16

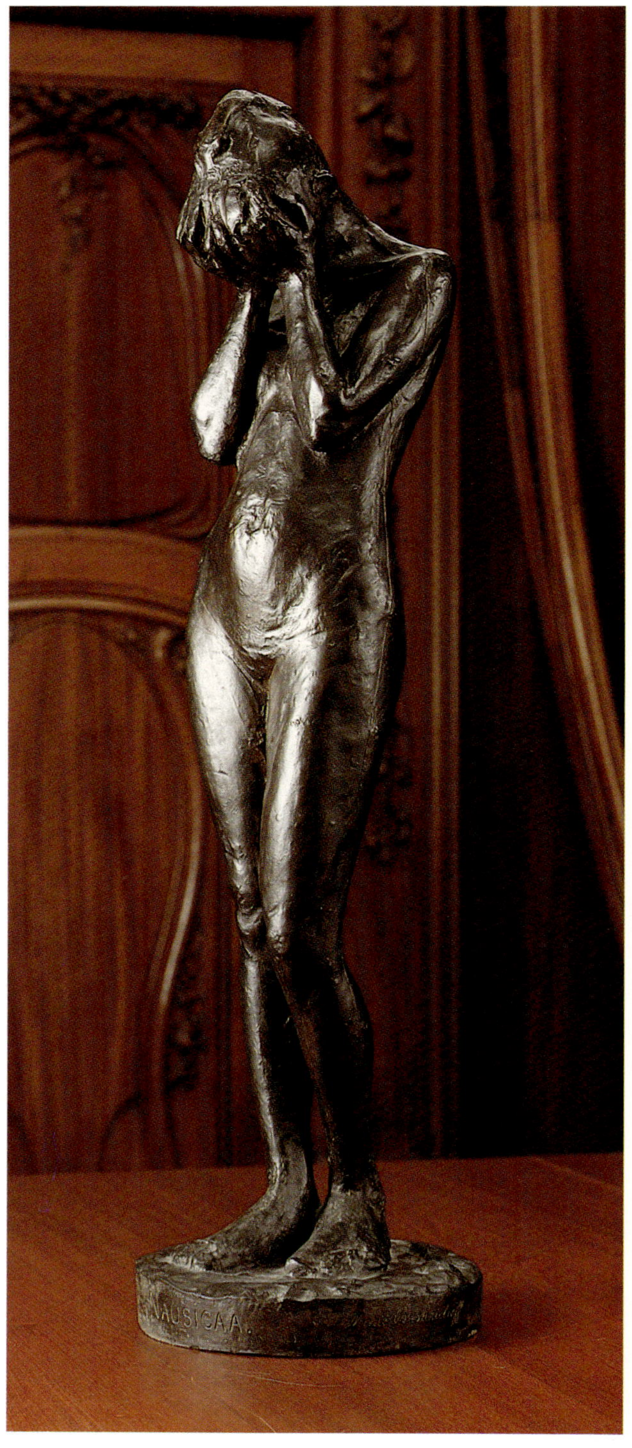

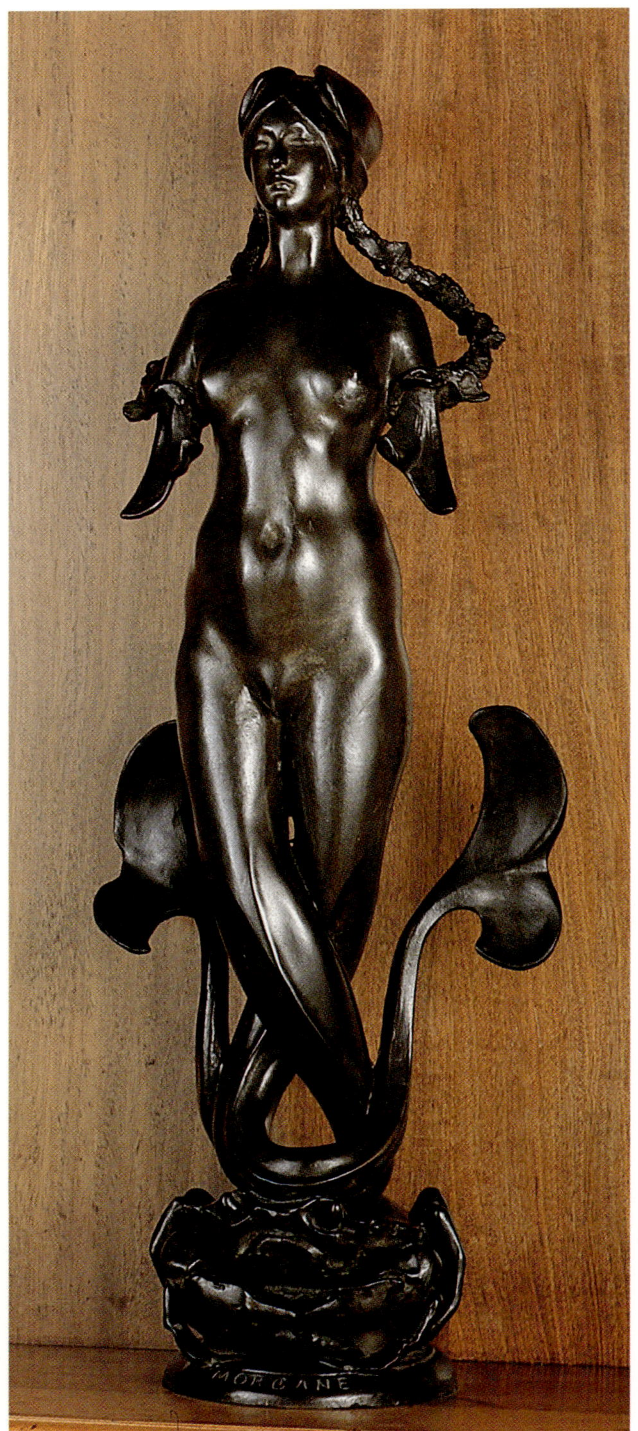

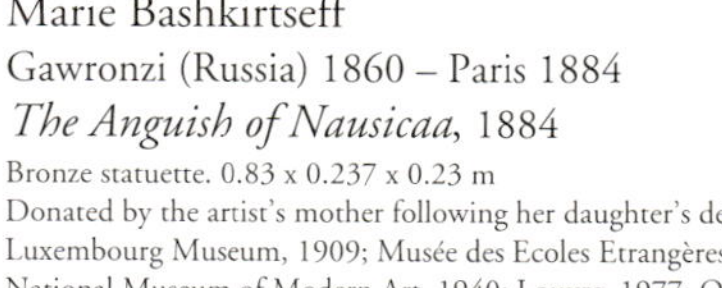

Marie Bashkirtseff
Gawronzi (Russia) 1860 – Paris 1884
The Anguish of Nausicaa, 1884
Bronze statuette. 0.83 x 0.237 x 0.23 m
Donated by the artist's mother following her daughter's death;
Luxembourg Museum, 1909; Musée des Ecoles Etrangères, 1922;
National Museum of Modern Art, 1940; Louvre, 1977; Orsay, 1986.
RF 3159

Pierre Roche
Paris 1855 – Paris 1922
Morgan le Fay, 1904
Bronze, lead and marble statuette. 0.83 x 0.265 x 0.16 m
Acquired by the Nation from the 1904 SNBA Salon;
Luxembourg Museum, 1904; National Museum of Modern Art,
1940; Louvre, 1977; Orsay, 1986.
RF 3281

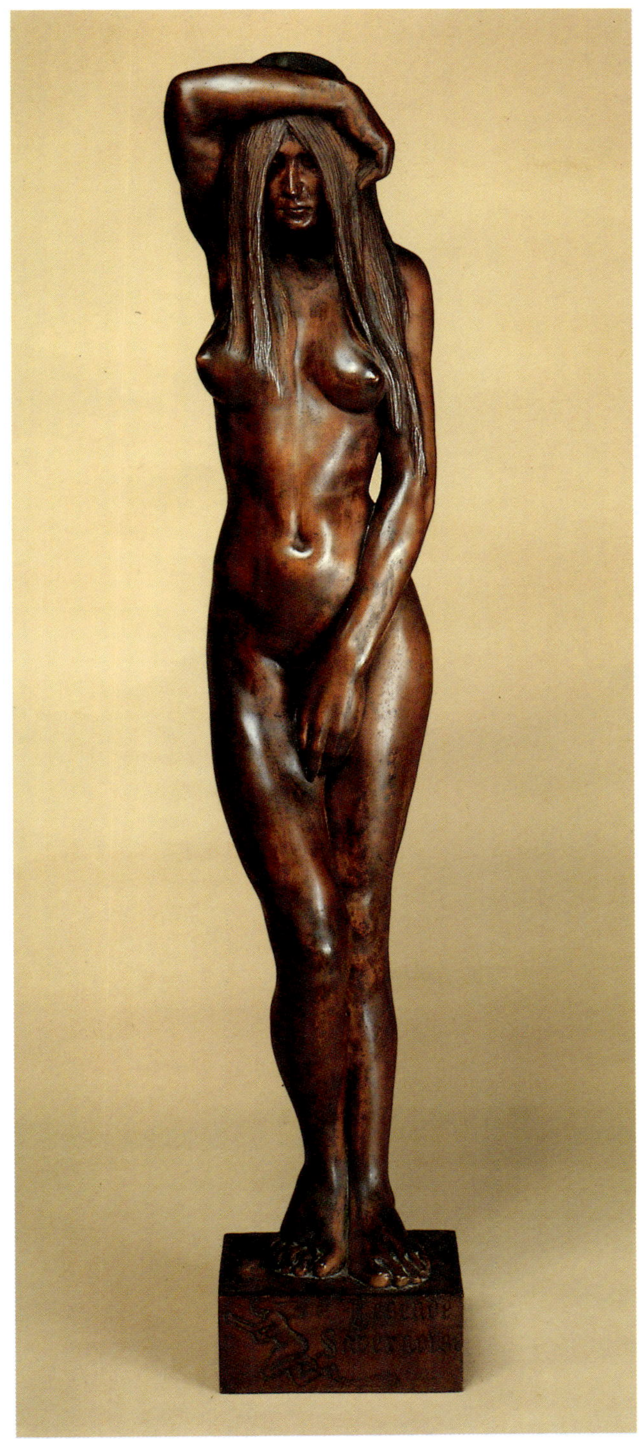

Rupert Carabin
Saverne 1862 – Strasbourg 1932
The Legend of Saverne, 1914
Pear-tree wood statuette. 0.829 x 0.174 x 0.18 m
Acquired by the Nation from the 1918 SNBA Salon; Luxembourg Museum, 1920; National Museum of Modern Art, 1940; Louvre, 1977; Orsay, 1986.
RF 3181

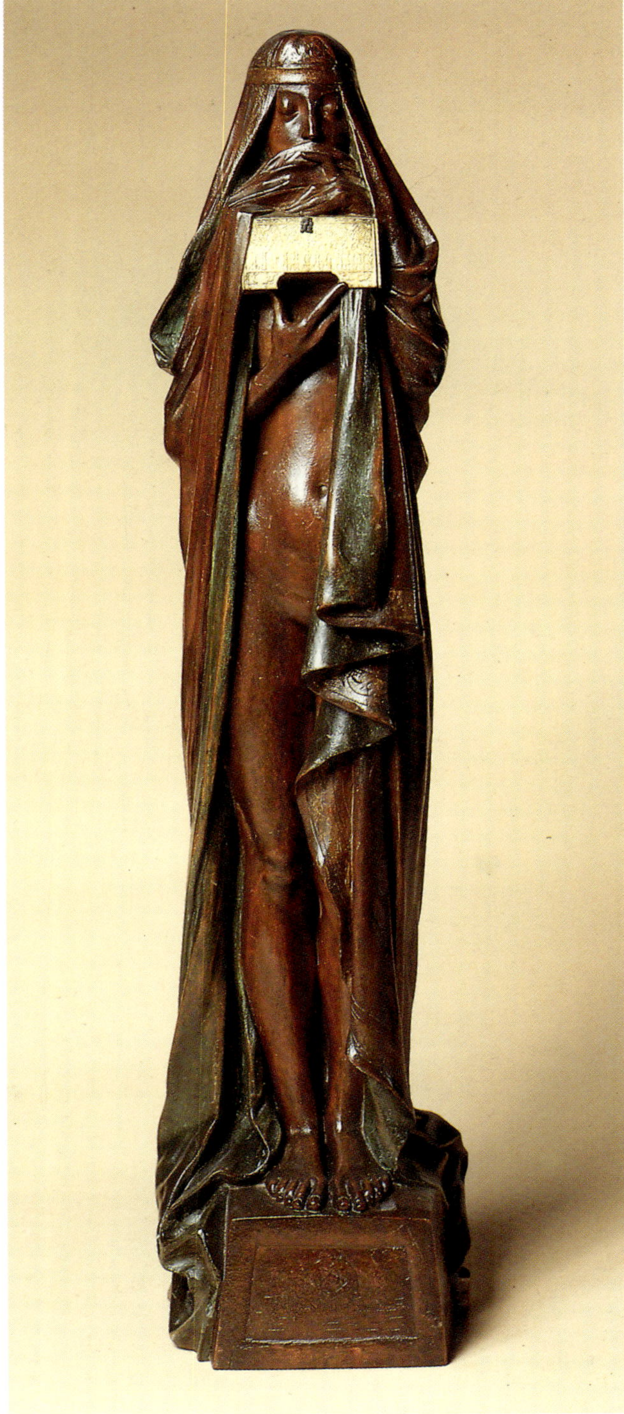

Fix-Masseau (Pierre-Félix Masseau)
Lyons 1869 – Paris 1937
The Secret, 1894
Polychromatic mahogany statuette, ivory casket. 0.76 x 0.175 x 0.18 m
Acquired by the Nation from the Objets d'Art section of the 1894 SNBA Salon; Lyon, Musée des Beaux-Arts, 1896; Louvre, 1982; Orsay, 1986.
RF 3638

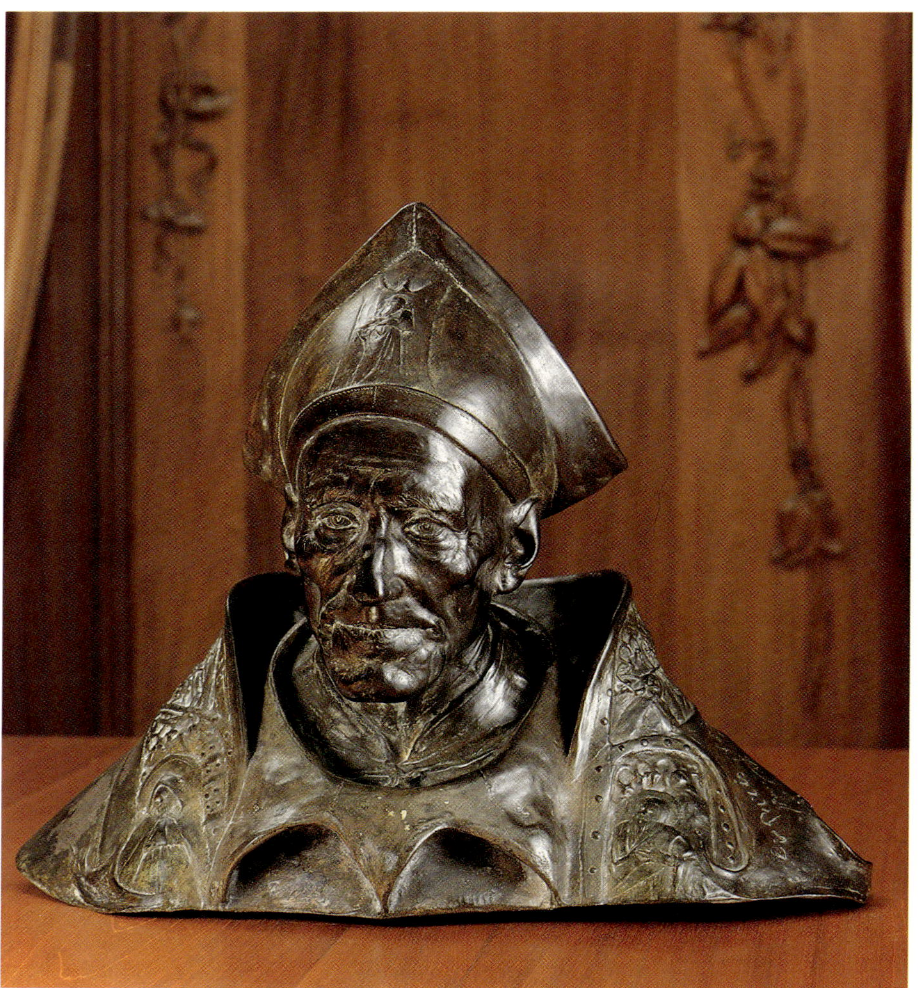

Jean Carriès
Lyons 1855 – Paris 1894
Bishop, 1883–9
Bronze bust cast by P. Bingen. 0.52 x 0.65 x 0.34 m
Acquired in 1889; Luxembourg Museum, 1891; Louvre, 1935; Orsay, 1986.
RF 881

Albert Bartholomé
Thiverval 1848 – Paris 1928
Tadamasa Hayashi (1856–1906), 1892
Bronze mask. 0.255 x 0.19 x 0.155 m
Donated by Les Amis du Musée d'Orsay, 1990.
RF 4303

Alexandre Charpentier
Paris 1856 – Neuilly 1909
Louis Welden Hawkins (painter, 1849–1910), 1893
Bronze mask. 0.26 x 0.21 x 0.12 m
Donated by Mrs Lomon-Hawkins, the model's grand-daughter, 1986.
RF 4185

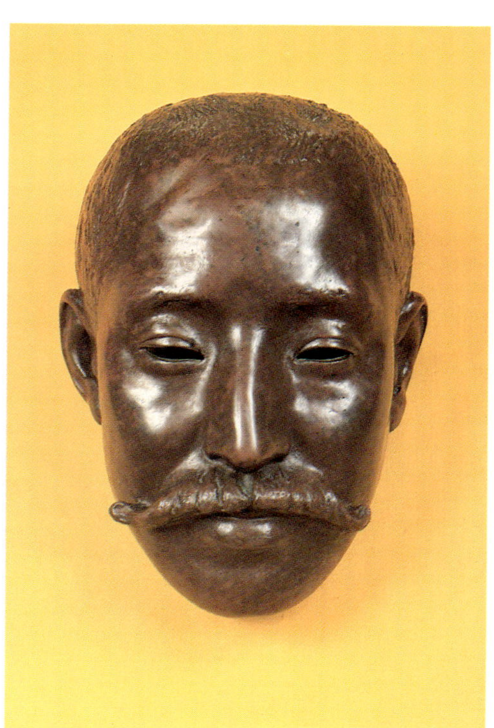

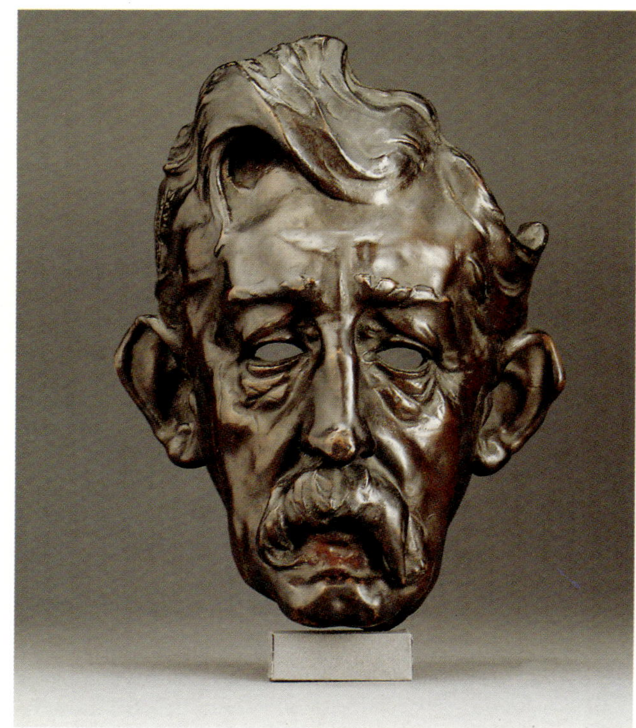

Carl Milles
Laga 1875 – Lindingö (Sweden) 1955
Young Girl Playing with Cat, c.1900
Bronze. 0.206 x 0.098 x 0.08 m
Donated by Mme David Nillet in memory of her husband, the painter David Nillet, 1933; Louvre, 1933; Orsay, 1986.
RF 2287

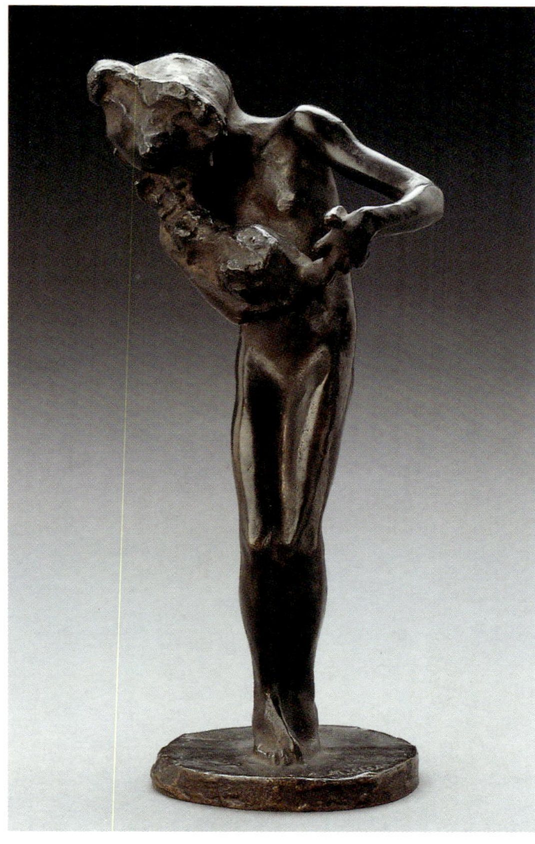

Albert Bartholomé
Thiverval 1848 – Paris 1928
Girl Crying, 1894
Bronze statue, 0.44 x 0.66 x 0.56 m
Acquired by the Nation from the 1894 SNBA Salon; Luxembourg Museum, 1895; Louvre, 1933; Orsay, 1986.
RF 1041

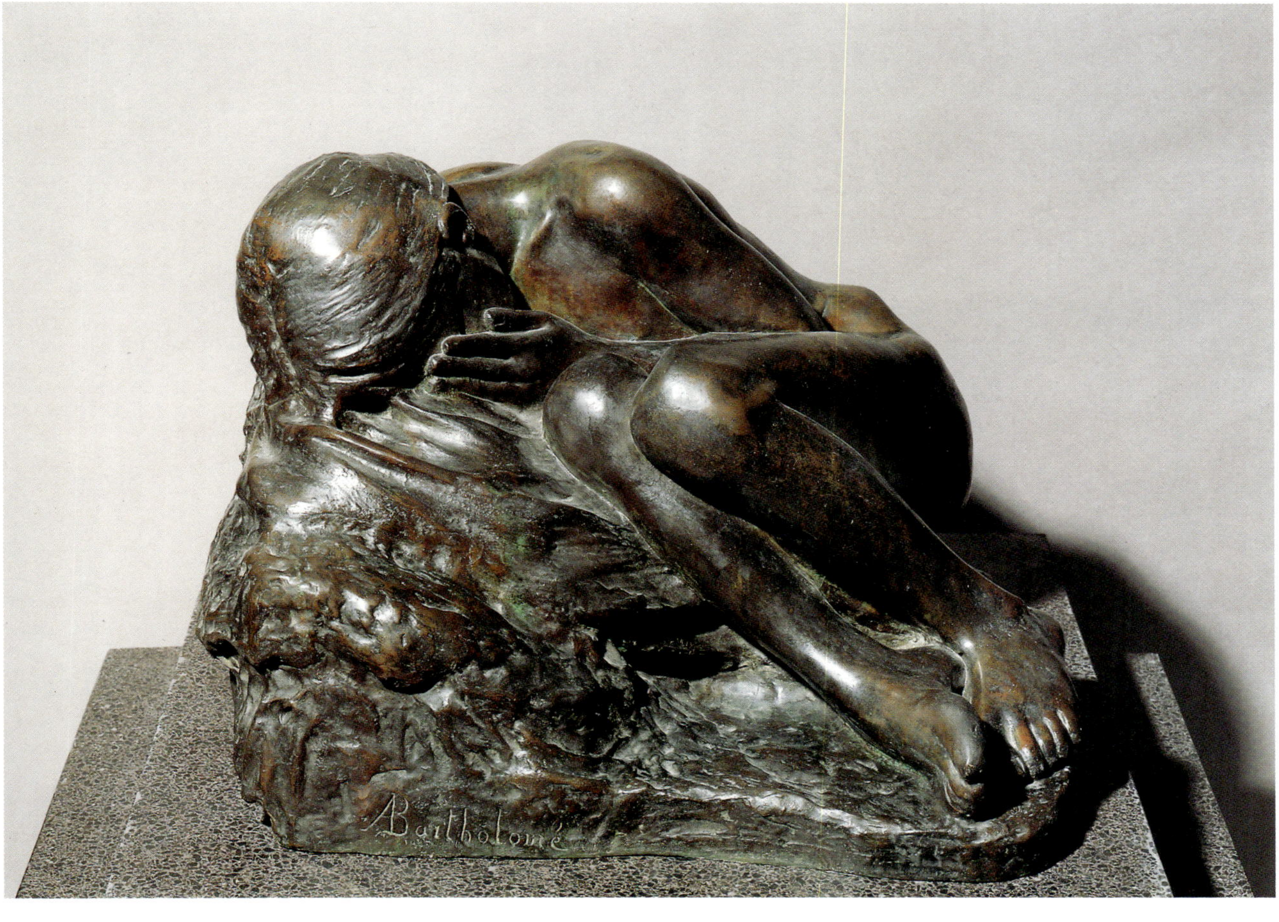

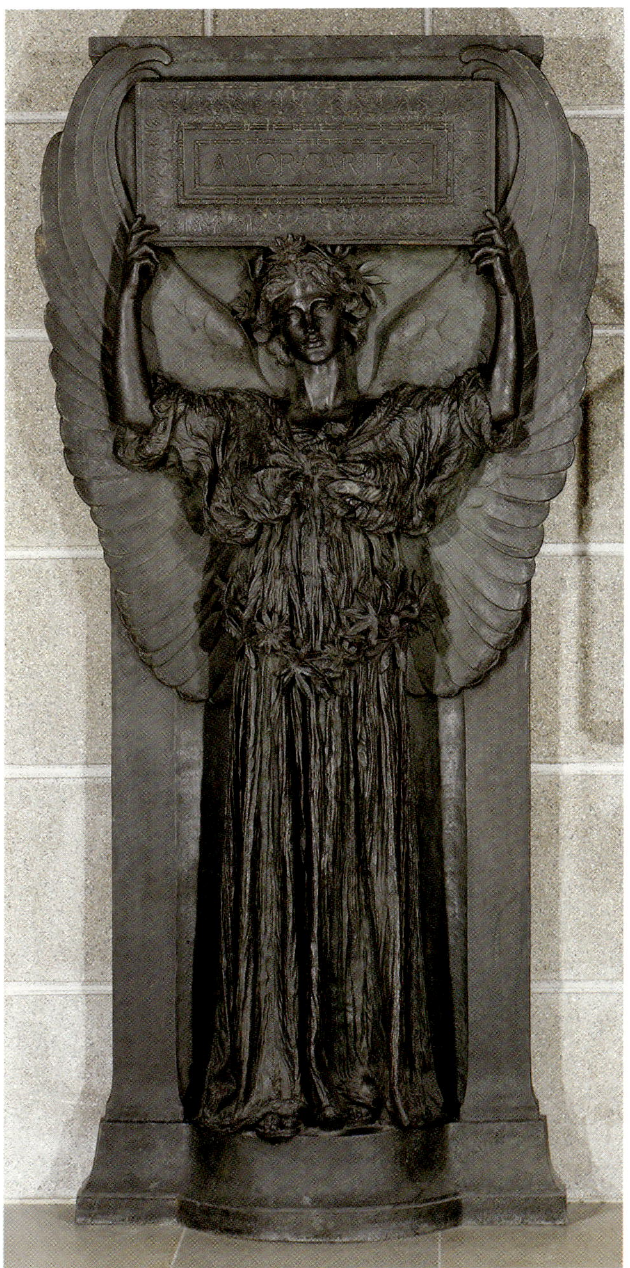

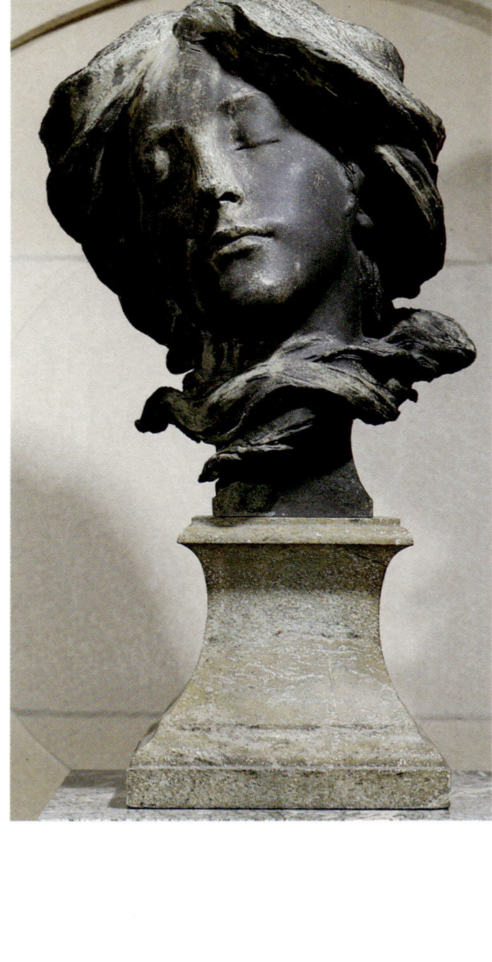

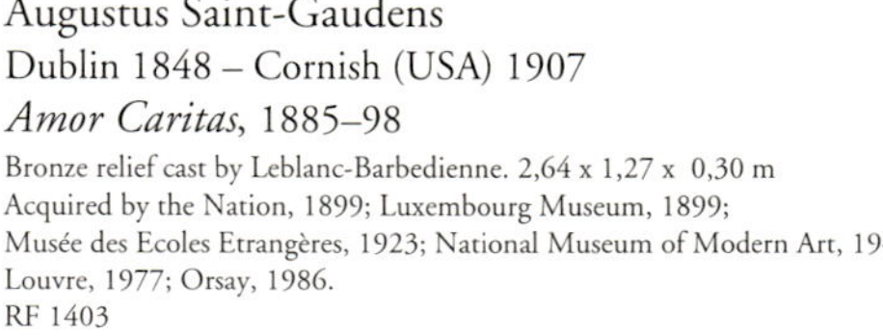
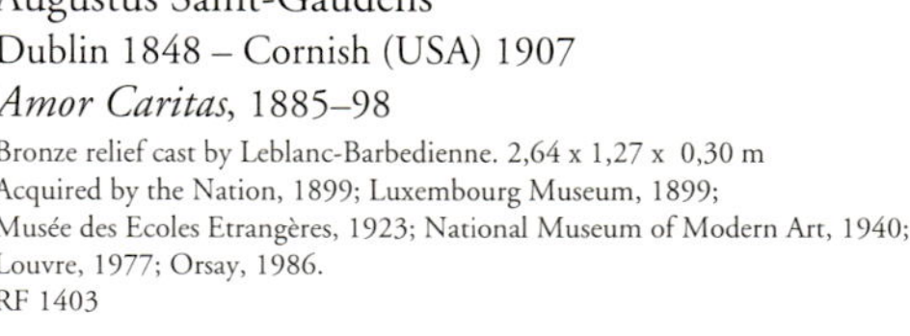

Augustus Saint-Gaudens
Dublin 1848 – Cornish (USA) 1907
Amor Caritas, 1885–98
Bronze relief cast by Leblanc-Barbedienne. 2,64 x 1,27 x 0,30 m
Acquired by the Nation, 1899; Luxembourg Museum, 1899;
Musée des Ecoles Etrangères, 1923; National Museum of Modern Art, 1940;
Louvre, 1977; Orsay, 1986.
RF 1403

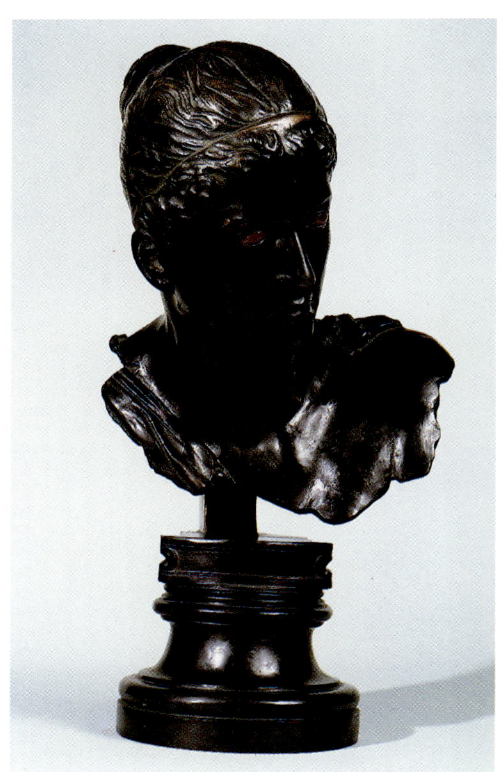

Max Klinger
Leipzig 1857 – Grossjena (Germany) 1920
Cassandra, 1886–1900
Bronze bust cast by H. Gladenback & Sons, Berlin, cornelian (?).
0.59 x 0.32 x 0.35 m
Acquired in 1990.
RF 4302

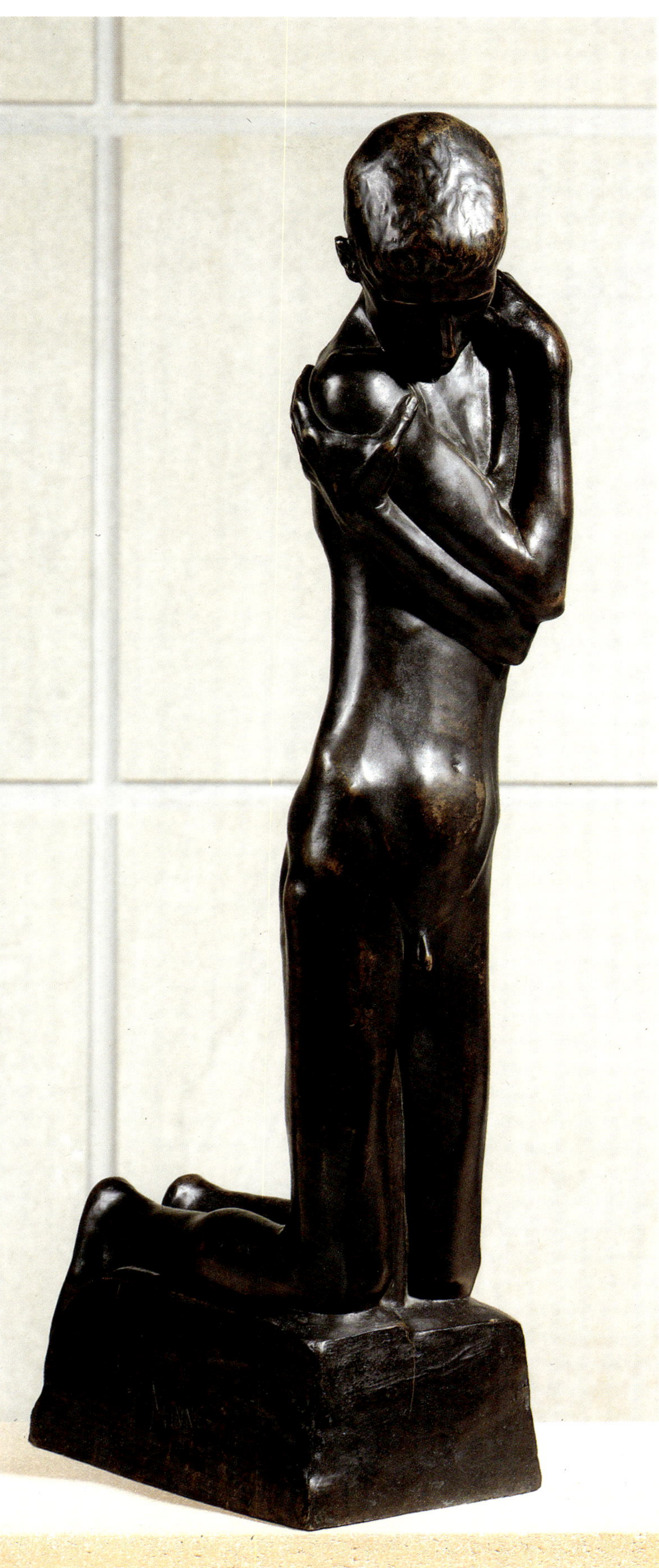

◁ Alfred Drury
London 1856 – Wimbledon (UK) 1944
Night Spirit, 1898–1905
Bronze head. 0.57 x 0.308 x 0.30 m
Acquired in 1984.
RF 3677

Georges Minne
Ghent 1866 – Laethem-Saint-Martin 1941
(Belgium)
Figure Kneeling at Fountain, 1898
Bronze statuette cast by J. Petermann, Brussels.
0.785 x 0.19 x 0.435 m
Donated by Enrique Mistler (under the title *Prodigal Child*), 1933;
Musée des Ecoles Etrangères, 1933; National Museum of Modern
Art, 1940; Louvre, 1977; Orsay, 1986.
RF 3256

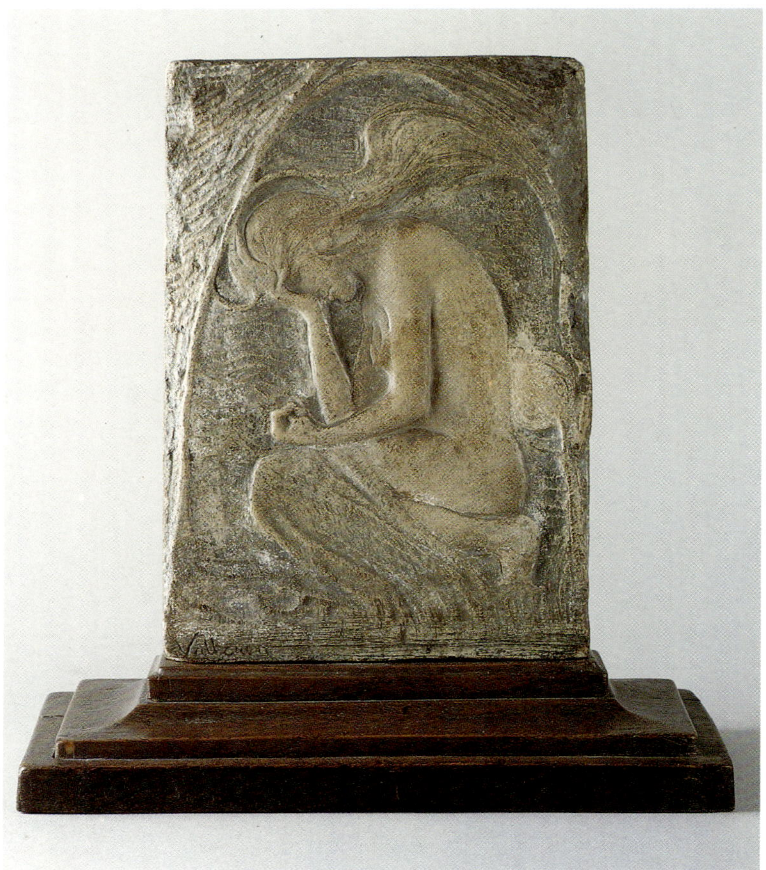

Ville Vallgren
Porvoo 1855 – Helsinki 1940 (Finland)
Anguish, c.1893
Polychromatic oolitic limestone. 0.35 x 0.244 x 0.55 m
Acquired in 1991.
RF 4371

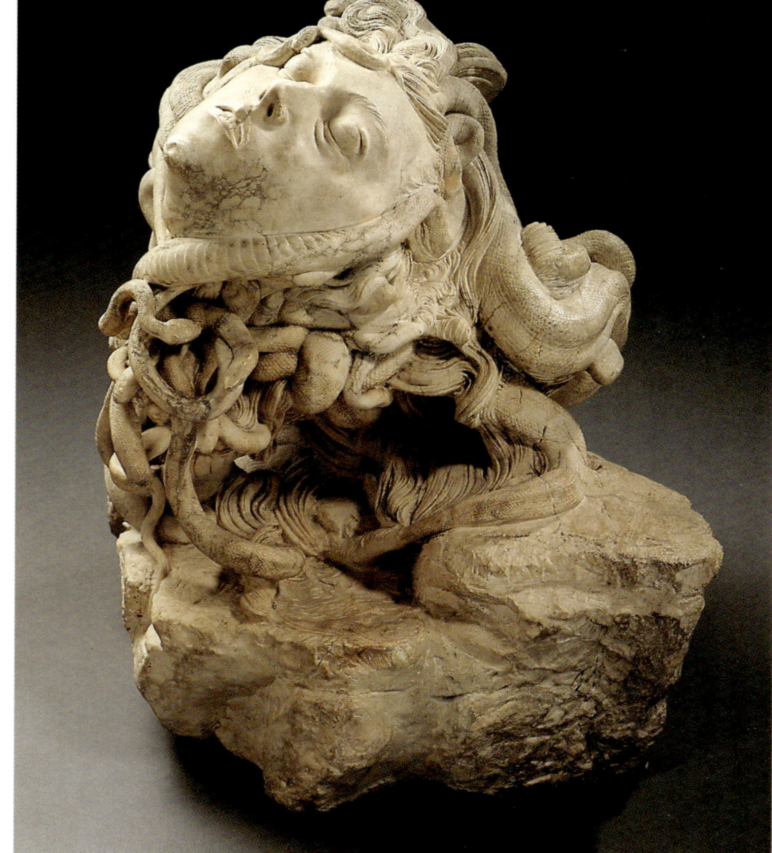

Paul Dardé
Olmet 1888 – Lodève 1963
Eternal Anguish, 1913
Gypsum group chiselled by the sculptor.
0.495 x 0.44 x 0.382 m
Acquired by the Nation, 1919; SAF Salon, 1920; Luxembourg Museum, 1920; National Museum of Modern Art, 1940; Louvre, 1977; Orsay, 1986.
RF 3853

Boleslas Biegas
Koziczyn (Poland) 1877 – Paris 1954
Sphinx, 1902
Plaster relief. 0.46 x 0.39 x 0.11 m
Acquired in 1987.
RF 4187

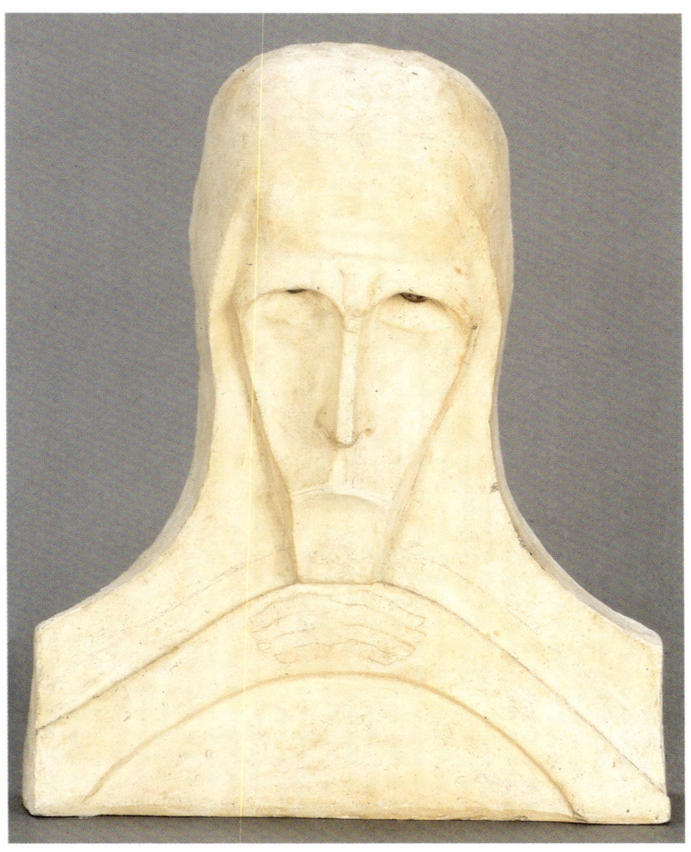

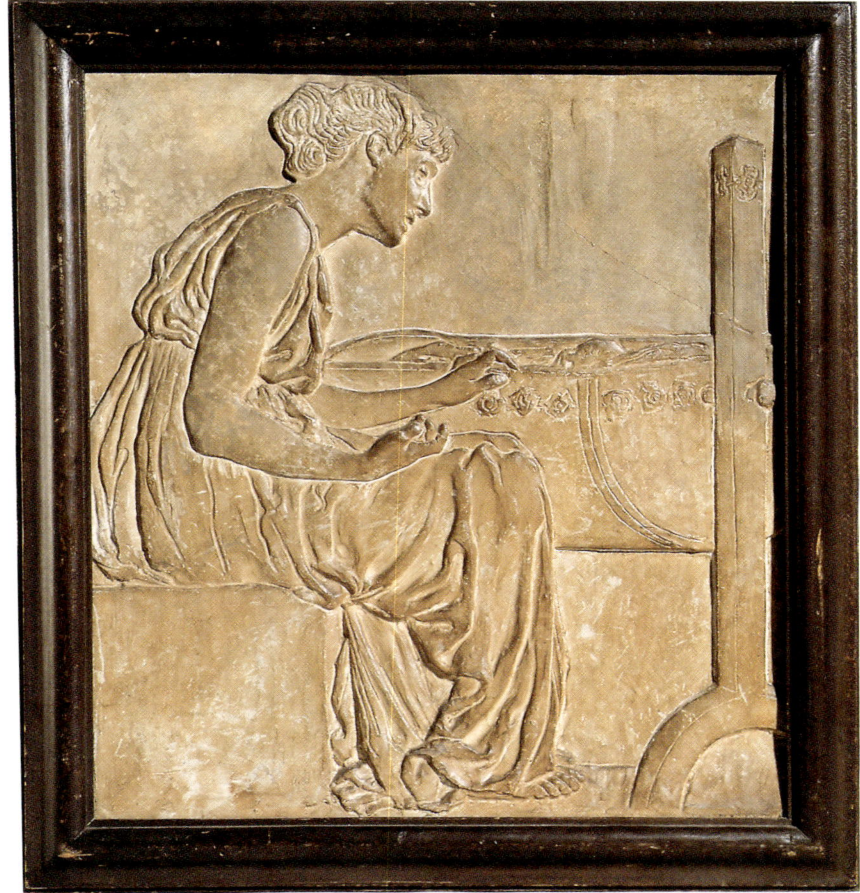

Leonardo Bistolfi
Casale Monferrato 1879 – Turin 1933 (Italy)
The Cradle, 1906
Plaster. 0.431 x 0.40 x 0.02 m
For the *Madonna di Campagna* war monument (1706), inaugurated 1906; destroyed during World War II.
Dedication on back to the moulder Michele Gilardini.
Acquired in 1992.
RF 4403

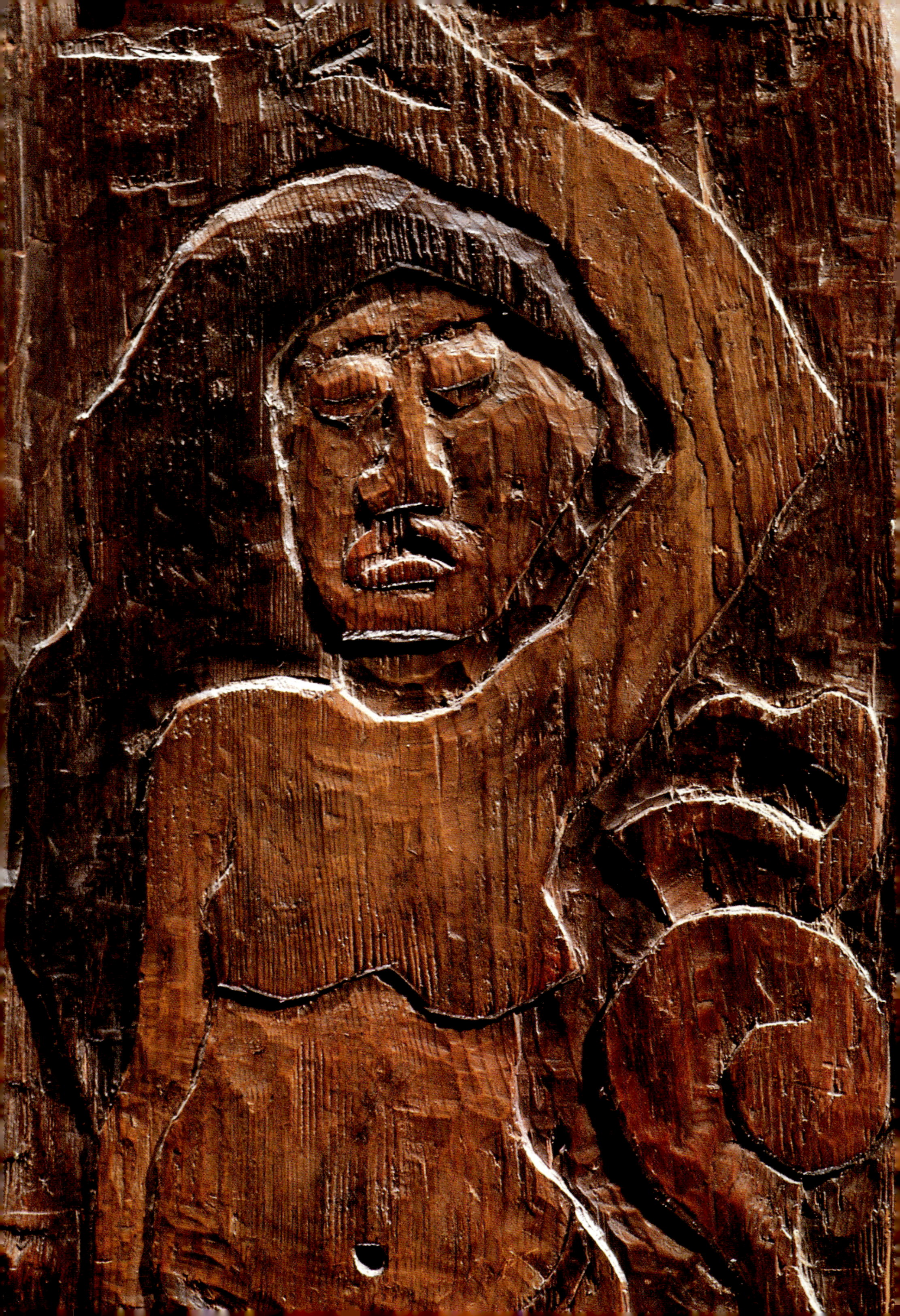

Primitivism

In February 1891 Albert Aurier called for a 'simple, spontaneous, primordial art, identical to primitive art, art as divined by the instinctive geniuses of humanity's earliest times'. Was this yet another 'historicity', now beamed on the ethnographer? Or was it the revelation of 'an attempt ... made to infuse into our pitiful, putrefied nation by that great artist of genius with the primitive soul and touch of the savage, Paul Gauguin'? Signs that a different kind of art was awakening were already perceptible early in the 19th century. As far back as 1838 David d'Angers noted in his notebooks: 'I've always noticed that people who have never learned to draw, if they want to give you an idea of something that has struck them, always find the most telling line to show you what has impressed them.' In 1848, in *Réflexions et menus propos d'un peintre genevois*, Rodolphe Toepffer asserted that a colossal stone head on Easter Island was as accomplished a work of art as Michelangelo's *Moses.* Although Daniel Defoe wrote *Robinson Crusoe* in 1719 and Jean-Jacques Rousseau celebrated 'the state of nature' in 1754, it was the reaction to industrial civilization that gave new force to Mallarmé's 'fly away, flee'. Gauguin, 'that lean, unleashed Wolf' (Degas), spent the first six years of his life in Peru, where his father had died on arrival in 1849. Nostalgia for this childhood perhaps explained his 'terrible yearning for the unknown that made him commit so many follies' (to Emile Bernard, August 1889). At the banquet preceding Gauguin's first trip to Tahiti, Mallarmé celebrated 'this superb vision, which, in the full tide of his talent, sends him into exile to plunge once more into faraway places and himself'.

Gauguin sought in distant climes what he bore within himself. In his correspondence, the word 'Wild' recurs again and again. In 1887 he wrote to his wife Mette, 'What I want above all is to flee Paris ... I am leaving for Panama to live in the *wild.*' In February 1888 he declared to the painter Emile Schuffenecker, 'I love Brittany, where I can find the wild, the primitive. When my wooden shoes resound against the granite soil, I hear that muted, flat, powerful tone I seek in painting.' Writing from Tahiti, he asked André Fontainas's indulgence for his 'folly and wildness' (1899). To Maurice Denis he described his 'Papuan art'. To Charles Morice he explained in 1901 that 'there [in the Marquesas Islands], this totally wild element, this complete solitude will give me before I die a final spurt of enthusiasm to revive my imagination and consummate my talent'. The very year he died he wrote from Atuana, again to Morice, 'I am a wild man. And civilized people sense this, for in my work there is nothing to astonish, to baffle, except this «wildness-in-spite-of-myself». That is why it is inimitable. A man's work explains the man.'

The Fauves began buying African and Oceanic masks in 1906, the year when the Gauguin retrospective at the Salon d'Automne displayed – in addition to the artist's paintings – twelve sculptures and fourteen ceramics, including the *Oviri* stoneware vase (acquired by the Musée d'Orsay in 1987). In 1907 Picasso's *Demoiselles d'Avignon* introduced Cubism, but the new techniques were already present in Gauguin's *House of Pleasure.*

Paul Gauguin
Paris 1848 –
Atuana (Hiva Hoa,
Marquesas Islands)
1903
House of Pleasure,
1901
Left panel (detail).
RF 2721

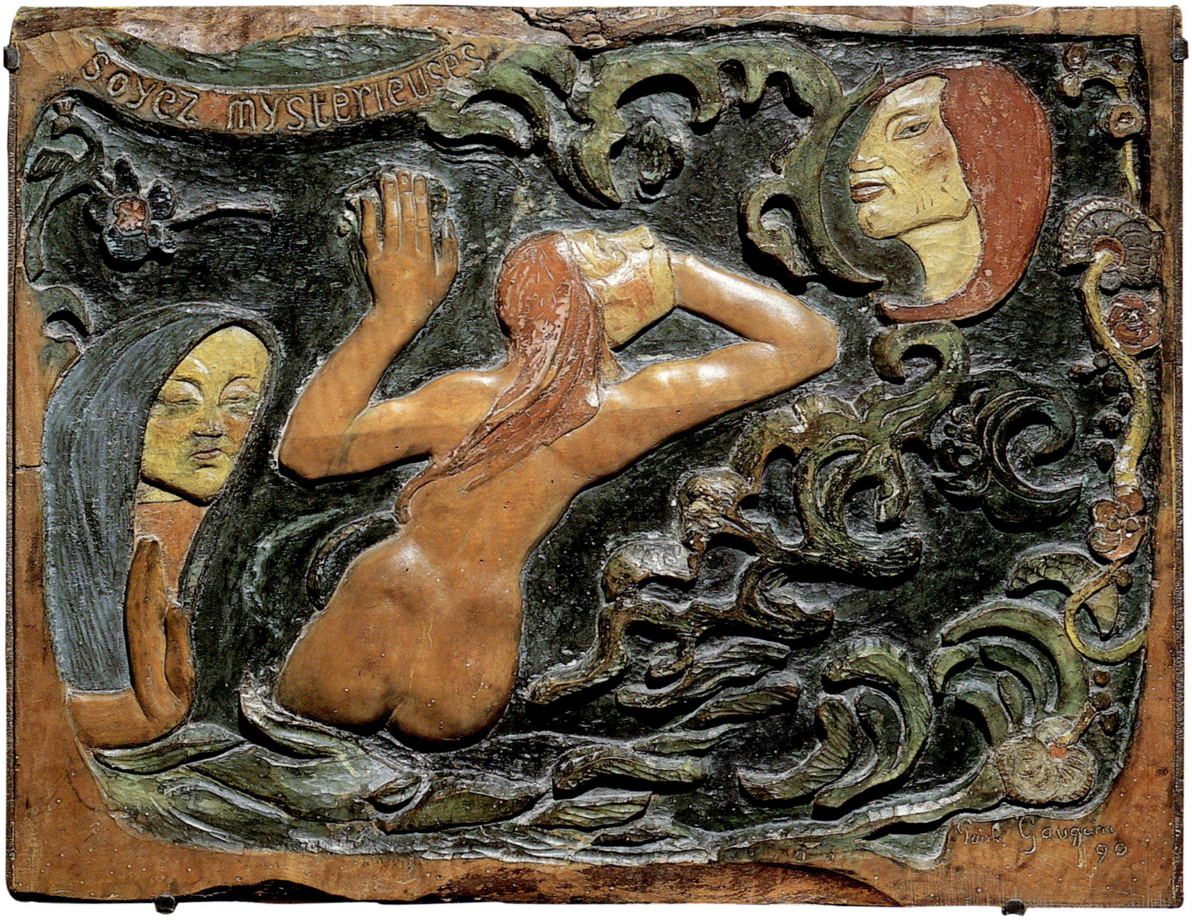

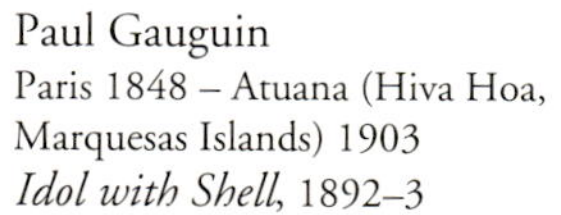

Paul Gauguin
Paris 1848 – Atuana (Hiva Hoa, Marquesas Islands) 1903
Idol with Shell, 1892–3
Ironwood (ua), mother-of-pearl, bone.
0.344 x 0.148 x 0.185 m
Daniel de Monfreid collection; acquired in 1951 with help from Mme Huc de Monfreid on condition that lifetime possession be retained by her;
Jeu de Paume, 1968; Orsay, 1986.
OA 9540

Paul Gauguin
Paris 1848 – Atuana
(Hiva Hoa, Marquesas Islands) 1903
Idol with Pearl, 1892–3
Painted and gilded tamanu wood with pearl and gold chain.
0.237 x 0.126 x 0.114 m
Daniel de Monfreid collection; donated by Mme Huc de Monfreid, 1951; Jeu de Paume, 1968; Orsay, 1986.
OA 9529

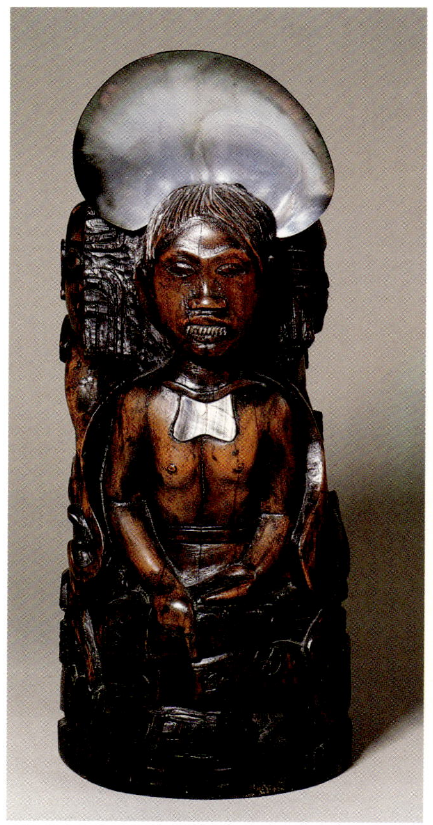

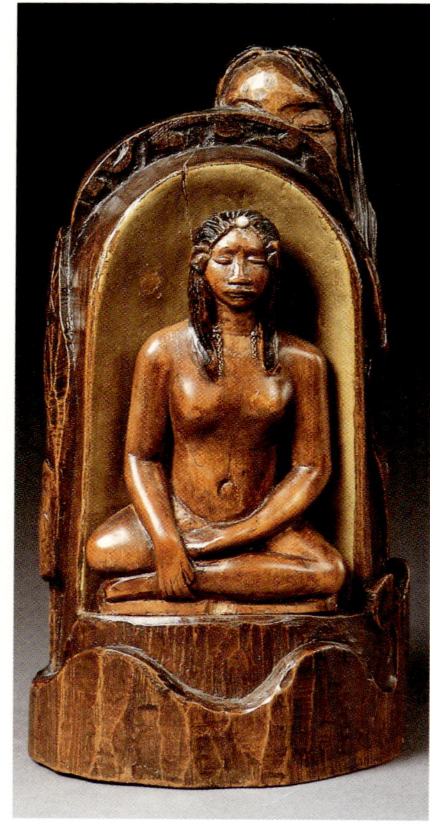

Paul Gauguin
Paris 1848 – Atuana
(Hiva Hoa, Marquesas Islands) 1903
Be Mysterious, 1890
Polychromatic linden-tree wood. 0.73 x 0.95 x 0.05 m
Gustave Fayet collection, Mme d'Andoque collection; acquired in 1979.
RF 3405

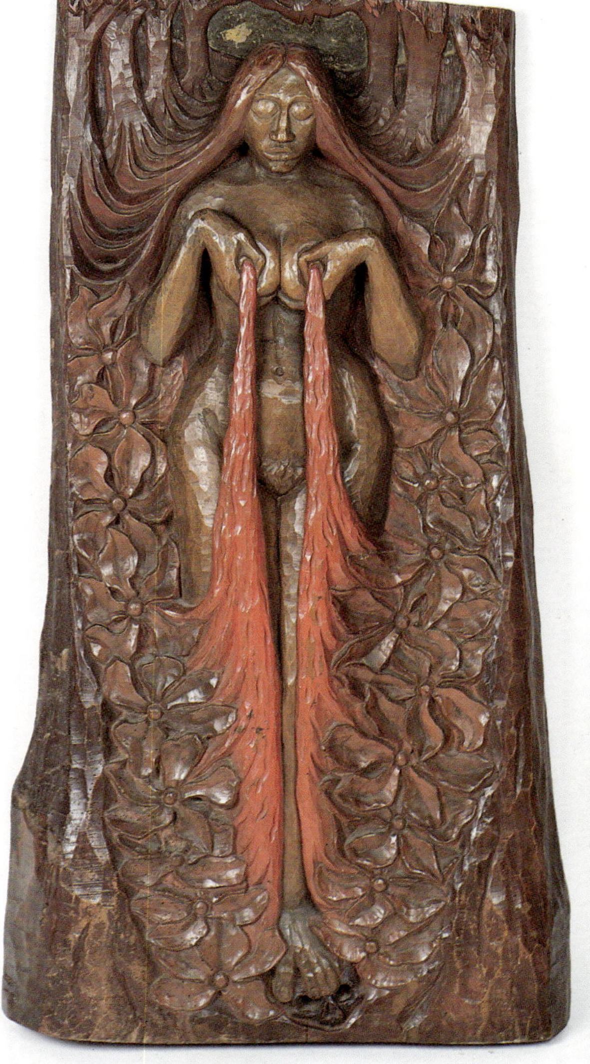

Georges Lacombe
Versailles 1868 – Saint-Nicolas-des-Bois 1916
Isis, 1893–4
Semi-polychromatic mahogany relief. 1.15 x 0.62 x 0.107 m
Salon des Indépendants, 1895; acquired in 1982.
RF 3627

Georges Lacombe
Versailles 1868 – Saint-Nicolas-des-Bois 1916
Existence, 1894–6
Walnut. 0.685 x 1.42 x 0.06 m
For the Nabis *L'Ergastère* bedhead (Lacombe Atelier, Versailles), *Exposition des Dix*, Vollard gallery, 1897; acquired from the artist's daughter, 1956; National Museum of Modern Art, 1956; Louvre, 1977; Orsay, 1986.
RF 3221

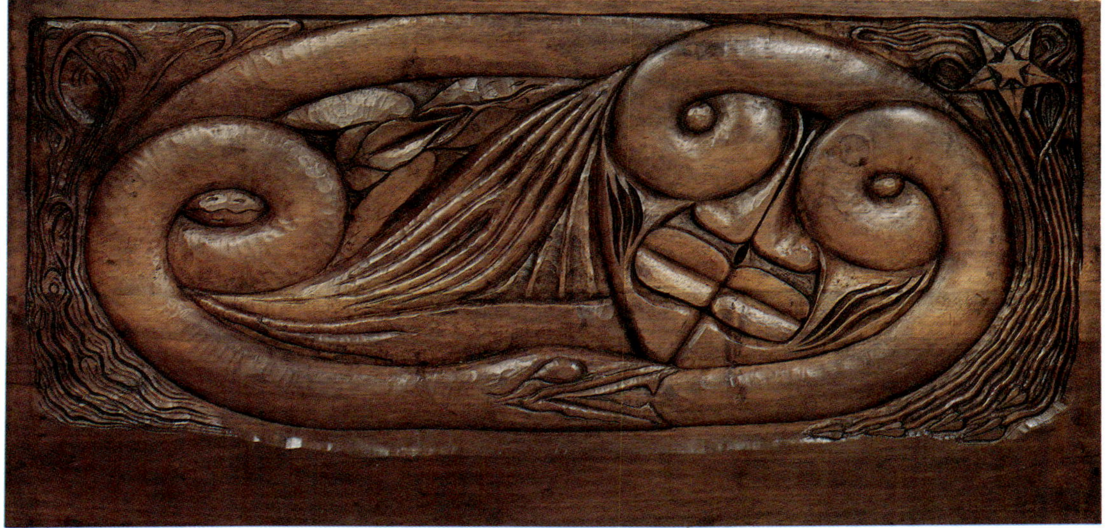

Gauguin carved the door jambs for his final hut from a wood that was not native to the island and which was probably imported from North America. The door was on the upper floor, as shown by the slot for a ramp in the right-hand panel. The self-conscious 'primitivism' of the carvings are accompanied by the written instructions to women – 'Be loving', 'Be mysterious' – which have been compared with Kant's 'categorical imperatives'.

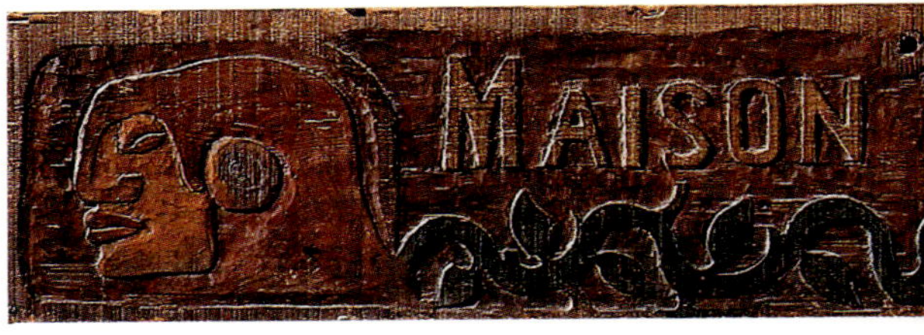

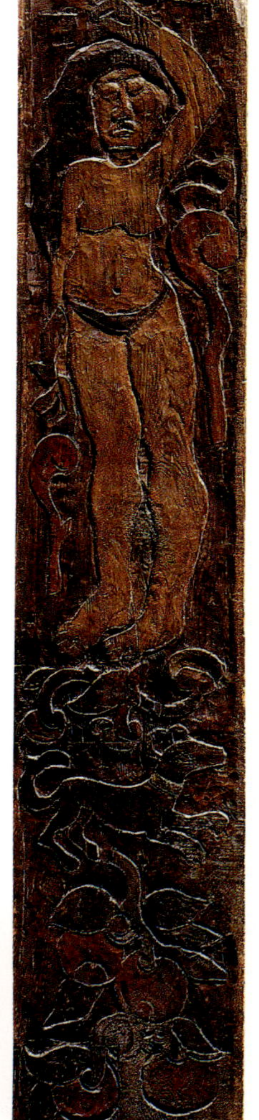

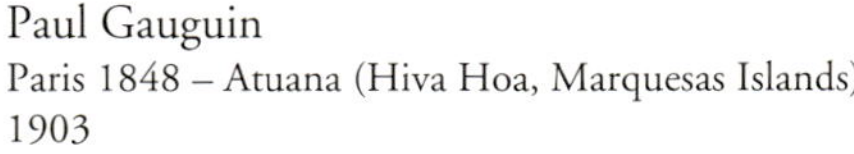

Paul Gauguin
Paris 1848 – Atuana (Hiva Hoa, Marquesas Islands) 1903
House of Pleasure, 1901
Polychromatic carving on giant sequoia wood. 2.40 x 5.62 x 0.03 m
Acquired by Victor Segalen at the auction on Papeete following Gauguin's death, 1903; acquired from the Segalen heirs, 1952; Jeu de Paume, 1958; Orsay, 1986. The fifth panel, with the signature 'PGO', was not acquired by the Musée d'Orsay until 1990.
RF 2720–2723, RF 4290

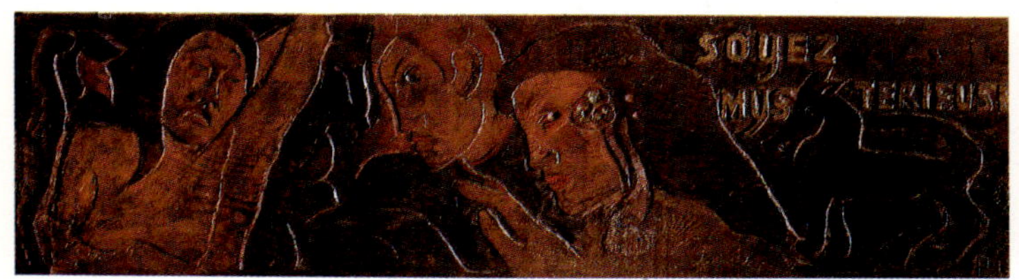

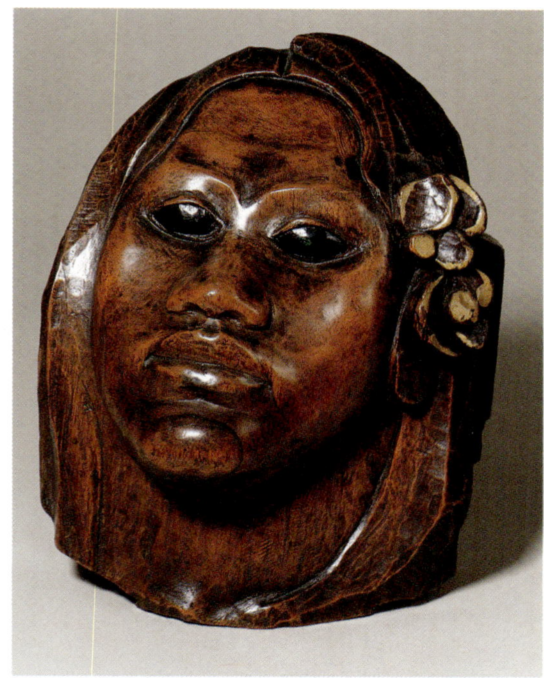

Paul Gauguin
Paris 1848 – Atuana (Hiva Hoa, Marquesas Islands) 1903
Tehura Mask, 1891–3
Polychromatic pua wood. 0.222 x 0.078 x 0.126 m
Gift from Gauguin to Mme Daniel de Monfreid; donated by Mme Huc de Monfreid on condition of retaining possession during her lifetime, 1951; Jeu de Paume, 1968; Orsay, 1986.
RF 9528

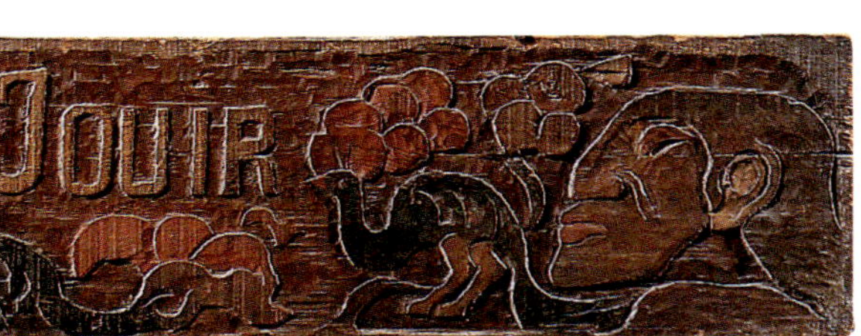

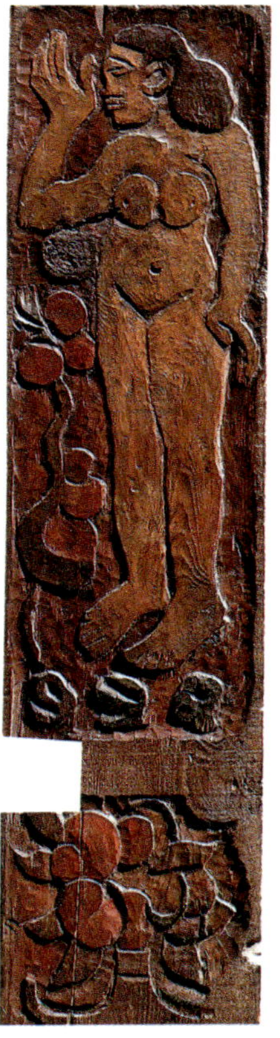

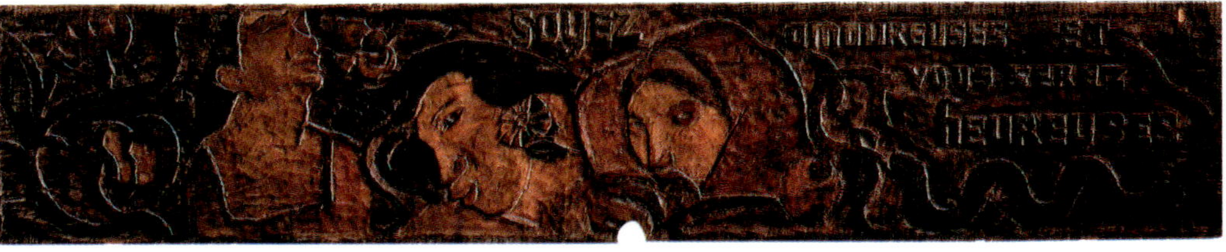

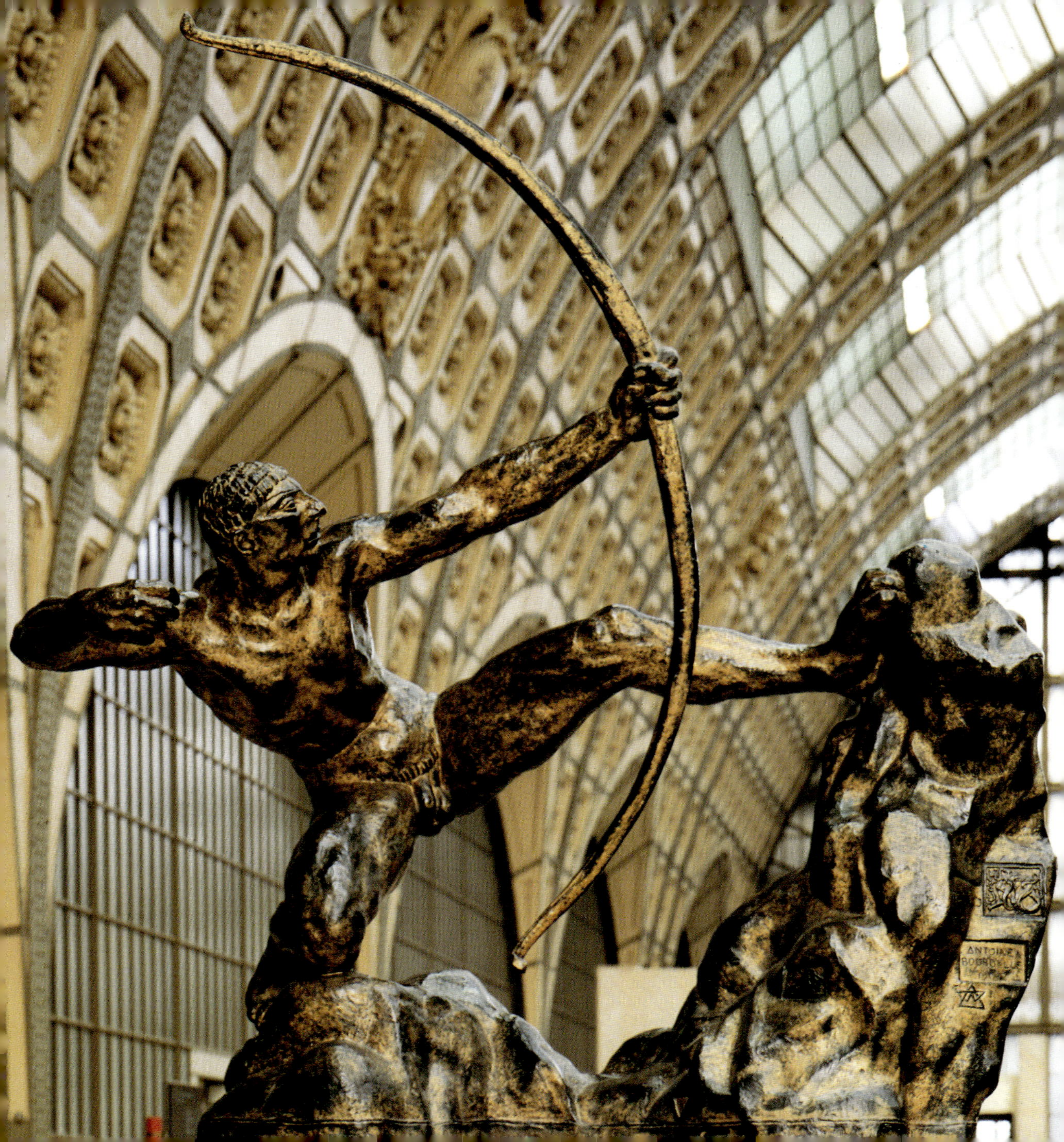
ANTOINE

A Return to Style

Bourdelle, a pupil and assistant of Rodin, rejected his master's romantic expressionism in about 1900 and reverted to an architectural style. 'Bourdelle is first and foremost an architect', as André Suarès said; this is borne out by such colossal constructions as the *Monument to General Alvéar* (1913–22), *Virgin at the Offertory* (1922–3), *France* (1923–5) and, above all, by his respect for the verticality of walls. Returning to classical Greek and Roman models, Bourdelle did not break up surfaces the way Rodin did. He respected the context surrounding his large Théâtre des Champs-Elysées friezes (1911–13) by sculpting simplified, stylized figures of *Apollo* and *The Muses* using flattened, angular lines. This is the style which, when purged of the final vestiges of expressionism, became Art Deco. The focus had shifted from emotion to subject, and mythology returned in force. *Apollo* heralds the emergence of Bourdelle's personal style through a return (again!) to classical antiquity. *Hercules the Archer* projects strength through the extension of lines braced against resistance. Fidelity is symbolized by the massive monumentality of *Penelope.*

Bartholomé simplified in response to current taste, but the great forerunner was Maillol. In an article written for the *Gazette des Beaux-Arts* (1905), 'Promenade au Salon d'Automne', Gide tells of his arrival 'in a vast room, in the centre of which rests M. Maillol's great seated woman. She is beautiful; she does not symbolize anything; it is a silent work. I believe we would have to go far back in time to find such complete indifference to any concern other than the simple manifestation of beauty.' It was in these terms that Gide compared Maillol's *Mediterranean* with Rodin's 'gasping, anxious, symbolic, pathetically clamorous' works.

The shift in emphasis from subject to material – as indicated by Maillol's titles – was to validate the 'chiselling directly into the stone' theory. The artist's hand was to be restored to its rightful place in the creative process. There should be no more interference from assistants, chisellers, modellers and casters who – according to Charles Blanc (1867) – took the original model and created statues that were copies. Paul Valéry, two of whose sculptures have recently been acquired by the Musée d'Orsay (1995, donated by Valéry's children), went so far as to inscribe this theory on the pediment of the new Trocadero Palace (1937): 'I am the guardian of works/from the artist's prodigal hand/equal and rival of his mind/one is nought without the other.' Sculpting directly into the material was popular for a time (1919–25), until it became obvious that what counts is the result, not the method. Even Joseph Bernard, the son of a master stone-cutter who pioneered the theory and was one of its best practitioners, refused to serve as a priest in what Pierre du Colombier called a 'fanatic cult'. However, despite their regressiveness, the final historicist trend based on the theory that artists should work directly with the raw material, and its ancillary morality of art through effort, did bear within them the seeds of modernity. The 'vital principle of materials' (Henry Van de Velde, *Formules de la beauté architectonique moderne*, Brussels, 1917) and the emphasis on the creative process both contributed to the birth of abstract sculpture.

Emile-Antoine Bourdelle
Montauban 1861 – Le Vesinet 1929
Hercules the Archer Killing the Stymphalian Birds, 1909
Gilded bronze group cast by Alexis Rudier. 2.48 x 2.47 x 1.23 m
2nd version, 1923 (dated 1909); acquired in 1926; Luxembourg Museum, 1926; National Museum of Modern Art, 1940; Louvre, 1977; Orsay, 1986.
RF 3174

Emile-Antoine Bourdelle
Montauban 1861 – Le Vesinet 1929
Apollo, 1909
Gilded bronze head cast by Alexis Rudier.
0.674 x 0.272 x 0.253 m
Dufet-Bourdelle Donation, 1989.
RF 4283

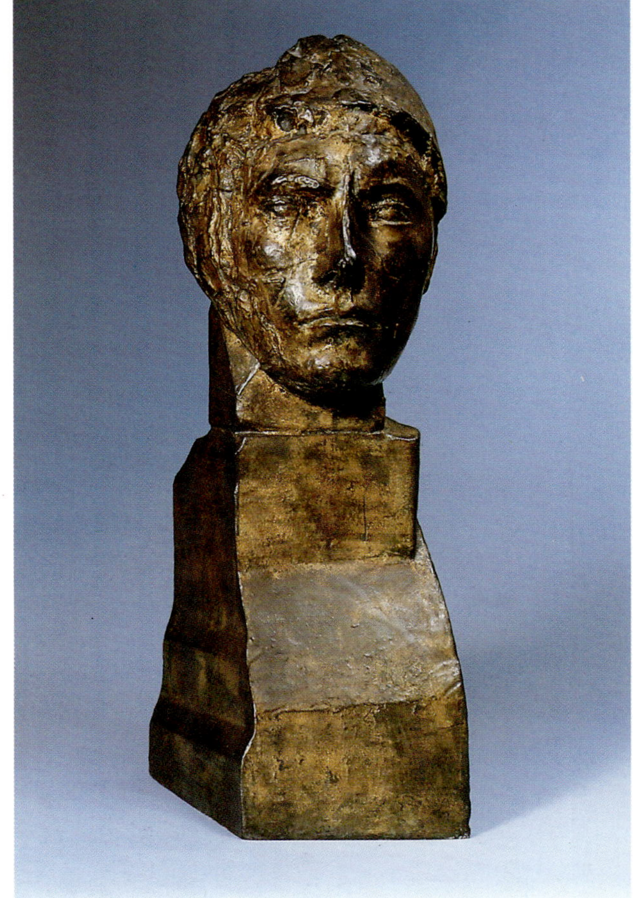

Emile-Antoine Bourdelle ▷
Montauban 1861 – Le Vesinet 1929
Victory and *Self-Discipline*, 1914–15
Bronze statues cast by Alexis Rudier.
3.72 x 1.15 x 1.15 m and 3.72 x 1.10 x 1.10 m
Two of the four *Virtues* from the Buenos Aires (Argentina) *Alvéar Monument*, 1913–22;
acquired in 1934; National Museum of Modern Art, 1934;
Orsay, 1986.
RF 3179-3178

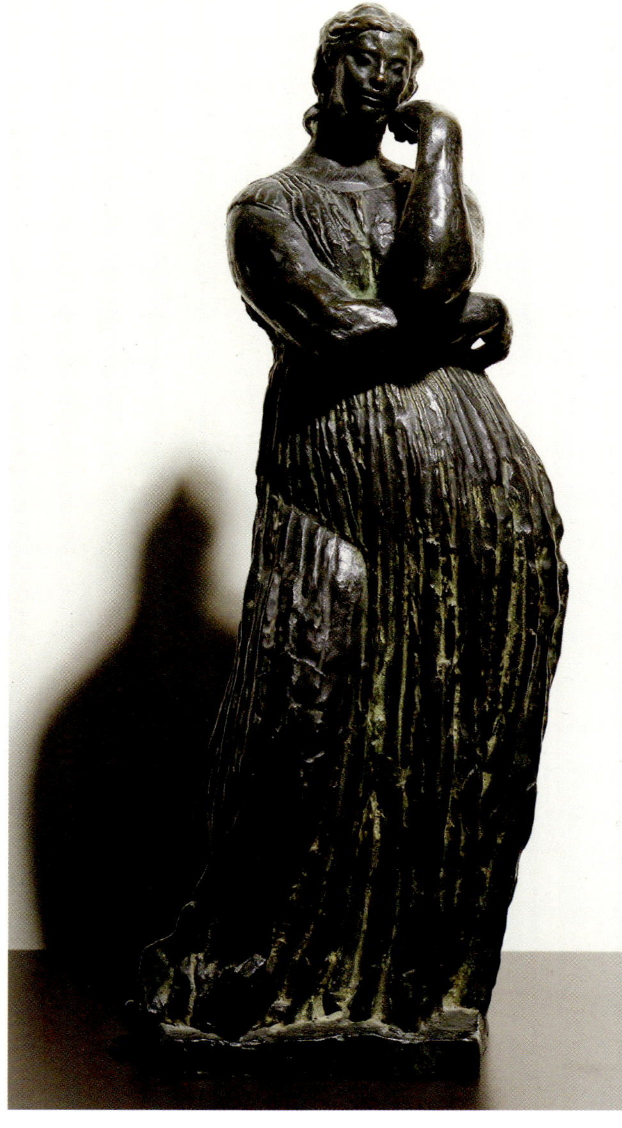

Emile-Antoine Bourdelle
Montauban 1861 – Le Vesinet 1929
Penelope, 1907–26
Bronze statuette from the French National Bronze Foundry.
0.60 x 0.22 x 0.175 m
Acquired by the Nation from the Salon du Franc, 1926;
Luxembourg Museum, 1926; National Museum of Modern Art, 1940;
Ministry of Culture, 1970; Orsay, 1986.
RF 3177

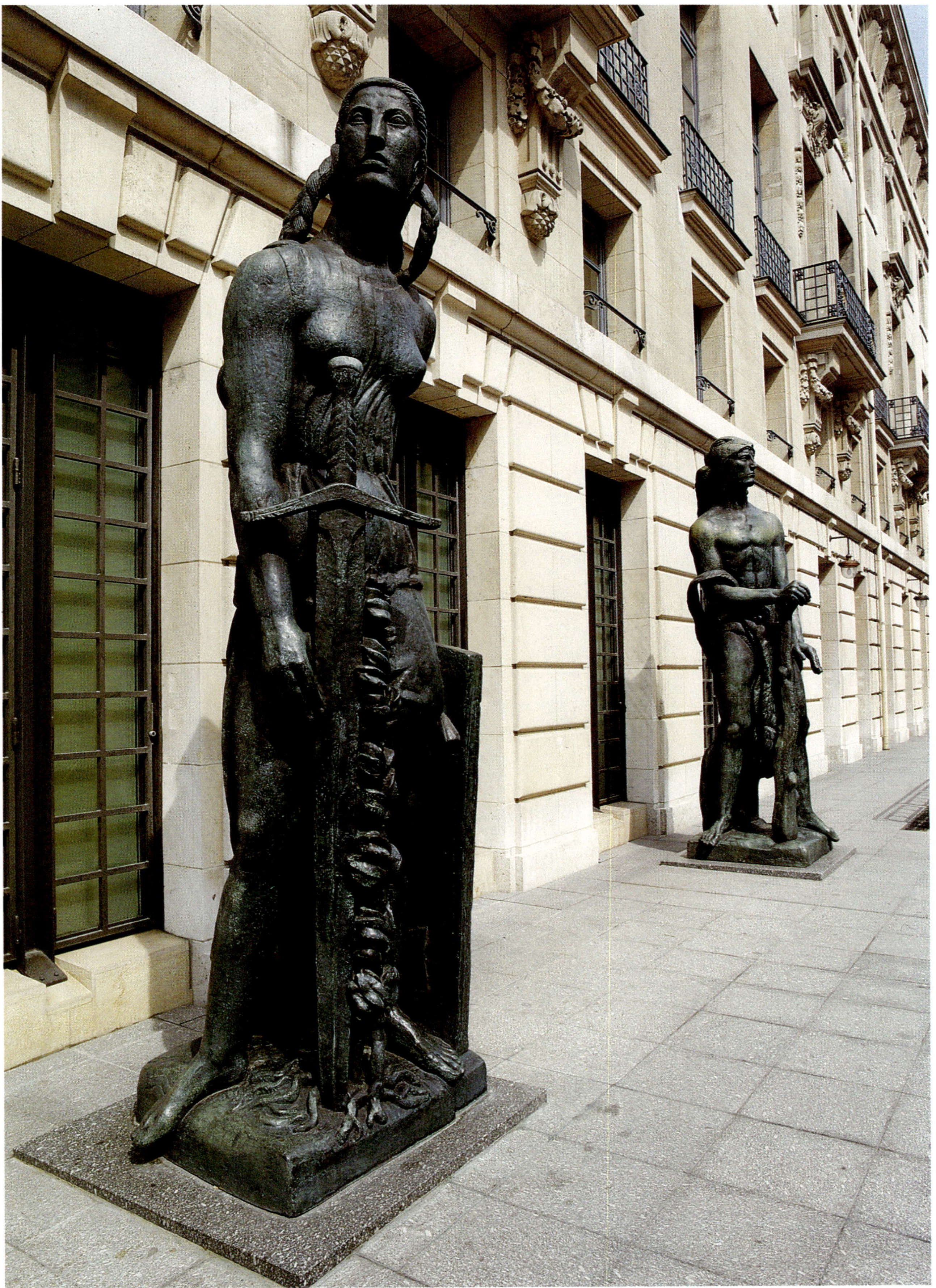

Albert Bartholomé
Thiverval 1848 – Paris 1928
Glory, 1907–10
Plaster statue. 2.26 x 0.87 x 0.82 m
Model for the right-hand section of *Monument to Jean-Jacques Rousseau* (1712–1778); commissioned 1907; inaugurated at Pantheon, 1912; Le Mans Museum, 1927; Orsay, 1985.
RF 3739

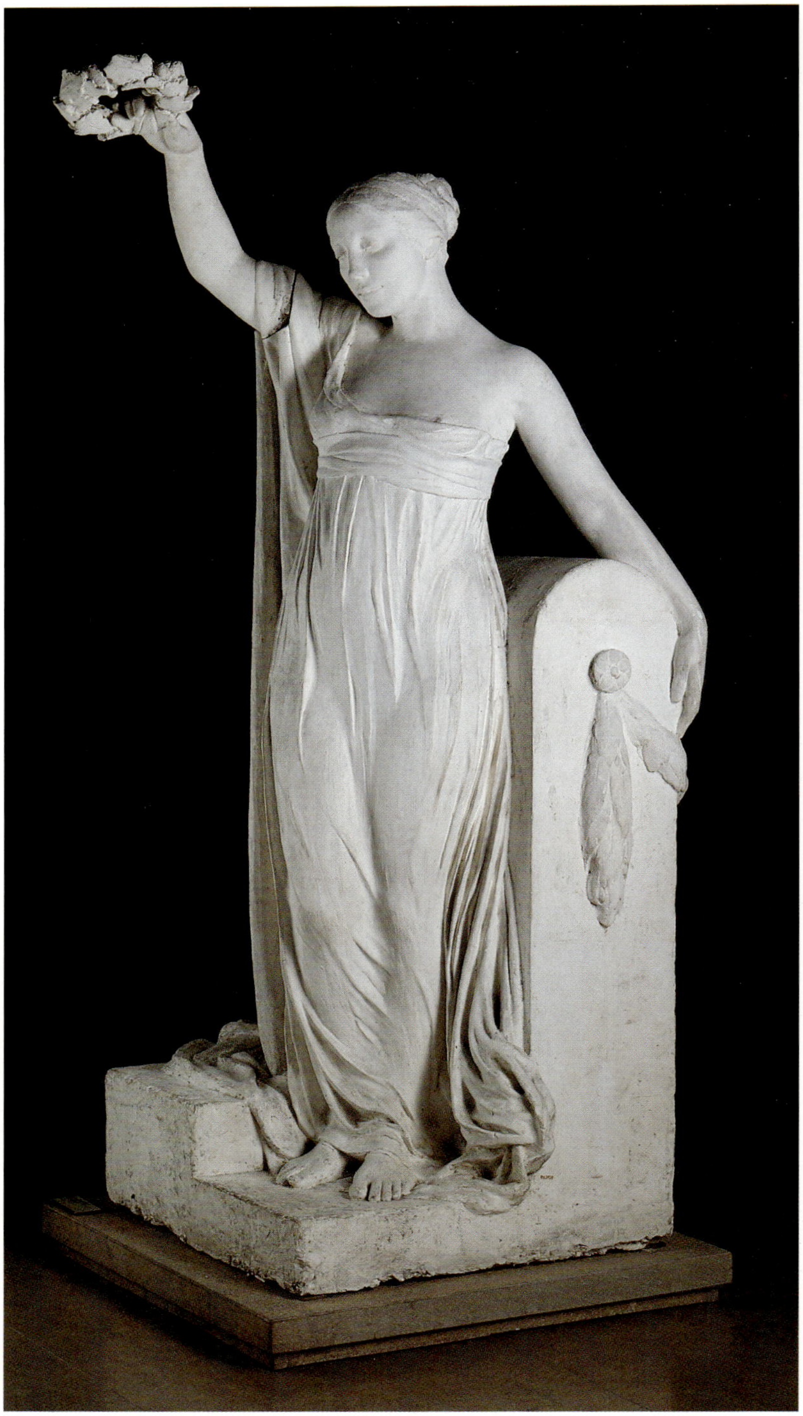

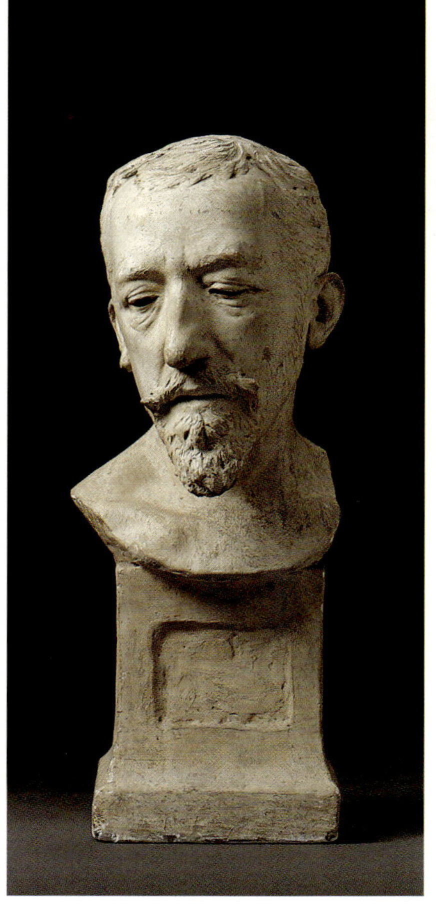

Albert Bartholomé
Thiverval 1848 – Paris 1928
Federico Zandomenighi (1841–1917), *painter friend of Degas*, 1890
Plaster bust. 0.56 x 0.25 x 0.21 m
Acquired in 1984.
RF 3675

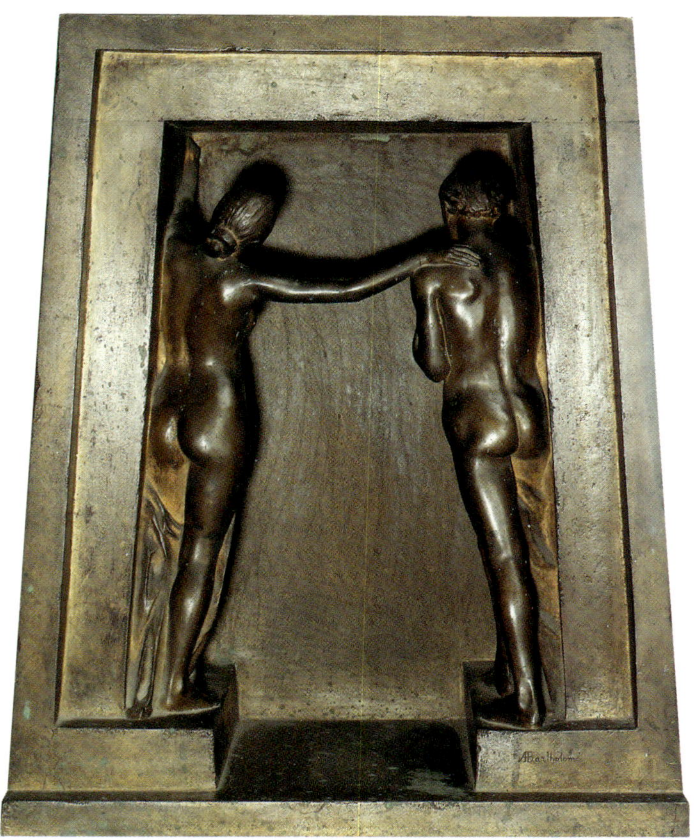

Albert Bartholomé
Thiverval 1848 – Paris 1928
Monument to the Dead
(Père Lachaise Cemetery, reduction of centre section), 1889–99
Haut-relief bronze cast by Siot-Decauville.
0.578 x 0.458 x 0.276 m
Provenance unknown.
RF 3881

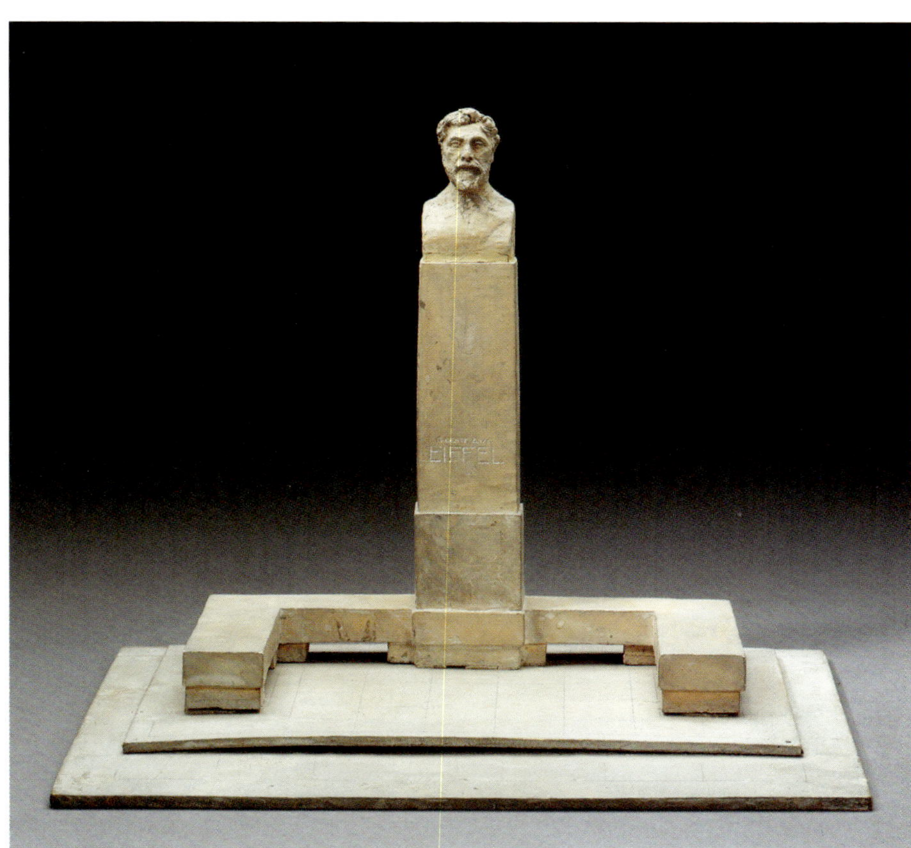

Emile-Antoine Bourdelle
Montauban 1861 – Le Vesinet 1929
Monument to Gustave Eiffel
(1832–1923), 1900–27
Plaster, cardboard and wood model.
0.22 x 0.27 x 0.253 m
Monument inaugurated on the north-east pillar of the Eiffel Tower, 1929; donated by Eiffel's heirs, Mlle Solange Granet, Mme Bernard Granet and her children Clémence, Amélie and Augustin, 1981.
RF 3613

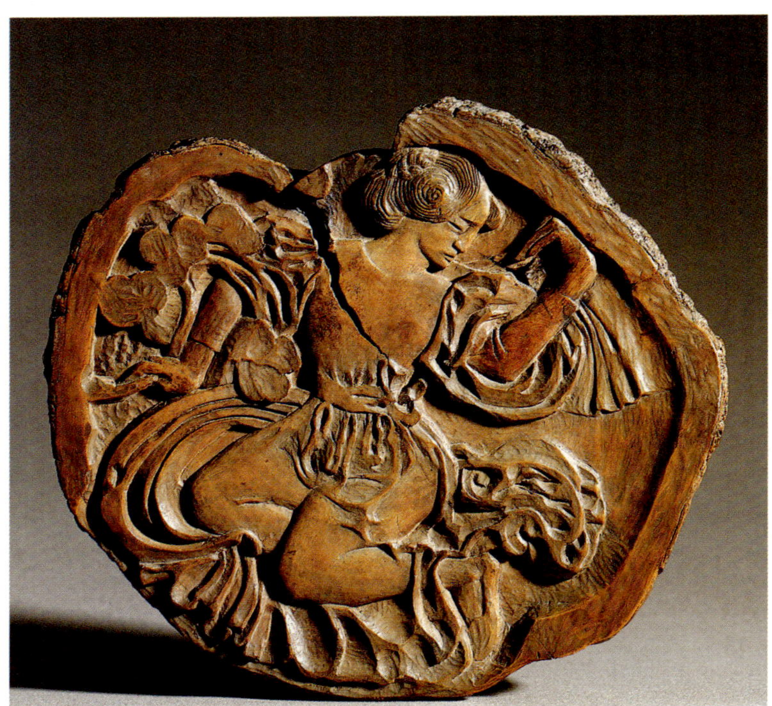

Aristide Maillol
Banyuls-sur-Mer 1861 – Banyuls-sur-Mer 1944
Dancer, 1895
Pear-tree wood, 0.22 x 0.245 x 0.05 m
Mme Thadée Natanson bequest, 1953; National Museum of Modern Art, 1953; Louvre, 1977; Orsay, 1986.
RF 3232

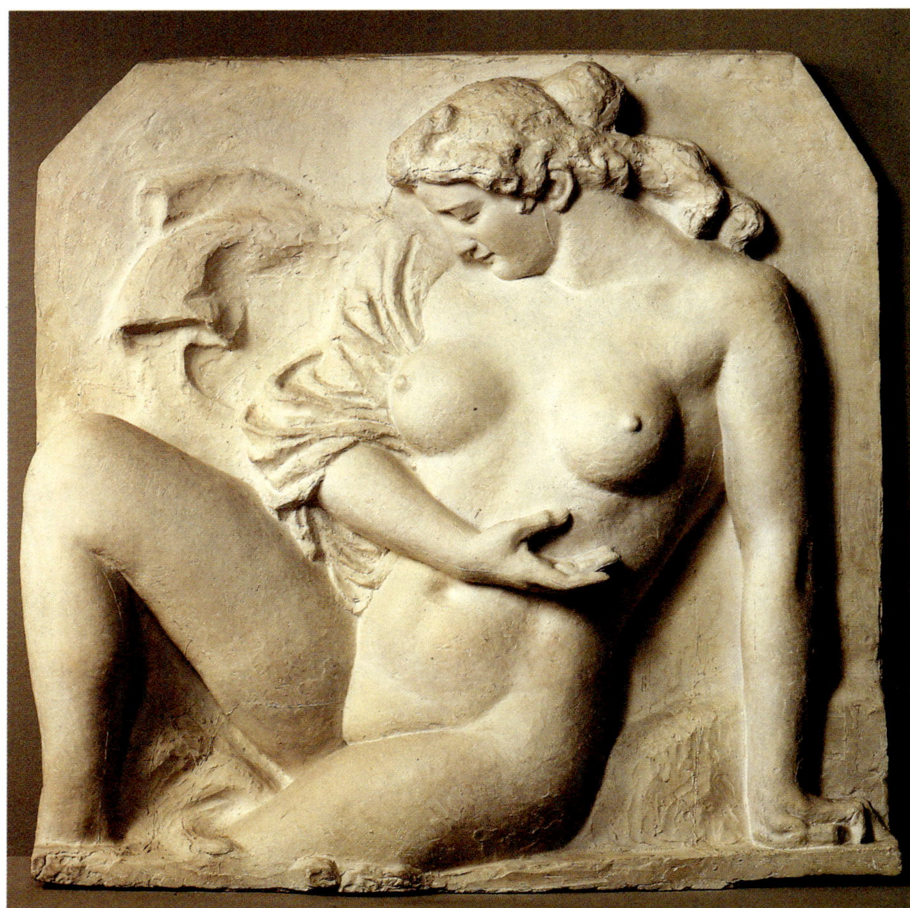

Aristide Maillol
Banyuls-sur-Mer 1861 –
Banyuls-sur-Mer 1944
Bather or *The Wave*,
1896–1900
Plaster relief. 0.93 x 1.03 x 0.25 m
Etienne Moreau-Nelaton bequest, 1927; Museum of Decorative Arts Depository; Orsay, 1986.
RF 3628

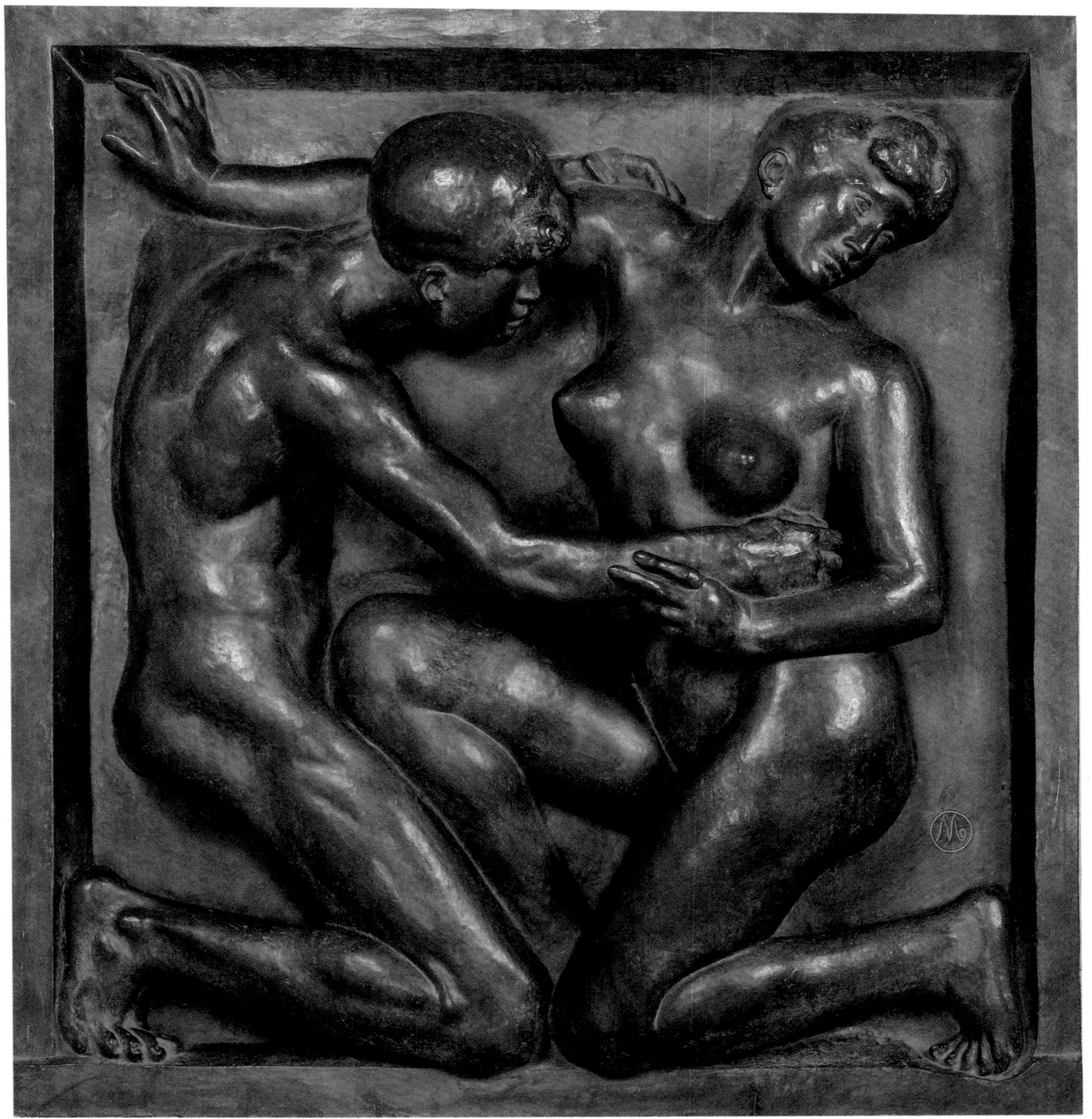

Aristide Maillol
Banyuls-sur-Mer 1861 – Banyuls-sur-Mer 1944
Desire, 1905–7
Lead relief cast by Alexis Rudier. 1.20 x 1.15 x 0.25 m
Artistic Heritage Commission, 1949; National Museum of Modern Art, 1951; Algiers Museum of Modern Art, 1951; Louvre, 1977; Orsay, 1986.
RFR 14

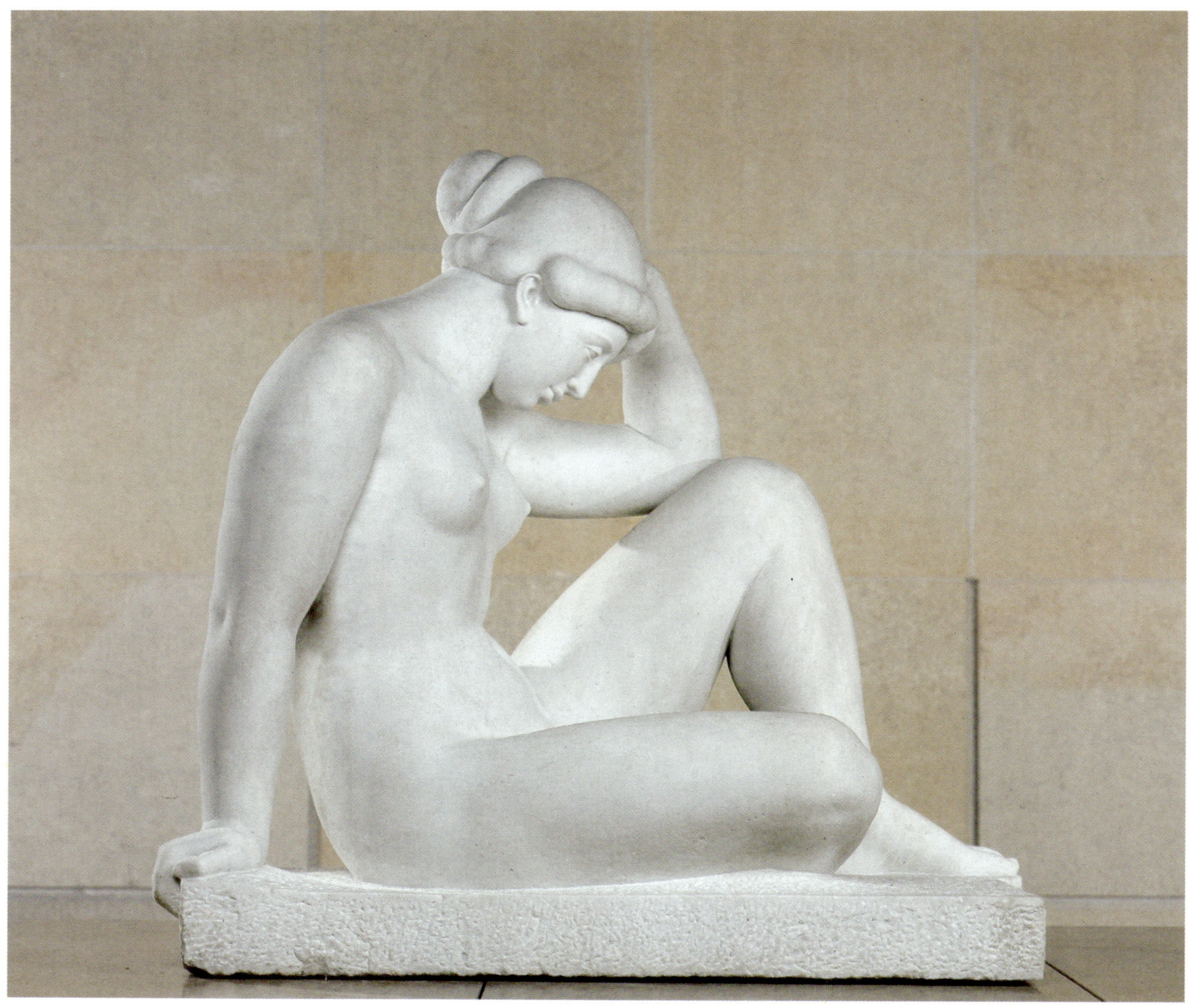

Aristide Maillol
Banyuls-sur-Mer 1861 – Banyuls-sur-Mer 1944
Mediterranean or *Thought,* 1905–27
Marble statue. 1.10 x 1.17 x 0.68 m
Commissioned by the Nation, 1923; Tuileries Gardens, 1929; National Museum of Modern Art, 1965; Louvre, 1977; Orsay, 1986.
RF 3248

'How lovely is the light on that shoulder! How lovely the shadow on that brow! No thought defiles it; no passion storms within that powerful breast.'

André Gide, 1905.

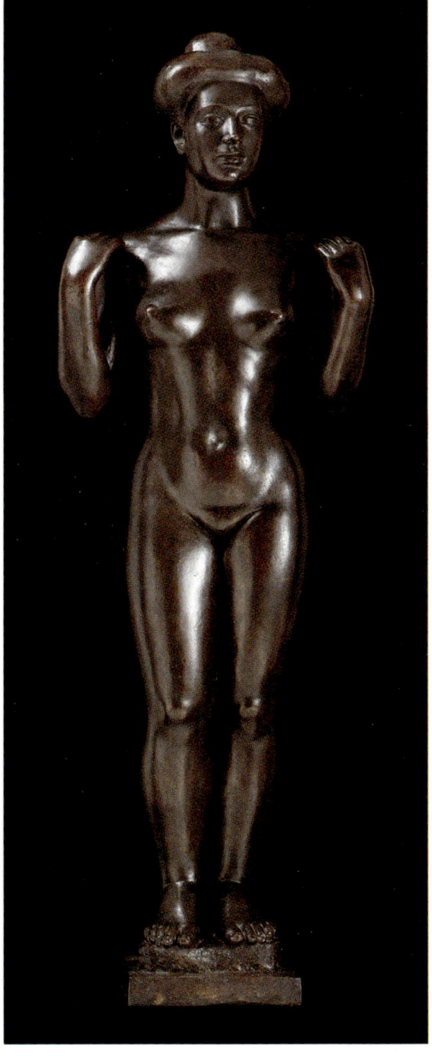

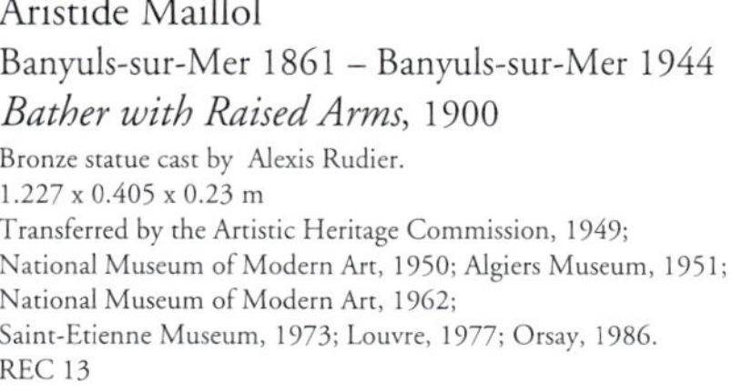

Aristide Maillol
Banyuls-sur-Mer 1861 – Banyuls-sur-Mer 1944
Bather with Raised Arms, 1900
Bronze statue cast by Alexis Rudier.
1.227 x 0.405 x 0.23 m
Transferred by the Artistic Heritage Commission, 1949;
National Museum of Modern Art, 1950; Algiers Museum, 1951;
National Museum of Modern Art, 1962;
Saint-Etienne Museum, 1973; Louvre, 1977; Orsay, 1986.
REC 13

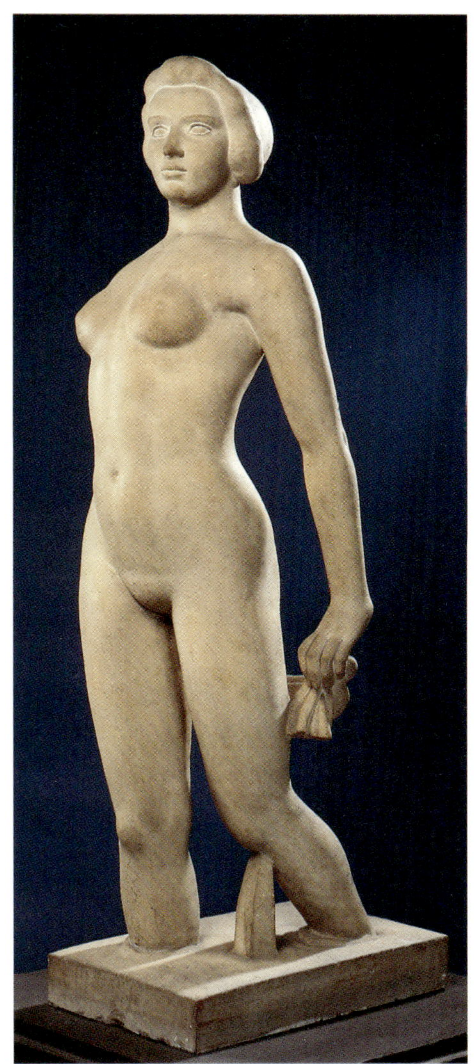

Aristide Maillol
Banyuls-sur-Mer 1861 – Banyuls-sur-Mer 1944
Ile-de-France, 1925–33
Stone statue. 1.52 x 0.49 x 0.575 m
From *Young Girl Walking on Water*, 1910–25; acquired in 1933;
Luxembourg Museum, 1933; National Museum of
Modern Art, 1940; Louvre, 1977; Orsay, 1986.
RF 3246

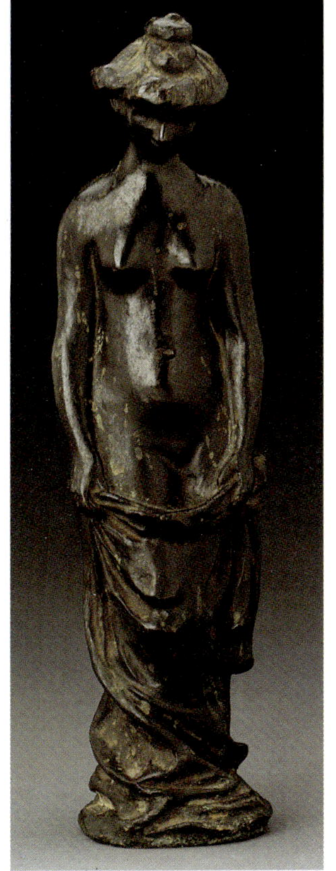

Félix Vallotton
Lausanne (Switzerland) 1865 – Paris 1925
Woman Holding Chemise, 1904
Bronze statuette cast by A.A. Hébrard (7).
0.302 x 0.082 x 0.087 m
Acquired in 1992.
RF 4404

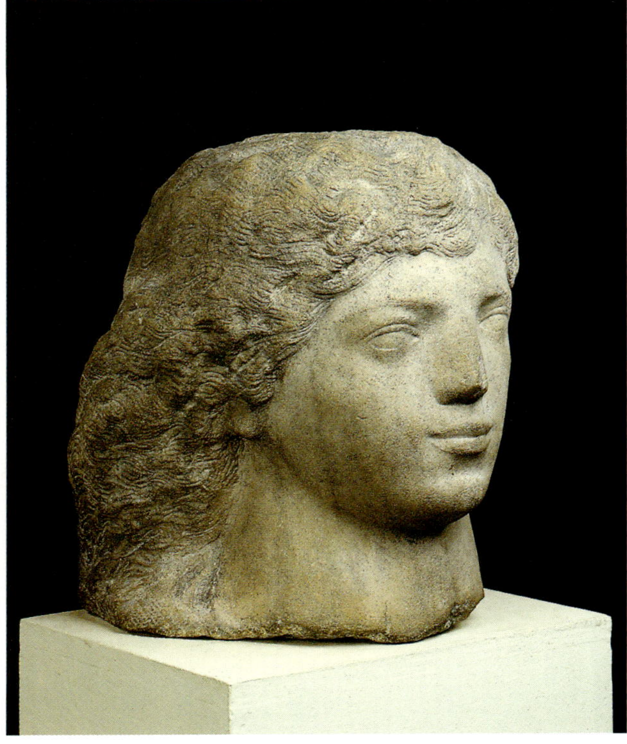

Joseph Bernard
Vienne 1866 – Boulogne-Billancourt 1931
Effort Towards Nature, c.1907
Lens stone head, chiselled by sculptor.
0.32 x 0.29 x 0.315 m
Gift from Jean Bernard, the artist's son, 1980.
RF 3513

Joseph Bernard ▷
Vienne 1866 – Boulogne-Billancourt 1931
The Dance (detail), 1911–3
Marble relief, chiselled by sculptor. 0.85 x 5.25 m
Music Room in the Hôtel Nocard (Neuilly-sur-Seine);
gift from Jean Bernard, the artist's son, 1980.
RF 3514

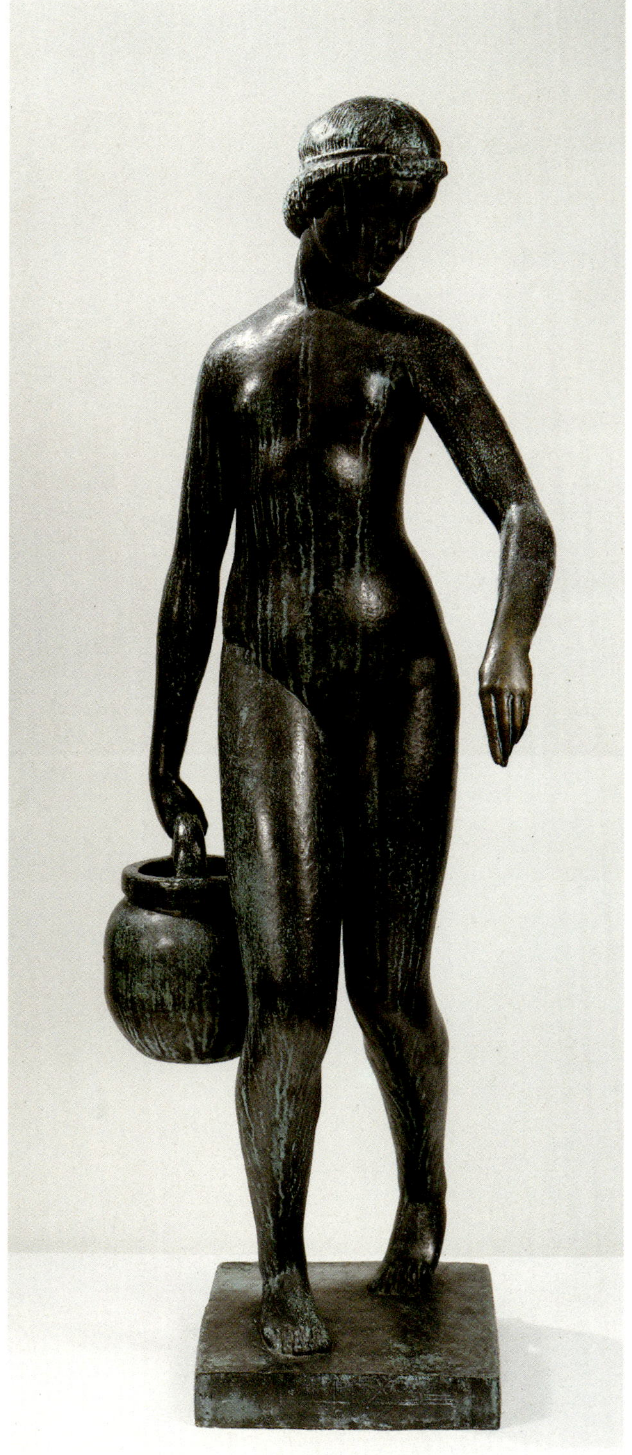

Joseph Bernard
Vienne 1866 – Boulogne-Billancourt 1931
The Water Carrier, 1912
Bronze statue cast by A.A. Hébrard.
1.75 x 0.40 x 0.52 m
Plaster, 1908; Salon d'Automne, 1912; acquired by the Nation, 1917; Luxembourg Museum, 1918; National Museum of Modern Art, 1940; Louvre, 1977; Orsay, 1986.
RF 3161

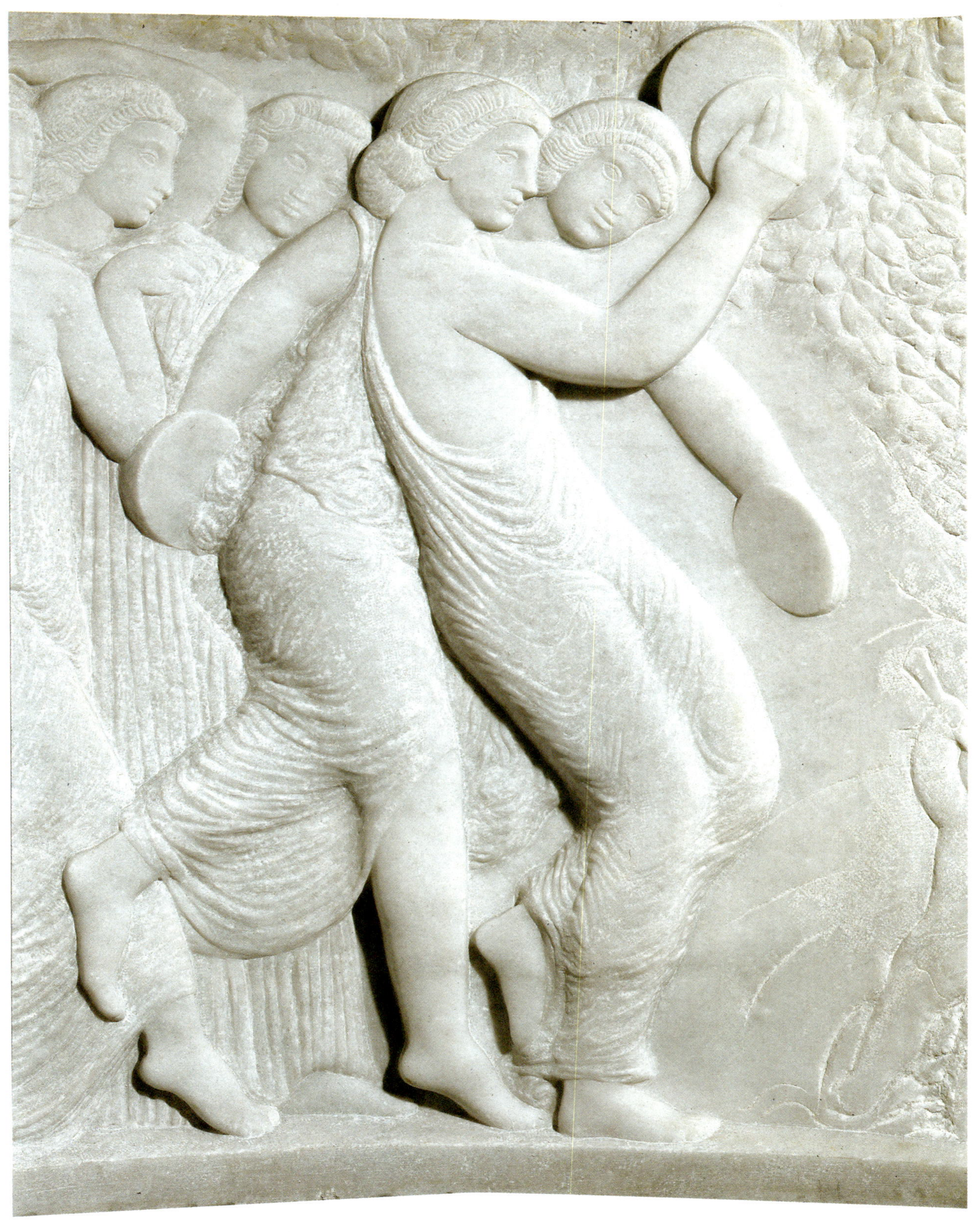

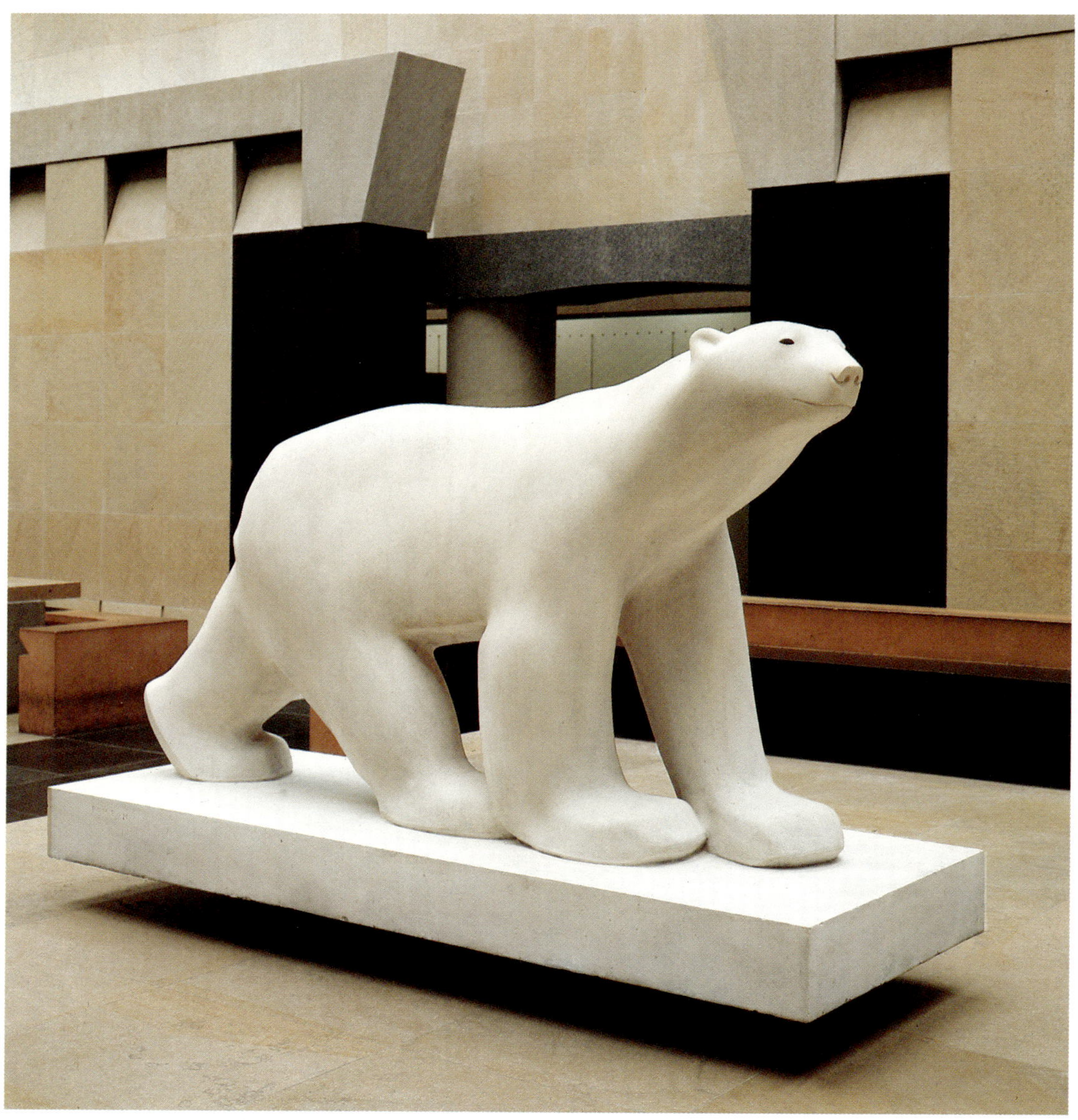

François Pompon
Saulieu 1855 – Paris 1933
White Bear, 1918–29
Lens stone statue chiselled by the Supérys of Malakoff.
1.63 x 0.90 x 2.51 m
Commissioned 1927 from the plaster shown at the Salon d'Automne (1922);
Luxembourg Museum, 1929;
National Museum of Modern Art, 1939; Orsay, 1986.
RF 3269

Index of proper names

Page numbers in roman type refer to text, in italics to illustrations.

ACKNOWLEDGMENTS

The sculptures at the Musée d'Orsay were sought, discovered, assembled, exchanged, acquired, transported, restored, displayed, studied, and documented by a trio that in 1978 comprised Antoinette Le Normand (the future Mme Romain, today Head Curator of Sculpture for the Paris and Meudon Rodin Museums); Laure de Margerie; and myself. We would again like to thank Jean Jenger, who obtained the Trocadéro animals, thus making it possible to recreate the 1878 group with the «Continents;» Jean-Loup Roubert who contributed the studies of the Paris Opera; and Michel Laclotte who negotiated for the contributions from the Rodin Museum, which was directed by Monique Laurent at the time.
For the present work, we would like to offer our thanks for the assistance provided by Luce Abelès, Alain Beausire, Dominique Becker, without whom this book would not exist; by the energetic Catherine Berthoud and Catherine Chevillot, who joined the Musée d'Orsay Sculpture team in 1990; and by Jean Coudane, Marie-Laure Crosnier-Leconte, Chantal Desmazières, the ever-patient Jérôme Faucheux, Brigitte Labat-Poussin, Antoinette Le Normand-Romain, Laure de Margerie, and René-Gabriel Ojeda, whose talent as a photographer triumphed over every technical problem.

PHOTOGRAPHIC CREDITS

Archives Nationales, Paris: p. 11g
Musée d'Orsay, Archives: pp. 6, 8, 9, 10, 11d, 12, 13d-photo J.Purcell, 13g 14, 15, 16, 17, 26h
© Réunion des Musées Nationaux: pp. 20, 21h, 29h, 30, 32h, 32bd, 34h, 38, 40, 41, 46, 49, 52b, 52h, 54bg, 64, 65hd, 65hg, 66, 72d, 78, 80h, 86b, 90h, 91, 93hd, 93hg, 99, 100bg, 102bd, 105h, 106, 108bd, 108h, 109h, 110-111b, 111h, 114b, 117h, 122g Photos Arnaudet: pp. 22-23b, 54bd, 80bd, 102hd
Photo Bellot: p. 60h
Photos Bernard: pp. 36b, 61, 116h
Photos Blot: pp. 18, 44, 104h, 115
Photo Blot & Lewandowski: p. 24
Photo Jean: p. 29m
Photos Jean & Blot: pp. 47h, 65b, 76, 109b
Photo Legiewski: p. 54h
Photos Lewandowski: pp. 29b, 34b, 48d, 55, 70d, 70g, 71d, 71g, 72g, 74, 75b, 83b, 85, 87, 96, 98d, 98g, 100h, 102g, 104b, 105b, 108bg, 112, 114h
Photo Morin: p. 124
Photos Ojéda: pp. 21b, 23h, 26b, 27, 28, 33b, 33h, 35, 36h, 37b, 37h, 42b, 43, 51, 53h, 56, 58b, 58h, 59, 60b, 62b, 62h, 63, 67, 68, 73, 75h, 77, 80bg, 81, 82, 84b, 84h, 88, 90b, 94b, 94h, 95, 100bd, 101h, 116b, 117b, 121g, 121m
Photos Schormans: pp. 22hd, 22hg, 32bg, 42h, 47b, 47h, 48g, 48m, 50, 53b, 86h, 92b, 92h, 99d, 101b, 103, 118b, 118h, 119, 120, 121d, 122d, 123
Photos Schormans & Bellot: pp. 83h, 93b

Every effort has been made to credit all photos properly, and to inform all photographers and/or copyright-holders. We apologize for any inadvertant omissions, and request that those involved make themselves known to us.

Printed in Italy by Editoriale
Colour Separation: Intégral Concept
Dépôt légal: May 1998